P9-DWH-917

SUNBELT

RETIREMENT

By the same author

The Fires of Autumn : *Sexual Activity in the Middle and Later Years*
The Illustrated Encyclopedia of Better Health (co-author)
The Wealth Management Handbook (co-author)
The Complete Retirement Planning Book

SUNBELT

RETIREMENT

The Complete State-by-State Guide to Retiring in the South and West of the United States

PETER A. DICKINSON

E. P. DUTTON | NEW YORK

Copyright © 1980 by Peter A. Dickinson
All rights reserved. Printed in the U.S.A.

No part of this publication may be reproduced or transmitted
in any form or by any means, electronic or mechanical, including
photocopy, recording or any information storage and retrieval
system now known or to be invented, without permission in writing
from the publisher, except by a reviewer who wishes to quote brief
passages in connection with a review written for inclusion in a
magazine, newspaper or broadcast.

Library of Congress Cataloging in Publication Data
Dickinson, Peter A
Sunbelt retirement.
1. Retirement, Places of—The West.
2. Retirement, Places of—Southern States.   I. Title.
HQ1062.D53 1978   301.43′5   77-10961
ISBN: 0-525-93123-6 (cloth)
0-525-93107-4 (paper)

Published simultaneously in Canada by
Fitzhenry & Whiteside, Limited, Toronto
10 9 8

CONTENTS

ACKNOWLEDGMENTS

I couldn't have written this book without the help of many people. My thanks to the scores of retirees, gerontologists, doctors, tax assessors, builders, and chambers of commerce directors who supplied material; to Nan Pose, Larchmont, N.Y., who did some basic research and typed the manuscript; to H. "Pat" Brigham, who took a research trip throughout Southern California to refresh my impressions; to Charles Weikel, Berkeley, Calif., and Patsy Edwards, Los Angeles, who supplied additional material for the chapter on Southern California; to Bernard Sloan, Larchmont, N.Y., who helped prepare material for Chapters XV and XVI; and to these state Commission on Aging personnel who worked closely with me: George L. Lentz, Deputy Director, North Carolina Office for Aging; Courtney Carson, Director of Public Affairs, and Harry R. Bryan, Director, South Carolina Commission on Aging; Ralph Dobbs, Georgia Department of Industry and Trade, and Joel Turner, Community Education Specialist, Georgia Office on Aging; Dale Ottman, Acting Deputy Director, Florida Division on Aging, and Harry Richards, Florida Council on Aging; Joan B. McMillan, Area Agency on Aging Director, and Fran Batten, Community Coordinator, South Alabama Regional Planning Commission; Robert Leigh, Research Analyst, Mississippi Council on Aging; Priscilla R. Engolia, Director for Aging, and John Raglin, Research Statistician, Bureau of Aging Services, Louisiana Department of Health and Human Resources; Phil S. Peters, Director, Office on Aging and Adult Services, Arkansas; Vernon McDaniel, Executive Director of the Governor's Committee on Aging, State of Texas; Robert A. Mondragon, Director, and Edythe Pierson, member, Pre-Retirement Planning Committee, New Mexico Commission on Aging; Robert G. Thomas, Acting Chief, Bureau of Aging, State of Arizona; Janet Levy, Director, Department of Aging, State of California; Renji Goto, Director, Executive Office on Aging, State of Hawaii. My special gratitude to my wife, Brigitte, who as reference librarian supplied me with an endless stream of facts, and who as a spouse, provided an infinite amount of patience.

PETER A. DICKINSON

January 1983
Larchmont, N.Y.

PREFACE TO THE 1983 EDITION

The Sunbelt is the most dynamic area of the United States—growing twice as fast as the rest of the country. Taxes, cost of living, housing, medical facilities are changing to meet changing conditions. Thus, the facts and figures reported in the 1982 edition have multiplied along with the population. That's why I've *updated* this new edition to bring you the latest data.

Basic details and impressions remain the same; a rise in taxes or housing costs doesn't change a place overnight. And, hopefully, you'll share my impressions of places mentioned here after you've visited them. I've done some "home work" for you so you'll know what to expect when you visit a state, what towns may be best suited to you, what to look (out) for, and where to get further information. If you want to find *your* place in the Sunbelt, *Sunbelt Retirement* will help you find your way.

Peter A. Dickinson

January 1983
Larchmont, N.Y.

PRINCIPAL RETIREMENT AREAS OF THE UNITED STATES

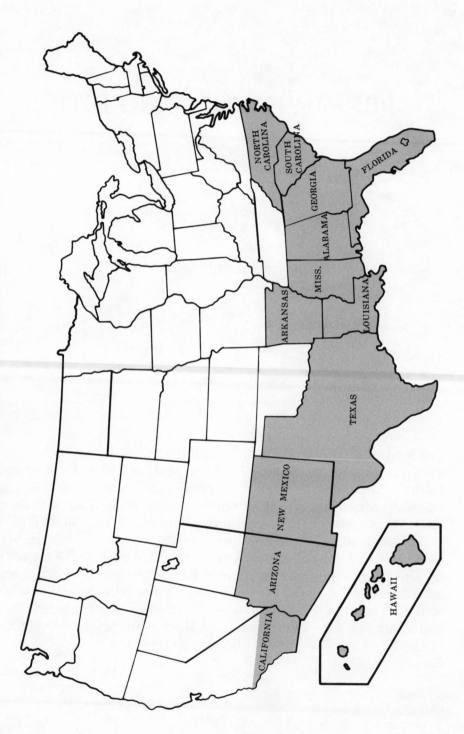

NORTH CAROLINA

SOUTH CAROLINA

GEORGIA

FLORIDA

ALABAMA

MISS.

LOUISIANA

ARKANSAS

TEXAS

NEW MEXICO

ARIZONA

CALIFORNIA

HAWAII

I.

WHY A

PLACE IN THE SUN?

I took a deep breath of soft, clean air, loosened my tie, and smiled back at the sun. Once again I was in Greensboro, N.C., on my final tour of the Sunbelt states to complete this book.

As I drove from Greensboro toward Chapel Hill and Raleigh, I naturally slowed down to 55 miles an hour. And during the next 6 weeks—when I drove 7,000 crisscrossed miles through the Sunbelt—I came to understand more than ever why this area is the new retirement mecca.

When I speak of the Sunbelt, I mean those states in the South and West of the United States including *North Carolina, South Carolina, Georgia, Florida, Alabama, Mississippi, Louisiana, Arkansas, Texas, New Mexico, Arizona, Southern California* (from Santa Barbara south), and *Hawaii.* Here snow is rare, winter is short, and the weather is mild and sunny, with an average annual temperature of 55° Fahrenheit.

The Sunbelt is the new American frontier—in people, places, politics, and retirement. Whatever you're looking for—lower cost of living, improved health, new friends and activities—you'll find it more easily in the Sunbelt than in any other part of the United States. You'll also have more choices of housing; variations in climate; differences in life styles. Decide what you want to do and where you want to do it, and you've found *your* place in the sun.

The Sunbelt is luring people twice as fast as the rest of the country. According to the latest Census Bureau estimates, most Americans now live in the South and West. In the 1980s, 6 of our largest cities will be in the area from Texas to California (Los Angeles, Houston, Dallas, San Diego, San Antonio, and Phoenix), and the South and West will have a majority of seats in the U.S. House of Representatives for the first time in history. The Sunbelt will be dictating to the rest of the country, both economically and politically.[1]

Many Sunbelters will be seniors. Already, California has supplanted New York as the state with the most residents aged 65 or older (over 2,000,000) and Florida, with some 17 percent of its population over 65, leads in the percentage of seniors.

What draws people to the Sunbelt? Long before Jimmy Carter was elected president, the Sunbelt had been shifting from a rural to an urban society, from blue-collar to white-collar jobs, from agriculture to industry, and from racial tension to racial relaxation.

During the past 10 years, 76 percent of all new manufacturing jobs in the United States were in the Sunbelt states. Between now and the year 2000, experts predict this region will produce two thirds of the growth in jobs and more than half the country's increase in income. Of the 500 largest corporations in America, 114 are now based in the Sunbelt, compared with only 79 a decade ago. These include Shell Oil, Houston; Lockheed, Burbank, Cal.; Dresser Industries, Dallas; Cone Mills, Greensboro, N.C.[2]

Many new Sunbelt companies are in service-related industries such as market distribution. These businesses are drawing the intellectual elite from the North and East; while one fourth of the Ph.D.'s in the country are educated in the Great Lakes region, only 1 in 6 now works there; increasing numbers of professionals are seeking their place in the Sunbelt states.[3] Many new companies are settling in rural or suburban communities, rapidly changing the landscape of the South and West. Although the Sunbelt states contain some 26 percent of the entire land mass of the U.S., only approximately 23 percent of the country's harvested land is now in this region. The Sunbelt is now 59.9 percent urban versus 73.7 percent for the rest of the U.S. (See table I.)

The Sunbelt is also becoming more racially integrated. While the percentage of black Americans living in the Sunbelt fell from 78 percent in 1900 to 43 percent in 1975, some 46.3 percent of all black pupils in the

TABLE I
URBAN vs. RURAL POPULATIONS OF THE SUNBELT STATES

Area	% Urban Population	% Rural Population
UNITED STATES	73.7	26.3
North Carolina	48.0	52
South Carolina	54.1	45.9
Georgia	62.3	37.7
Florida	84.3	15.7
Alabama	60.0	40.0
Mississippi	47.3	52.7
Arkansas	51.6	48.4
Louisiana	68.6	31.4
Texas	79.6	20.4
New Mexico	72.2	27.8
Arizona	83.8	16.2
California	91.3	7.7
Hawaii	86.5	13.5
AVERAGE SUNBELT	68.4	31.5

Source: U.S. Bureau of Census, 1980. The same census figures show that the Sunbelt has more old towns with fewer than 7,500 residents than any other region of the country.

South attended schools that were predominantly white, compared to 31.8 percent in the Border states and 28.3 percent in the North and West.[4]

Change stimulates change, and the Sunbelt is now setting the pace for the future. New people, new industry, new ideas, new activities generate a dynamism and pride in achievement that fuels progress in all areas. And the Sunbelt states have incentives that are attracting young people with dreams as well as older people with money.

I saw new food processing plants in North Carolina; pulp mills in South Carolina; aluminum plants near New Orleans; petrochemical facilities along the Mississippi River; aircraft plants in Georgia; shipbuilding along the Gulf Coast; steel in Alabama; and a space crescent stretching from Cape Kennedy, Fla. to Huntsville, Ala. to rocket-testing sites in Houston, Texas. I also saw signs of international industry—a Sperry Rand electronics plant in St. Petersburg, Fla.; a Volvo assembly plant near Chesapeake, Va.; and a Michelin factory in Spartanburg, S.C.

While industrial gases affected my breathing in some places, I could still savor the spice of piney woods; the fragrance of orange blossoms;

the perfume of magnolias. And nowhere did the jackhammer subdue the Ozark twang, the sandpiper's chirp, or the humming velvet nights.

The Senior Power of Politics

Senior Power packs a wallop in the Sunbelt. Already, over-50 voters are numerous enough to swing any issue and elect any candidate; in the next few years seniors will have even more power. After the 1980 census, the South and West held a majority of House seats for the first time in U.S. history—51 percent. By the year 2000, the Sunbelt may hold as many as 55 percent of the seats. Florida will jump from 15 to 25 seats by the century's end, Texas from 24 to 29, Arizona from 4 to 7, and California from 43 to 45. In contrast, New York is expected to lose 8 of its 39 House seats and Pennsylvania, Ohio, and Illinois will each lose 4 seats. A count of all 29 states in the South and West, including the District of Columbia, shows that they now represent 271 (or 50.3 percent) of the 538 electoral votes cast. That proportion is projected to grow to 53 percent by 1984 and 56 percent by the year 2004.[5]

The federal government is recognizing this power shift and is pumping money southward. In the 1976 fiscal year, the Southeast received $9.5 billion *more* in federal aid than it paid in taxes and the West received $8.7 billion *more*. This federal money was spent not only for military bases and defense industries in the Sunbelt; much of it was paid in Social Security pensions to retirees who may have spent their working years in the North but were now drawing their benefits in the South.[6] Adding up defense contracts, government employee salaries, welfare outlays, public works and other federal spending, the Sunbelt received $1.14 for every $1.00 sent to Washington in taxes, while 9 Northeastern states received only 86 cents and 12 Midwestern states received only 76 cents per dollar.[7]

Business and industry are responding to this growing political and economic power and are building housing, providing recreational equipment, and sponsoring programs catering to seniors. In each Sunbelt state, I called upon the state commissioner on aging, who showed me ambitious new programs in health, housing, nutrition, transportation, education, and recreation—all appealing to the new Senior Power bloc.

1. WHAT THE SUNBELT OFFERS YOU

The following is a brief introduction to the unique advantages of these Southern and Western states.

The Sunbelt Costs Less

Because living is easier in the Sunbelt, costs are lower. Using a Bureau of Labor Statistics index where 100 represents the average cost of living for retired couples in the urban U.S., cities and towns in the West and South (except for Los Angeles and Honolulu) score consistently in the 80s and 90s:

SUNBELT COST INDEX FOR A RETIRED COUPLE*

AREA	AREA COST INDEXES		
	Lower Budget	Intermediate Budget	Higher Budget
URBAN U.S.	100	100	100
Metropolitan areas[1]	102	104	104
Non-metropolitan areas[2]	93	89	87
SOUTH			
Atlanta, Ga.	91	92	92
Austin, Tex.	92	93	94
Baton Rouge, La.	89	89	90
Dallas, Tex.	92	93	97
Durham, N.C.	98	97	94
Houston, Tex.	95	95	98
Orlando, Fla.	97	94	92
Non-metropolitan areas	90	86	84
WEST			
Bakersfield, Cal.	93	93	93
Los Angeles–Long Beach, Cal.	101	100	104
San Diego, Cal.	99	97	99
Honolulu, Hi.	115	114	112
Non-metropolitan areas	94	88	86

* The retired couple is defined as a husband age 65 or older, and his wife. They are assumed to be self-supporting, in reasonably good health, and able to take care of themselves. Budgets include food, housing, transportation, clothing, personal care, and medical care, but *not* personal income taxes. Annual budgets are projected to 1983 prices; Lower—$7,800; Intermediate—$11,700; Higher, $18,720.

[1]—over 50,000 population

[2]—2,500 to 50,000 population

Source: U.S. Bureau of Labor Statistics.

Taking the Intermediate Budget ($11,700) as an example, here's what a retired couple in 1983 would pay for major items in these Sunbelt cities:

COSTS FOR RETIRED COUPLE IN MAJOR SUNBELT CITIES

CITY	Food	Housing	Transportation	Other	Total
Atlanta, Ga.	$3,440	$3,112	$1,063	$3,214	$10,802
Austin, Tex.	$3,060	$3,596	$1,125	$3,182	$10,963
Bakersfield, Calif.	$3,177	$3,431	$1,145	$3,111	$10,864
Baton Rouge, La.	$3,458	$2,739	$1,122	$3,099	$10,418
Dallas, Tex.	$3,150	$3,393	$1,173	$3,199	$10,915
Durham, NC	$3,393	$3,364	$1,099	$3,321	$11,077
Honolulu, Hi.	$4,222	$4,251	$2,132	$3,423	$14,028
Los Angeles, Cal.	$3,301	$3,921	$1,223	$3,298	$11,743
Orlando, Fla.	$3,050	$3,710	$1,134	$3,117	$11,011
San Diego, Cal.	$3,238	$3,767	$1,177	$3,221	$11,403
URBAN U.S.	$3,461	$3,968	$1,044	$3,228	$11,700

Taxes are also generally lower in the Sunbelt states. Here are average annual taxes that a family with an income of $10,000 would pay in the Sunbelt states, based on combined state and local rates:

STATE (rank in U.S.)[1]	Ind. Income	Gen. Sales	Resident	Other[2]	Total
Alabama (28)	$250	$258	$164	$143	$ 815
Arizona (35)	$150	$158	$307	$153	$ 768
Arkansas (39)	$160	$129	$225	$186	$ 700
California (24)	$ 60	$158	$512	$145	$ 875
Florida (47)	——	$112	$225	$155	$ 492
Georgia (32)	$ 80	$185	$348	$172	$ 784
Hawaii (4)	$350	$175	$550	$150	$1225
Louisiana (48)	$ 50	$176	$123	$113	$ 462
Mississippi (41)	$ 40	$237	$205	$176	$ 658
New Mexico (36)	$ 80	$200	$328	$130	$ 738
North Carolina (21)	$260	$156	$348	$134	$ 898
South Carolina (23)	$160	$172	$246	$152	$ 730
Texas (43)	——	$136	$307	$169	$ 612

[1] —states ranked from highest to lowest. The higher the number, the lower the tax burden.

[2] —auto, gasoline, associated vehicle taxes; cigarette excise taxes.

Source: Statistical Abstract for the U.S.

All Sunbelt states offer some tax relief to the elderly, usually according to income (see the chapter on the individual state). However, you must have established legal residency in the state, and you must apply for the exemption.

The Sunbelt Is Healthier

Doctors tell me that the body functions best when the temperature is about 66° F. with a relative humidity of about 55 percent. This temperature and humidity allow the body chemistry to function at maximum efficiency and without strain. The temperature-humidity index, a combination of these two factors, ideally should be *under* 72. Above that you begin to feel uncomfortable as your body strains to adjust. Ideally, there should be a gently blowing breeze and beaming sunshine. You'll find most of this "perfect" weather in the Sunbelt states:

CITY	Average Temp. F. Winter	Summer	Sunny Days	Humid- ity %	Precipita- tion (ins.)	Aver. Wind (mph)
Montgomery, Ala.	55.1	76.0	233	71.8	47.1	1.5
Phoenix, Ariz.	60.5	96.4	289	33.5	10.87	7.3
Little Rock, Ark.	41.3	82.1	212	69.3	47.08	6.0
Los Angeles, Cal.	60.6	72.5	293	63.3	6.54	7.8
Miami, Fla.	72.1	79.7	252	76.25	63.11	9.3
Atlanta, Ga.	50.2	71.5	206	70.8	50.61	9.2
Honolulu, Hi.	72.9	79.6	244	68.8	26.90	13.2
New Orleans, La.	59.7	77.5	234	78.8	63.98	8.5
Jackson, Miss.	55.0	77.4	226	76.0	50.03	7.4
Albuquerque, N.M.	44.0	69.4	271	42.3	16.5	9.7
Raleigh, N.C.	47.8	69.1	201	70.5	55.74	8.6
Columbia, S.C.	53.1	73.1	216	75.5	55.51	7.6
Austin, Tex.	57.9	79.0	221	67.5	26.07	9.0

Source: U.S. Department of Commerce—National Oceanic and Atmospheric Administration. Based on standard thirty-year period, 1941 to 1970.

A good climate makes fewer demands upon your body and pocketbook. Diabetes appears more controllable in hot climes, and stress diseases —ulcers, certain heart problems, hardening of the arteries—are less frequent in warm zones. Doctors frequently recommend Southern California, Florida, Georgia, South Carolina, North Carolina; the Gulf coast of Alabama, Mississippi, Louisiana, and Texas; the southern parts of Arizona and New Mexico for people suffering from arthritis, rheumatism, emphysema, sinus, respiratory problems, hypertension, and heart problems.

The milder weather also makes you feel and behave better psychologically because changes in weather affect your pulse rate, urine, body temperature, and metabolic processes. According to Dr. Clarence E. Mills of the University of Cincinnati, falling barometric pressure causes body tissues to swell, reducing blood flow. This, in turn, places a slight pressure on the brain, prompting some people to behave peculiarly. Other researchers have learned that a sudden rise in temperature within a low-pressure area stimulates aggressive and destructive acts.[8]

Extreme heat and cold also affect health. After studying hospital admission records, Dr. George E. Burch of Tulane University found that more heart attack victims were admitted to hospitals and died in August than in any other month. And related studies by the Metropolitan Life Insurance Company show that acute respiratory disease occurs $4\frac{1}{2}$ times more frequently in January than in July, and that February and March are the worst months for circulatory diseases. Leukemia strikes more often in winter and rheumatic fever reaches its yearly high in April.[9]

Northern cities—with their noise, congestion, and pollution—strain nerves and the body. Colds and other respiratory diseases abound as soon as winter sets in and people are forced to stay indoors in artificially heated air. It's not surprising that over 50 percent of all deaths in the U.S. occur during the winter months.[10]

The older you are the more sense it makes to seek a place in the Sunbelt. If you're contemplating a change of climate for health reasons, consult your doctor first. He knows your medical history and emotional

RATIO OF PHYSICIANS TO RESIDENTS IN SUNBELT STATES			
State	*Population*	*No. Physicians*	*Residents per Phys.*
North Carolina	5,525,000	7,591	728
South Carolina	2,867,000	3,489	821
Georgia	5,048,000	6,794	743
Florida	8,824,000	14,604	604
Alabama	3,690,000	4,071	906
Mississippi	2,389,000	2,424	985
Louisiana	3,921,000	5,457	718
Arkansas	2,144,000	2,303	930
Texas	12,830,000	18,421	696
New Mexico	1,190,000	1,714	694
Arizona	2,296,000	4,117	557
California	21,896,000	47,223	463
Hawaii	895,000	1,534	583
UNITED STATES	217,700,000	378,572	575

Source: Division of Health Manpower and Facilities, U.S. Dept. HEW

patterns, and will help you evaluate whether or not a move may be helpful for you. Also, realize that even within states of the Sunbelt, you're likely to find many climatic variations. So moving to Arizona for your health works only if you find the right spot in that state.

Be sure to investigate the availability of doctors and hospitals in your new location. This is especially important in rural areas. Although I found excellent health facilities in New Bern, N.C., and Fairhope, Ala., for example, I noted that some towns, such as Deming, N.M., had signs pleading: DEMING NEEDS DOCTORS! Note that the U.S. Department of Health, Education and Welfare classifies any ratio of residents to primary care physicians *higher than 750 to 1* as critical.

The Sunbelt Has a Stimulating Social Environment

Social life in the Sunbelt states is centered more on personal interaction than on social or economic status. Sunbelters value the individual stand and personal contact; men aren't just friends, they're "good ol' boys." "Southern hospitality" is a way of life that can charm even the most confirmed Northerner. And if you think you'll miss the folks back home, chances are that other Northerners or Midwesterners have chosen the same place to retire that you did—and for the same reasons.

Entertaining is less formal than in other parts of the country; many activities are centered in the outdoors, which is always close by. You can enjoy golf, tennis, lawn bowling, shuffleboard, and boating at low or no cost all year round. And you'll find abundant and intriguing new flora and fauna if you're nature-minded. In fact, *you should be outdoors-oriented or nature-minded if you move to the Sunbelt.*

You'll find many opportunities to continue learning in the Sunbelt. Colleges such as the universities of Texas, North Carolina, and South Carolina offer free or low-cost classes for seniors, and most community colleges will provide a course and instructor if 10 or more seniors sign up. Especially popular are the minicourse and weekend learning experiences offered by many schools as well as by professional, business, and religious organizations and museums.

The Sunbelt Offers More Housing at Lower Cost

I visited retirees living in housing ranging from mobile homes to houseboats, cabins to mansions, condominiums to single-family houses. I saw neat stucco-and-frame two-and-three-bedroom houses being auc-

SEMIPRIVATE DAILY ROOM RATES IN SUNBELT HOSPITALS

STATE & Cities	*Average Semiprivate Daily Rate*
NORTH CAROLINA	
Raleigh	$135.39
Charlotte	$137.59
Wilmington	$131.62
Asheville	$139.40
State Average = $152.29	
SOUTH CAROLINA	
Columbia	$149.60
Spartanburg	$106.24
Charleston	$100.95
Greenville	$100.20
State Average = $141.82	
GEORGIA	
Atlanta	$189.39
Athens	$153.49
Augusta	$159.12
Savannah	$168.35
Columbus	$158.59
State Average = $170.59	
FLORIDA	
Jacksonville	$181.79
Pensacola	$150.85
Gainesville	$162.19
Orlando	$175.34
Miami	$208.44
Ft. Lauderdale	$191.13
Tampa	$178.32
St. Petersburg	$209.10
Ft. Myers	$194.60
State Average = $197.63	
ALABAMA	
Birmingham	$170.48
Huntsville	$152.81
Montgomery	$155.14
Dothan	$132.54
Mobile	$136.44
State Average = $157.86	
MISSISSIPPI	
Jackson	$118.11
Gulfport	$143.92
State Average = $119.90	

STATE & Cities	Average Semiprivate Daily Rate
LOUISIANA	
New Orleans	$170.76
Hammond	$112.21
Lafayette	$129.25
Lake Charles	$135.71
Baton Rouge	$134.18
Shreveport	$122.14
Monroe	$134.24
Alexandria	$117.58
State Average = $154.33	
ARKANSAS	
Pine Bluff	$127.41
Hot Springs	$114.65
Little Rock	$161.40
Batesville	$118.31
Fayetteville	$155.18
Ft. Smith	$143.00
State Average = $147.96	
TEXAS	
Tyler	$137.25
Wichita Falls	$163.44
San Angelo	$129.68
San Antonio	$157.12
Corpus Christi	$175.90
McAllen	$177.11
Austin	$143.58
Midland	$152.85
El Paso	$143.51
State Average = $165.98	
NEW MEXICO	
Albuquerque	$175.42
Santa Fe	$204.27
Truth or Consequences	$151.26
Clovis	$175.65
Roswell	$180.30
State Average = $192.51	
ARIZONA	
Phoenix	$194.70
Tucson	$185.62
Flagstaff	$160.89
Prescott	$168.97
Kingman	$158.59
State Average = $196.66	

STATE & Cities	*Average Semiprivate Daily Rate*
CALIFORNIA	
Los Angeles	$323.43
Santa Monica	$312.19
Long Beach	$267.06
San Diego	$259.16
Palm Springs	$262.36
San Bernardino	$252.72
Riverside	$234.20
Santa Ana	$271.43
Ventura	$203.28
Santa Barbara	$262.64

State Average = $264.84

HAWAII	
Honolulu	$226.52

U.S. AVERAGE = $221.81

Source: Health Insurance Association of America. Rates prevailing in 1983.

tioned off at an abandoned U.S. Air Force base in Roswell, N.M. for as low as $7,000. Generally, two-and-three-bedroom retirement houses sell for 25–50 percent less in the Sunbelt than in the North and East. Costs range from $30,000 to $45,000 and up in the Sunbelt versus $50,000 to $65,000 and up in the rest of the country. One- and-two bedroom apartments rent for $200 to $300 and up a month in the Sunbelt compared to $250 to $400 and up in the rest of the country.

Housing in the Sunbelt costs less and gives you more freedom because you don't *need as much shelter* and you *spend more time outdoors.* Sunbelt houses don't require full basements for central heating systems (space, floor, or wall heaters or simple heat pumps suffice), nor do they require as much insulation or enclosed garages.

For instance, our house in the San Diego area had only 1,000 square feet indoors, but an additional 800 square feet in patio outdoors. The roof extended over this patio, and living room doors led to it. We could and did spend much time in this "outdoor living room." And when we needed heat indoors, we used wall heaters or the fireplace. We just parked our car outside, no garage or covering.

It usually costs less to build a house in the Sunbelt. The National Association of Home Builders estimates that the average new home sells for around $40 per square foot of living space. Recent average prices of new homes in the Sunbelt compare favorably.

State	Average selling price per square foot living space
Alabama	$34.47
Arizona	$36.65
Arkansas	$38.35
California	$49.14
Florida	$32.69
Georgia	$41.37
Hawaii	$43.05
Louisiana	$31.45
Mississippi	$33.50
New Mexico	$31.45
North Carolina	$36.19
South Carolina	$35.52
Texas	$36.43

The Sunbelt also offers more housing projects suited to retirement. In Myrtle Beach, S.C., Clearwater, Fla., and Tucson, Ariz., for example, I saw Planned Unit Developments (PUDs) that feature groups of single-family houses, townhouses, apartments, or mobile homes surrounding a garden, swimming pool, or recreation area. These "clustered" homes provide ample open-space areas. The homeowners, through a cooperative association, work together to maintain pleasant landscaping and an attractive environment. Many PUDs include a golf course, bowling green, and tennis courts.

While PUDs require city, county, and state approval and are often financed by the U.S. Department of Housing and Urban Development (HUD) and the Federal Housing Administration (FHA), these agencies don't guarantee that you'll get your money's worth. Your protection is in the records of the government agencies that review, investigate, and finally approve the project. Individual developers are obligated to show you these documents if you request to see them. The Community Associations Institute, 1832 M Street, N.W., Washington, D.C. 20036, offers a booklet for $1.00 explaining condominiums and PUDs.

The U.S. Department of Agriculture's Farmers Home Administration gives lower income persons and families an opportunity to finance a home in a community with a population of 20,000 or less, if the applicant can show he is a responsible citizen without enough assets to qualify for a suitable loan from existing commercial loan sources such as banks or savings and loan associations. For further information, check the telephone directory under the heading "U.S. Government—Department of Agriculture—Farmers Home Administration." This office supplies the name, address, and telephone number of the agent to consult about loans, conditions, eligibility, and other matters. The Farmers Home Administration programs have over 30 unusual loan plans in rural areas for buying or building a home, replacing a roof, and making other major repairs. Check to see if you qualify.

For housing in other Sunbelt areas, send for these catalogs:

United Farm Agency
612 West 47th Street
Kansas City, MO 64112

Strout Realty
Plaza Towers
Springfield, MO 65804

The Sunbelt Provides Service for Seniors

In every Sunbelt state I visited the commissioner on aging. Each Sunbelt state has state, area, and local subagencies on aging that work directly with local and community groups on programs with and for older people: housing, health, transportation, nutrition, recreation, and legal services. While many programs are aimed at helping the poorer elderly, other services such as transportation (minibuses) and nutrition (a hot meal for which seniors pay what they can afford) appeal to the more affluent, as they are convenient and often serve as social meeting places.

For instance—in conjunction with the Division on Aging, the Florida State Employment Service operates an Older Workers Special Program, which finds jobs for older people, and the Florida Insurance Commission provides free counseling to seniors on all insurance matters and will even collect from insurance companies that hedge on payments. The University of Alabama's Center for the Study of Aging has organized a Consortium of Educators in Gerontology (the social science of aging), which coordinates the sharing of information, resources, and expertise in the field of aging in the state. In Louisiana, the Bureau on Aging Services holds many public hearings and sponsors Senior Day rallies at the Governor's Conference on Aging. Louisiana's outstanding Information and Referral Services provide information for over 10,000 seniors a month, and its Outreach program brings people in need in touch with available services. The Georgia Office on Aging has a tie-line service that provides seniors with toll-free advice on any problem. The Texas Governor's Committee on Aging offers a Senior Texans Employment Program (STEP) that employs the elderly for community service projects. The Mississippi Council on Aging has a team that travels the state in a mobile office unit and informs seniors of available services. The Arizona Council for Senior Citizens has been a leader in the battle to obtain equal rights and opportunities for retirees.

Each individual state chapter in this book has more details on these and other aspects of life in the Sunbelt. There is a unique *rating scale* at the end of each chapter to help you tell at a glance if the location in question meets your own standards and needs.

II.

WHERE DO YOU

START LOOKING?

I once loved a city—San Francisco. And I laughed when an older man (about my age now) said: "Your love for San Francisco is as young as your heart and as strong as your nerves."

I still love San Francisco, but it's grown older and so have I. It demands more and I can give less. I want peace and quiet; it generates noise and confusion.

No, I don't think I'll retire in San Francisco. But I'd like to retire *near* there, or perhaps near Atlanta, Mobile, or Phoenix—near enough for an occasional meal at a restaurant or an evening at the theater. But I want to go in when I want—and stay away when I want.

No matter where we were born, as we grow older most of us seek the relaxation of the country rather than the tension of the city. Even youngsters are escaping the cities for the simpler life of the country. And many places that slumbered for years are now awakening to find themselves much sought-after retirement communities. For example, Kingman, Ariz. Until a few years ago, this town, located in northwestern Arizona along U.S. Route 66 (I-40) was only a truck stop on the way to Los Angeles (250 miles west) or Las Vegas (102 miles northwest). Sitting on a high plateau, elevation 3,336, and surrounded by plenty of open land, Kingman had plenty of room to grow. And grow it did—from a population of 4,525 in 1960 to over 15,000 today. Much of this growth is due to attractions in the surrounding area, including Bullhead City and Lake Havasu City, home of the reconstructed London Bridge. About 25 percent of the residents are now retired and think nothing of driving to the Lake Mead Recreation Area (98 miles) or to Las Vegas or Los Angeles for shopping and entertainment.

The same growth occurred in retirement towns like Scottsdale, Ariz. (near Phoenix) and many other smaller towns near large cities. But before examining specific retirement communities, let's look at the main regions of the Sunbelt.

1. THE MAIN REGIONS OF THE SUNBELT

The Sunbelt breaks down into several regions which share similar geographic and environmental features. However, climate not only changes from north to south and from seacoast to mountains; it can change within a few horizontal miles or a few hundred vertical feet: *for every 1,000 feet of altitude, the average temperature drops 5° F.; and for every 75 miles south you go, the average temperature increases 1° F.*

Keeping these variations in mind, here are the general areas and aspects of the Sunbelt:

Coastal Plains

These cover major tidewater areas of the Sunbelt from North Carolina south to Florida and west to Texas. In North Carolina the Coastal Plain is 200 miles wide, but in Florida it narrows to under 100 miles and in Texas broadens to over 300 miles. The region contains such popular retirement towns as Edenton and New Bern, N.C.; Charleston and Hilton Head Island, S.C.; St. Simons and Jekyll Islands, Ga.; Daytona Beach, Palm Beach, Miami, Naples, Sarasota, St. Petersburg, Tallahassee, and Pensacola, Fla.; Fairhope, Point Clear, and Mobile, Ala.; Oceans Springs, Biloxi, and Pass Christian, Miss.; Abita Springs, Covington, and New Orleans, La.; Corpus Christi, Brownsville, Harlingen, and McAllen, Tex. With the exception of southern Florida, the coastal features are much the same—sandy barrier beaches separated from the mainland mainly by tidal lagoons or saltwater marshes. The land is fertile and flat, and it is here that much of the country's cotton, corn, tobacco, and even sugar cane grows. The altitude ranges from sea level to 345 feet near Lake Wales, Fla. Annual temperatures are

II:1 PHYSIOGRAPHIC REGIONS OF THE SOUTH

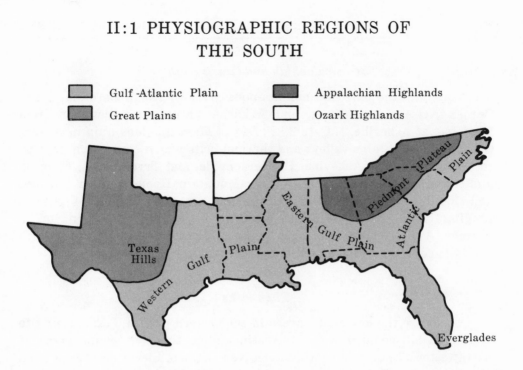

high, averaging 60° F. in Edenton, N.C.; 67.9° F. in Miami, Fla.; 72° F. in McAllen, Tex. Humidity is also unusually high, averaging 72.5 percent annually in Miami and 75.5 percent annually in New Orleans.

The Piedmont

This area lies just west-northwest of the Coastal Plain in North Carolina, South Carolina, and Georgia. It is 150 miles wide in North Carolina but narrows as it descends south. The land is heavily forested, with deciduous trees in the flatter and lower (below 300 feet) elevations in the east and more evergreens in the higher elevations (above 2,000 feet) in the west. Many of the larger cities—Charlotte and Raleigh, N.C.; Columbia and Spartanburg, S.C.; Atlanta and Macon, Ga.—are located at or near the fall line, where the Piedmont slopes sharply from the Coastal Plain. The area also contains such popular retirement towns as Chapel Hill, Southern Pines, and Pinehurst, N.C.; Camden and Aiken, S.C.; Greensboro and Thomasville, Ga. Temperatures and humidity average 47.8° F. and 69 percent in Raleigh, N.C. and 51.3° F. and 70 percent in Atlanta, Ga.

The Appalachian and Ozark Highlands

These are the pine-clad mountainous areas of North Carolina, South Carolina, Georgia, Alabama, and Arkansas, ranging in elevation from 2,340 feet at Asheville, N.C. to 2,823 feet at Magazine Mountain in Arkansas. The area contains valleys and thermal belts which house such popular retirement areas as Asheville, Hendersonville, and Tryon, N.C.; Clemson and Greenville, S.C.; Dahlonega, Ga.; Mountain Home, Eureka Springs, and Mountain View, Ark. Temperatures and humidity reflect all 4 seasons, ranging from −7° F. to 99° F. in Asheville, N.C., to zero to 90° F. in Eureka Springs, Ark. Humidity averages around 60 percent in most areas, with rainfall averaging 50 inches annually.

The Plains

These are the low plains areas in the eastern part of Texas, rising to the Texas hill country west of Austin and to the high plains areas of northwestern Texas and southeastern New Mexico. Elevation ranges from 550 feet at Austin to 4,260 feet at Clovis, N.M. Much of this land borders the Rockies and other mountains, and has been formed by drainage and erosion from the higher elevations. This has created such areas as the Pecos Valley and the Texas Hill Country, where many popular retirement towns lie: Clovis, Roswell, Artesia, and Carlsbad, N.M.; San Angelo, Wichita Falls, Alpine, Kerrville, Fredericksburg, Highland Lakes, Austin, and San Antonio, Tex. Annual temperatures and humidity range from 52° F. in January to 84° F. in July and 30 to 80 percent humidity in San Antonio to 41° F. in January to 77.5° F. in July and 5 to 30 percent humidity in Clovis, N.M.

The Deserts

These are the Mojave desert of California and the Sonora desert of Arizona and parts of southwestern New Mexico. Elevation ranges from below sea level in areas such as Death Valley, Cal. and east of El Paso, Tex. to 3,700 feet near Wickenburg, Ariz. The land is drier than the rest of the Sunbelt (average rainfall is less than 10 inches annually) and sunnier (sun shines more than 292 days a year). Humidity averages around 40 percent annually. The area contains mainly desert flatlands with eroded gullies and canyons, and broken up here and there with clumps of mountains. Vegeta-

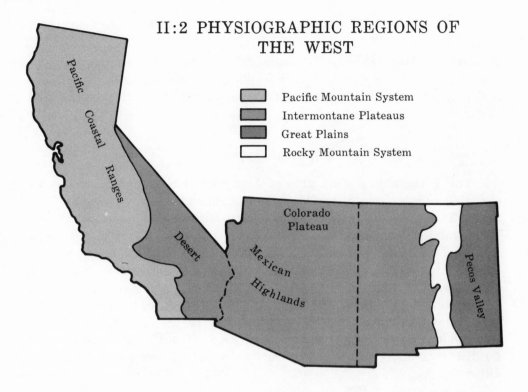

II:2 PHYSIOGRAPHIC REGIONS OF THE WEST

▨ Pacific Mountain System
▨ Intermontane Plateaus
■ Great Plains
☐ Rocky Mountain System

Pacific

Coastal Ranges

Desert

Colorado Plateau

Mexican Highlands

Pecos Valley

tion is sparse—mostly scrub bushes and desert cacti. However this area contains some of the most popular Sunbelt retirement communities: Hemet, Sun City, Riverside, Rancho Bernardo, and Palm Springs-Palm Desert, Cal.; Yuma, Green Valley, Tucson, Phoenix, Scottsdale, Mesa, and Cave Creek-Carefree, Ariz.; Alamogordo, Truth or Consequences, and Deming, N.M. Temperatures average in the 90s in the summer and in the 60s in the winter, and there's often a drop of 30 degrees or more between day and night.

The Southern California Coastal Areas

This is the area west of the coastal range of mountains from Santa Barbara south to the Mexican border. The area is green and lush toward the ocean and the climate is relatively stable; inland, the area becomes drier, the climate more extreme. This area contains the major coastal re-tirement areas of San Diego, Los Angeles, Escondido, and Santa Barbara. In the southern coastal areas around San Diego, the temperature averages 68° F. in summer and 57° F. in winter. Humidity stays at about 61 percent all year round, and about 10 inches of rain falls, mainly from December to March. Inland, around Escondido, the temperature averages in the middle 60s in the winter and in the high 80s in the summer. Nights are cool all year round and the humidity ranges from about 42 percent to 88 percent.

The Colorado Plateau

This is the high plateau area of Arizona and New Mexico, where the elevation ranges from about 4,240 feet at Sedona, Ariz., to almost 7,000 feet at Taos, N.M. The area is mountainous, with deep valleys and canyons (the Grand Canyon and Oak Creek Canyon), and high, dry plateaus, especially in northern parts. It contains favorite retirement areas such as Flagstaff, Kingman, Prescott, and Sedona, Ariz.; Albuquerque, Sante Fe, and Taos, N.M. It has a 4-season climate with summers averaging 70° F. and winters 58.6° F. and an average humidity of 45 percent in Prescott, Ariz. to an average of 25° F. in winter and 70° F. in summer with an average humidity of 45 percent in Sante Fe, N.M. Rain and snow average 50 inches annually in the lower elevations and 15 inches in the higher altitudes.

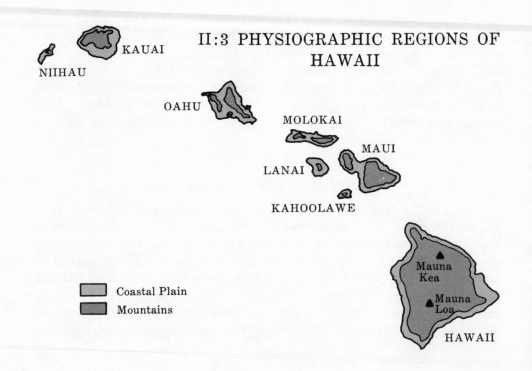

II:3 PHYSIOGRAPHIC REGIONS OF HAWAII

KAUAI
NIIHAU
OAHU
MOLOKAI
MAUI
LANAI
KAHOOLAWE
Mauna Kea
Mauna Loa
HAWAII

Coastal Plain
Mountains

The Hawaiian Islands

These islands lie in the north Pacific, 2,397 miles from San Francisco (5 hours by commercial jet). They consist of 8 major islands and 124 minor islands. The principal islands are Hawaii, the largest; Oahu, with Honolulu and Pearl Harbor; Lanai; Maui; Molokai; Kauai; Nihau; and Kahoolawe. The islands are volcanic; the highest point is Mauna Kea, on Hawaii, an extinct volcano 13,796 ft. above sea level. The average annual rainfall is 22.9 inches at Honolulu Airport, 133.57 inches at Hilo, and 486 inches atop Waialeale, a mountain on Kauai. Honolulu is subtropical (all-time range 57° F. to 88° F.), but Mauna Kea is often snowcapped. Relative humidity averages 71 percent annually, with 65 percent maximum possible sunshine.

2. VARIATIONS WITHIN EACH REGION

While the regions above share basic characteristics, each state offers varied climate and geography. In California, for example, I found summer temperatures of 60° F. on the ocean side of the coastal ridges and 105° F. just a few miles eastward on the other side. In Hawaii, on the trade wind slope of Mount Waialeale, the annual rainfall is 222 inches, but on the opposite slope just 10 miles away, it is only 15 inches.

In western North Carolina I've seen morning fog in summer and fall, while people a few hundred yards up the hillside were basking in sunshine. And in Arizona I've gone from winter to summer just driving down a mountain (from Prescott to Phoenix).

The following table summarizes the main physical and climatic characteristics of each region and the states that comprise them:

COASTAL PLAINS

STATES IN REGION	MAIN CHARACTERISTICS
North Carolina	high temperatures and humidity
South Carolina	sandy beaches
Georgia	saltwater marshes
Florida	tidal lagoons
Alabama	flat, fertile land
Mississippi	sea-level to 345 ft. elevation
Louisiana	
Texas	

THE PIEDMONT

STATES IN REGION
North Carolina
South Carolina
Georgia

MAIN CHARACTERISTICS
moderate temperatures and humidity
deciduous-evergreen forests
rolling hills
300 to 2,000 ft. elevation

APPALACHIAN-OZARK HIGHLANDS

STATES IN REGION
North Carolina
South Carolina
Georgia
Alabama
Arkansas

MAIN CHARACTERISTICS
four-season climate
pine-clad mountains
valleys and thermal belts
2,340 to 2,823 ft. elevations

THE PLAINS

STATES IN REGION
Texas
New Mexico

MAIN CHARACTERISTICS
moderate temperatures and humidity
eroded plateau areas
arid landscapes
550 to 4,260 ft. elevations

THE DESERTS

STATES IN REGION
New Mexico
Arizona
Southern California

MAIN CHARACTERISTICS
high temperatures but low humidity
sharp day-night temperature variations
desert flatlands
eroded gullies and canyons
scrub bushes and desert cacti
sea-level to 3,700 ft. elevations

SOUTHERN CALIFORNIA COASTAL AREA

STATES IN REGION
Southern California

MAIN CHARACTERISTICS
stable temperatures and humidity
coastal fog (sometimes smog)
lush growth near oceans
sea-level to 1,727 ft. elevation

COLORADO PLATEAU

STATES IN REGION
New Mexico
Arizona

MAIN CHARACTERISTICS
four-season climate
forested mountains
deep canyons
4,240 to 7,000 ft. elevation

HAWAIIAN ISLANDS

STATES IN REGION   MAIN CHARACTERISTICS
Hawaii   subtropical temperatures and humidity
                                    lush vegetation
                                    volcanic mountains
                                    extreme rainfall (some areas)
                                    sea-level to 13,796 ft. elevation

Cost of living and taxes also vary within each state. In Southern California, the cost of living (food, housing, medical care, transportation, and so on) is 10 to 20 percent higher on the coast than in the interior valleys.

Thus, your final choice of a place in the Sunbelt depends more on the *community* than it does on the state or region. Use the characteristics of each region and state as guides to the *right community* for you.

3. GUIDEPOSTS TO POINT THE WAY

In April 1974, Dr. Ben-chieh Liu of the Midwest Research Institute in Kansas City, Mo., and his associates launched a study to determine the quality of life in all the 243 Standard Metropolitan Statistical Areas (SMSAs) in the United States. Dr. Liu and his associates used five major components to measure quality of life: economic well-being; responsiveness and effectiveness of government; environmental quality; health and educational facilities; social well-being.

To add to this data, last year the Council on Municipal Performance analyzed pollution data for recent years in metropolitan areas and also rated cities for their responsiveness to citizen groups. And, in 1973, David and Holly Franke rated cities on the basis of freedom from crime (*Safe Places*, Arlington House).

The following list evaluates major retirement areas in the Sunbelt. It is based on the reports cited above plus my own travels and findings. These ratings are only guidelines—use the rating charts in Chapter III to make your own evaluations.

Population

Large	500,000 and over
Medium	200,000–500,000
Small	under 200,000

OVERALL RATINGS OF LARGE METROPOLITAN AREAS

Anaheim-Santa Ana-Garden Grove, Cal.	Excellent
Atlanta, Ga.	Good
Dallas, Tex.	Good
Fort Lauderdale-Hollywood, Fla.	Adequate
Fort Worth, Tex.	Adequate
Greensboro-Winston-Salem-High Point, N.C.	Poor
Honolulu, Hi.	Good
Houston, Tex.	Good
Jacksonville, Fla.	Adequate
Los Angeles-Long Beach, Cal.	Adequate
Miami, Fla.	Adequate
New Orleans, La.	Good
Phoenix, Ariz.	Adequate
San Antonio, Tex.	Good
San Bernardino-Riverside, Cal.	Adequate
San Diego, Cal.	Excellent
Tampa-St. Petersburg, Fla.	Adequate

OVERALL RATINGS OF MEDIUM METROPOLITAN AREAS

Albuquerque, N.M.	Good
Augusta, Ga.	Adequate
Austin, Tex.	Excellent
Bakersfield, Cal.	Good
Baton Rouge, La	Good
Charleston, S.C.	Good
Charlotte, N.C.	Adequate
Columbia, S.C.	Adequate
Columbus, Ga.	Adequate
Corpus Christi, Tex.	Adequate
El Paso, Tex.	Good
Fayetteville, N.C.	Good
Greenville, S.C.	Poor
Jackson, Miss.	Adequate
Little Rock, Ark.	Adequate
Macon, Ga.	Poor
Mobile, Ala.	Adequate
Montgomery, Ala.	Poor
Orlando, Fla.	Good

Pensacola, Fla.	Good
Raleigh, N.C.	Good
Santa Barbara, Cal.	Superior
Shreveport, La.	Poor
Tucson, Ariz.	Good
West Palm Beach, Fla.	Good

OVERALL RATINGS OF SMALL METROPOLITAN AREAS

Albany, Ga.	Poor
Asheville, N.C.	Good
Biloxi, Miss.	Adequate
Brownsville-Harlingen-San Benito, Tex.	Adequate
Durham, N.C.	Adequate
Fort Smith, Ark.	Adequate
Gainesville, Fla.	Good
Galveston, Tex.	Good
Lake Charles, La.	Adequate
McAllen, Tex.	Good
Midland, Tex.	Excellent
Monroe, La.	Adequate
Pine Bluff, Ark.	Adequate
San Angelo, Tex.	Good
Tallahassee, Fla.	Good
Tyler, Tex.	Excellent

III.

WHAT DO

YOU LOOK FOR?

Your housing is as personal as your dreams and as practical as your pocket-book. You and only you know what you need, want, and can afford. To help find *your* housing I suggest:

■ *Try to pinpoint the area* you'd like to settle in by studying Chapter II. Also write the Administration on Aging, Department of Health, Education and Welfare, Washington, D.C. 20201 or the U.S. Department of Housing and Urban Development (HUD) Information Center, 7th and D Streets, S.W., Washington, D.C. 20410 for housing suggestions. If health is a factor, check with your doctor.

■ After you've pinpointed the area, *write to the specific state units on aging.* They are located in the state capitals. Ask about location and availability of housing; cost of living and taxes; climate and environment; special facilities for seniors, including tax exemptions. Be as specific as possible.

■ Then *write to the chambers of commerce* of the various cities and towns you're interested in. No street address is necessary but the zip code is desirable. Again, specify what you're looking for. A friendly (or no) answer from the chamber of commerce will tell you whether the welcome mat is out.

■ *Subscribe to weekly or Sunday papers* to learn about the area's businesses; social life; cost of food, clothing, appliances; and real estate prices.

■ *Vacation there*—off-season as well as on. Get the pulse of the town; is it brisk in the morning but dull in the evening? Are weekdays somber and weekends lively?

■ *Get to know the people*—the postman, grocer, real estate agent, librarian, chamber of commerce people as well as the people you meet in clubs, town meetings, houses of worship—are they friendly or do they avoid strangers? How long would it take you to go from "stranger to neighbor" (two years is about average)?

■ *Rent before buying*. Rent a house, apartment, mobile home—the type housing you'd like—before buying. *Rent your home* "back home." If you decide you don't like your new community, you'll always have a place to retreat to.

1. HOW TO SIZE UP ANY COMMUNITY

You can judge any community by these categories: (1) climate and environment; (2) health aspects and facilities; (3) housing costs and availability; (4) cost of living; (5) leisure-time activities; (6) special services and facilities for seniors.

Below are specifics in each category. The more items you can check favorably, the better the community. Most important: *Is the new community better than your previous one* in those aspects that are important to you?

1. Climate and Environment

■ *Temperature.* Does the summer average between 66° and 71° F. _____? winter 63° and 71° F., depending upon clothing you can wear _____? Do nighttime temperatures average 50° to 56° F. for best sleeping _____?

■ *Humidity.* Does the relative humidity range from 30 percent to 70 percent with an average of 55 percent _____?

■ *Temperature-humidity index.* Does the index average *under* 72 (over that one starts to feel uncomfortable) _____?

- *Sunshine or clear days.* Are there at least 200 such days a year _____?

- *Elevation.* Under 6,000 feet but above sea level _____?

- *Scenery and views.* Does it have the vistas you like _____? Are there enough trees, flowers, other plants to your liking _____?

- *Pollution.* Is the air relatively free from smoke, pollution, smells _____?

- *Noise.* Is it quiet enough for you (both ground and air traffic) _____?

- *Shopping.* Are there adequate shops, stores for basic needs (food, clothing, housewares, drugs, laundry, shoe repair, TV and radio repair, restaurants, and so on) _____?

- *Services.* Are there adequate banks, postal, legal, and civic offices and services _____? Can you get a driver's license _____?

- *Police and fire protection.* Do you have local police and fire departments and is this reflected in insurance rates _____?

- *Transportation.* Is there adequate public transportation (buses, taxis) _____?

- *Surrounding area.* Are you near a larger town, city, shopping center that might have items you need and want and can't get locally _____? Is there convenient transportation to this area _____?

2. Health Aspects and Facilities

- *Health advantages.* Is the community noted for any outstanding health facilities or research centers, or natural attributes such as climate, mineral waters, and so on _____?

- *Water.* Is the water tasty and pure (try some) _____? Does sewerage seem adequate with few or no septic tanks _____? Is there an adequate supply for present and future needs of the community _____?

- *Hospitals.* Is there a community hospital or health maintenance organization that has enough beds (at least 5 per 1,000 population) _____?

- *Dentists, Doctors.* Are there doctors and dentists who will accept new patients (particularly you) _____? Is one on call at all times _____?

- *Nursing facilities.* Is there a nursing home in the area and/or adequate community home-care facilities (meals on wheels, visiting nurses, homemakers, and so on) _____?

■ *Clinics.* Are there community clinics and/or emergency care facilities _____?

■ *Specialists.* Does the community have specialists who can treat your particular problem _____?

3. Housing Costs and Availability

■ *Costs.* Are they in line with what you can afford _____?

■ *Availability.* Is there enough housing available for you to have two or three choices _____? Can you buy or rent?

■ *Variety.* Is there sufficient housing variety: single-family houses _____? apartments _____? co-ops and condominiums _____? mobile home parks _____? nonprofit housing for the elderly _____? retirement communities _____? retirement hotels _____? life-care housing _____? vacation homes _____?

4. Cost of Living

■ *Food.* Do food costs seem reasonable _____? Can you buy locally grown produce and meats from local farmers _____? Can you grow your own _____?

■ *Taxes.* Do taxes seem reasonable and can you afford them? Must you pay extra for services or are they covered by taxes _____? Do taxes go up every year _____? Have they just been raised or are they expected to be raised _____? Do county or other taxes fill the gap in taxes omitted by your community _____?

■ *Earning money.* Are there part-time jobs available (the more retirees, the more the competition) _____? Are there temporary help agencies _____? state employment offices with older worker specialists _____? nonprofit employment agencies specializing in finding jobs for seniors _____?

■ *Energy costs.* Are gas and electricity both available _____? Are the rates reasonable _____? Are they expected to rise soon _____? Is it possible that power or heating-cooling energy might be curtailed (brownouts or blackouts) _____? What happens to power during storms _____?

■ *Services.* Are there plumbers, handymen, carpenters, repairmen of all kinds _____? Are their services reasonably priced _____? Can you get someone to do "odd jobs" at reasonable rates _____?

5. Leisure-Time Activities

■ *Cultural facilities.* Are there libraries _____? art galleries or museums _____? theaters _____? FM classical stations and public service TV programs available _____? local TV, radio, and newspapers _____?

■ *Social activities.* Are there clubs of your choice _____? houses of worship _____? service clubs or chapters you might belong to _____?

■ *Educational opportunities.* Are there adult education courses or classes available in local schools _____? informal classes at libraries, senior centers, Y's, churches, clubs, etc. _____? craft and hobby courses and facilities _____?

■ *Outdoor recreation.* Are there parks _____? swimming pools _____? horseback, bike, and hiking trails _____? gardens and gardening facilities _____?

■ *Peer groups.* Are there people of your age _____? interests _____? ethnic background _____? occupational or academic interest _____? members of the opposite sex _____? members of the same sex _____?

6. Special Services and Facilities for Seniors

■ *Senior clubs.* Are there senior centers _____? other senior clubs _____? senior groups in churches and other mixed-age groups _____?

■ *Tax exemptions.* Are there special property-tax exemptions for seniors _____? personal tax exemptions _____? housing or homestead exemptions _____? discounts for seniors (entertainment, medicines, food, personal items, and so forth _____?

■ *Offices on aging.* Is there a local or area office on aging _____? counseling for seniors at various civic groups, service clubs, senior centers _____? active state office on aging (did they reply to your letter) _____?

■ *Special programs or services for seniors.* Are there such programs sponsored by local groups _____? Special transportation services (dial-a-

ride, public transportation discounts, limousine or other services for bank-
ing, shopping, and so on) _____?

Make your own checklist. Choose those items which are most important to you, and rate them: 1, vital; 2, important; 3, casually concerned.
Write the number on the line (use a minus sign if the answer is no). *Use
the same rating system for each community* you're interested in, then add
up the score. *Be sure to compare it with your present community;* you
might find that you're better off not moving.

ESTABLISHING LEGAL RESIDENCY

If you move to a Sunbelt state, you should *establish legal residency*
and make sure *your will conforms to your new state's law.* If you don't,
both your old and new state could claim a share of your estate in the
form of death taxes.

Generally, you can establish legal residency in one of several ways:

1. Filing a Declaration of Domicile with the Clerk of the County
   or State Court.

2. Registering to vote.

3. Remaining in the state for 6 months or more.

4. Engaging in trade, profession, or occupation in the state or
   accepting employment in other than seasonal agricultural work.

5. Declaring yourself a resident for the purpose of obtaining at
   resident rates any state license or tuition fees at any educational
   institution maintained by public funds.

If you're in doubt about your new state's law, check with your
local lawyer, banker, city officials, library, state or local agency on
aging. The rules aren't complicated, but it's wise to make sure you've
taken the necessary steps to assure that you're a legal resident. Don't
forget to notify the tax authorities of your previous state that you
have legally changed residence.

---

2. OTHER POINTS TO CHECK

1. *Can you get a good location?* If you're selecting a homesite, choose
the southeast or south side of a mountain or hill to protect you from cold
north and northwest winds. The same applies to apartments: Pick a
southern or southeasterly apartment to give you more sun and fewer
weather extremes.

2. *Are you at the right elevation?* If you want to escape ground fog or pollution, you should be 300 to 500 feet above ground level. In apartments, a higher floor means less noise and a better view, but perhaps higher rent. And, remember, annual mean temperature decreases about 5° F. for every 1,000 feet of elevation. On a mountain ridge 2,000 feet high and at right angles to the storm winds of winter, select the lee side part way up.

3. *What about sound control?* Sound travels in annoying ways, and you might find you're in a "noise zone" even if you're on a hill. This is particularly important if your homesite is near a freeway. You might want to eliminate outside noise while enhancing indoor acoustics.

4. *Is it safe?* Your housing should have some sort of alarm device, smoke detector, and automatic dialer system on telephones to summon help if needed.

5. *Does your housing have the right layout?* In terms of general layout, your housing should have these features:

- *all rooms on one floor*—no thresholds or walking hazards;

- *doors and halls wide enough* to accommodate a wheelchair;

- *lighting*—perhaps three times as much lighting as for younger families, including good lighting in all hallways and near stairs;

- *nonslip surfaces*—unglazed ceramic tile, unwaxed vinyl or vinyl asbestos in kitchen and bathroom; rugs and carpets firmly anchored;

- *heating and cooling*—central heating and cooling to supply 70–75-degree temperatures (winter and summer) in each room;

- *separate sleeping quarters*—you should have one or more bedrooms (or a sleeping alcove) to allow privacy and permit sick care.

6. *Do you know how to buy country property?* Buying a "farmette" in the country can be more difficult than buying a house in the city. Ask your librarian or send for *Buying Country Property* by Herbert R. Moral ($3 from Garden Way Publishing Company, Charlotte, VT 05445).

7. *Are you getting bitten by a land shark?* Never buy land for speculation and never buy land site unseen. Don't take "promised developments" at face value; find out any restrictions on building, construction, landscaping. Be sure to get, read, and *understand* the property report that the U.S. Department of Housing and Urban Development requires builders to provide to prospective buyers. Most important: *Try to find the real value of*

the land. Land in a development may be priced at 15 to 100 times its actual value. Find out what land is selling for around your property; the county tax assessor should know.

If you have any questions about buying land, contact the Federal Office of Interstate Land Sales Registration, 451 Seventh Street, S.W., Washington, D.C. 20411. Some states have real estate offices that can help you. For California land write to Real Estate Department, 714 P Street, Sacramento, CA 95814. Florida, write to Division of Land Sales and Condominiums, 310 South Calhoun, Brock Bldg., Tallahassee, FL 32304.

8. *Have you taken energy needs and crises into account?* Any location that depends upon natural gas (which recently went up in price and may be in short supply) or that is without adequate electricity may be in for trouble. Areas of the Sunbelt that depend upon enormous amounts of electricity for air conditioning (such as Southern California, Arizona, New Mexico, Florida, and so on) may be subject to "rolling blackouts" in which utilities are forced to shut down several hours a day to conserve fuel. If you're building a home and would need these services *be sure you can get a guaranteed fuel supply,* perhaps by inserting a contingency clause in your contract. Also, be wary of any location that requires you to travel far in your own car; a gasoline shortage and the inevitable rise in gasoline prices could leave you high and dry.

If you build a house in the Sunbelt, consider installing solar heating. You can install these units for $2,000 to $6,000, and your investment will be paid off within 10 years because of your savings in oil, gas, or electricity. *You'll never have to worry about an energy shortage,* although you'll need some backup equipment for cloudy days. Many Sunbelt states— including Arizona, New Mexico, and Texas—have already passed some sort of tax incentive for installing solar energy. For details on solar heating get these publications from the Government Printing Office, Washington, D.C. 20402: "Solar Heating and Cooling" ($1.50) ; "Solar Dwelling Design Concepts" ($2.30) ; "Making the Most of Your Energy Dollars in Home Heating and Cooling" (70 cents) ; "In the Bank—Or Up the Chimney. A Dollars and Cents Guide to Energy-Saving Home Improvements" ($1.70).

For further information contact the federally financed National Solar Heating and Cooling Information Center, Post Office Box 1607, Rockville, MD 20850; Solar Energy Industries Association, 1001 Connecticut Ave., N.W., Washington, D.C. 20036; and Acorn Structures, Inc., Post Office Box 250, Concord, MA 97142. Acorn Industries has developed houses with solar heating that cost $43,500 and up, with solar equipment valued at $7,500.

9. *Always try it before you buy it.* If you rent in your new community while renting your home "back home" you can evaluate your new house at your leisure and still have the option of returning "home" if you aren't satisfied. Another idea is to *swap houses* with someone in your new area. Four major home-exchange clubs will let you list your home, for a fee of about $15.00, in their directories, then leave it to you to exchange letters and make any arrangements. Write to:

Vacation Exchange Club
350 Broadway
New York, NY 10013

Interchange Home Exchange
888 Seventh Ave., Suite 400
New York, NY 10019

Holiday Home Exchange Bureau
Post Office Box 878
Belen, NM 87002

Adventures in Living
Post Office Box 278
Winnetka, IL 60093

and ask for details. Note that the deadlines for listings are about 6 months in advance of the time you might want to swap.

10. As a general rule, *don't buy into a retirement or vacation community that has been in existence for less than six or seven years.* New condominiums or retirement communities may set maintenance and recreation charges low at first to attract tenants, but once the place is established they may turn recreation facilities over to tenants (who then must pay higher charges) and/or raise maintenance charges. Talk to people living there to find out what's happened to property values, whether the buildings and facilities have deteriorated unreasonably, and what sort of people the community is attracting. Retirement communities are shaped by the people who live there; make sure they're "your kind." Retirees of the same religion, ethnic background, economic status, even job interest often retire in the same place—and exclude others. You should be part of the "in group"—whatever the stripe.

I've applied the above standards to all the places I've visited and written about. I've lived, worked, or visited in all these areas, and have just returned from an extensive "refresher" tour of the Sunbelt. Here now are my state-by-state reports on Sunbelt retirement.

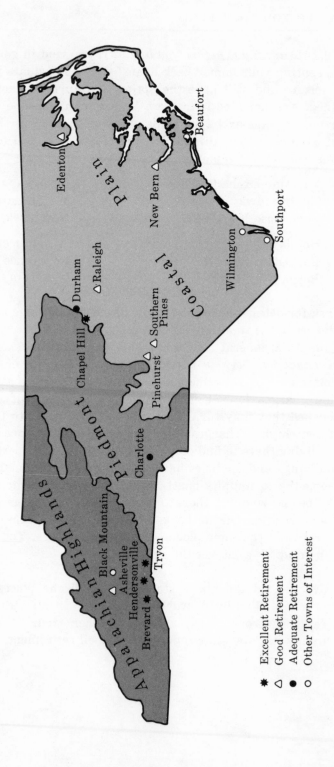

NORTH CAROLINA

Appalachian Highlands

Black Mountain
Asheville
Hendersonville
Brevard
Tryon

Piedmont

Chapel Hill
Durham
Raleigh
Charlotte
Pinehurst
Southern Pines

Coastal Plain

Edenton
New Bern
Beaufort
Wilmington
Southport

★ Excellent Retirement
△ Good Retirement
● Adequate Retirement
○ Other Towns of Interest

IV.

NORTH CAROLINA—

BETWEEN SOUTHERN DREAMS

AND NORTHERN REALITIES

North Carolina is not a state of extremes. It's predominantly middle income with moderate values. As a Northerner I could feel "at home" here.

North Carolina was one of the first states to rejoin the Union after the Civil War, and it led the South in racial relaxation and economic progression. It has more variety of trees than all of Europe: chiefly pine in the Coastal Plains and hardwood in the Piedmont region. But it also contains exotic flora: the flowering crepe myrtle, the chinaberry, yaupon trees, Venus's-flytrap, mountain laurel, flame azalea, wild orchid, and kudzu vine. This natural beauty makes it an oasis between Northern realities and Southern dreams—a day's drive from families in the North and resorts in the South.

Some 13.2 percent of the Tarheel State's population is age 60 or over. About 50 percent of the retirees live in the central Piedmont area, 30 percent in the Appalachian Highlands, and 20 percent in the Coastal regions. Each segment of the state offers unique advantages to retirees.

The Moderating Climate

The temperature seldom gets over 90° F. or under 30°, and the average year-round temperature for the state as a whole is 59° F. with 69 percent humidity. However, North Carolina offers a wide range of moderate climates; the warmest part is the southeastern low country around Southport and Wilmington, and the coldest part is 6,684-foot Mt. Mitchell in Yancey County. Average temperatures for the 3 principal regions:

	Spring	Summer	Fall	Winter
Coastal Plain annual average: 61° F.	60° F.	77° F.	60° F.	44° F.
Piedmont Plateau annual average: 59.5° F.	59° F.	77° F.	60° F.	42° F.
Appalachian Highlands annual average: 55° F.	54° F.	71° F.	56° F.	38° F.

The Modest Cost of Living

To live comfortably in North Carolina, I estimate a retired couple should have an annual income of about $10,000. Food costs would comprise 29.6 percent of the total ($2,960), housing (mortgage or rent, furnishings and household operation) 33.9 percent ($3,390), transportation 8.9 percent ($890), and other (medical care, personal care, clothing) 27.6 percent ($2,760).

North Carolina has the highest overall taxes in the South (approximately $898 annually on a $10,000 income), which break down as follows:

State income tax—3 percent on first $2,000, rising to 7 percent over $10,000. Heads of household (including single people *without* dependents) get a $2,000 exemption; if two single adults share an apartment, one is entitled to $2,000 exemption, the other to $1,000; single people a $1,000 exemption; taxpayers over age 65 get an additional $1,000 exemption.

Property taxes (per $100 actual value)—the state does not levy such taxes, but counties and cities do. The average county tax is about 71 cents per $100; city tax, 73 cents; some rural fire districts, 10 cents. Combined average tax per $100 value totals approximately $1.53 on property within cities and towns. Counties and cities have exemptions for seniors if income is $9,000 or less. Assessed values of real property vary from about 50 to 90% of current market value due to the 8-year cycle of revaluation.

Intangibles tax—classes of property and rates per $100:

CLASSES OF PROPERTY	RATES PER $100
money on deposit	10 cents
money on hand	25 cents
notes and bonds receivable	25 cents
market value of shares of stock owned on Dec. 31 of each year to the extent the issuing corporation is conducting business outside North Carolina	25 cents
interest on foreign trust	25 cents
deposit with insurance company	10 cents

Retail sales tax—3 percent on most items; many counties add an additional 1 percent. Tax does not apply to prescription medicines, false teeth, eyeglasses, or utility services. Motor vehicles, boats and airplanes are taxed at 2% subject to a $120 maximum; the 1% local tax does not apply.

An Abundance of Housing

Housing in North Carolina ranges from picturesque shacks to tidy brick houses to antebellum mansions with graceful porches guarded by stately pillars. Some housing costs $25,000, but most new two- to three-bedroom homes start at approximately $35,000. Average two- to three-bedroom retirement housing costs approximately $40,000. Prices are highest in resort areas of the coasts and mountains, e.g., Blowing Rock. Here, $45,000 is typical for a retirement home and property taxes run about $1,100 a year. Prices are lower in remote rural areas in the western mountains around Brevard, where homes sell for about $30,000.

The High Quality of Medical Care

North Carolina has excellent medical facilities. These include the famed Duke University Center for the Study on Aging at Durham, the 486-bed University of North Carolina Medical School Hospital at Chapel Hill, the 724-bed Asheville Community Hospital plus the new 640-bed Asheville Veterans Hospital and Orthopedic Hospital, the 891-bed Charlotte Memorial Hospital and 507-bed Presbyterian Hospital, and the 2,765-bed Raleigh Mental Hospital. Smaller communities also have good medical facilities: the New Bern Community Hospital has 259 beds and 80 doctors; Black Mountain has the Highland Farms Retirement Health Community where there is 1 registered nurse for every 6 residents. The state has 161 hospitals with 34,441 beds; 231 nursing homes with 13,890 beds; 607 personal care homes with 8,225 beds. There are 7,591 doctors in the state, an average of about 1 doctor per 728 residents.

Culture Is King

With over 50 colleges and universities, North Carolina leads the Sunbelt in the number of adult education courses and classes. In fact, the state leads the country in the number of Ph.D.'s per 100,000 population. The famed "Research Triangle" of Durham-Raleigh-Chapel Hill claims 708 Ph.D.'s per 100,000 population, compared to New York City, which has only

119 per 100,000 population and Boston, which has only 264 per 100,000 population. Retirees are among the active scholars: the University of North Carolina in Charlotte waives fees for its Senior Scholars program and seniors at Fayette State College earn degrees through a combination of weekend classes and independent studies. The Sandhills Community College in Southern Pines-Pinehurst has a continuing education division which offers courses ranging from bridge to estate planning. Included are several courses specially for seniors: health and nutrition, arts and crafts, and retirement planning. Other communities offer educational and cultural opportunities, e.g., the State Museum of Art and State Symphony Orchestra in Raleigh; the Transylvanian Music Center at Brevard; the educational TV and classical music stations in Chapel Hill. Most community colleges will offer a course on any subject for which 10 or more students sign up and will either waive the fee for seniors or charge minimum fees. Writers, artists, musicians, scientists, doctors, lawyers, and other professionals have traditionally retired in North Carolina just for the intellectual advantages.

Leading Services for Seniors

North Carolina leads the Sunbelt states in the number of senior projects, with 54 projects covering nutrition, health, housing, transportation, financial and legal assistance, recreation, cultural activities, telephone reassurance, information and referral, homemaker service, shopping assistance. Besides the progressive State Office for Aging, North Carolina has some 90 councils on aging that provide a hot meal program, transportation and other services, as well as recreation. Most popular is the daily hot meal program, which is open to anyone over age 60. Seniors contribute what they wish or what they can. Even those who can afford restaurant meals like to come to these centrally located nutrition sites because they can meet friends as well as get a low-cost nutritious meal.

North Carolina is also the first state in the South to offer prepaid legal services to groups or businesses of 10 or more persons for $65 to $75 a month per family.

For more information on services for seniors, write:

Executive Director
North Carolina Division on Aging
708 Hillsborough St.
Raleigh, NC 27603

For a booklet outlining state taxes, write:

> Secretary, Department of Revenue
> Box 25000
> Raleigh, NC 27602

1. THE COAST—"DOWN YONDER" FOR RETIREMENT

Tarheel residents refer to Coastal (eastern) North Carolina as "Down Yonder." It covers about a third of the state and includes 338 miles of beaches. Many seaside resorts—Atlantic Beach, Pine Knoll Shores, Indian Beach—border on banks, offshore islands, and peninsulas, allowing residents access to rivers and sounds as well as the Atlantic Ocean. The Coastal area draws seniors who can vacation here during the winter months at low or no cost (Atlantic Beach has offered such free vacations). All developed oceanfront resorts and much of the Cape Hatteras National Seashore are linked to the mainland by toll-free bridges and causeways. A favorite sport here is to sail to Florida via the protected Inland Waterway.

Coastal North Carolina is a land of churches, barbecues, steamed clams, Brunswick stew, tobacco, peanuts, and livestock. The area boasts some 150 specialty seafood restaurants such as Tony's Sanitary Seafood Restaurant in Moorhead City where I ate a delicious flounder dinner for only $3. The tiny town of Calabash alone has some 18 seafood restaurants, and you can dine in turn-of-the-century atmosphere in restaurants like Henderson House in New Bern, which specializes in antiques and Old World charm.

"Down Yonder" is also a land of pine and white oak, the flowering crepe myrtle, the chinaberry and the yaupon tree. It is home to the Azalea Festival held each spring in Wilmington. The area has 115 all-weather tennis courts, 35 golf courses, 42 ocean-fishing piers, 18 art galleries, and 74 antique shops.

Bogue Banks, lying east-west from Beaufort Inlet is the site of such popular resorts as Atlantic Beach, Pine Knoll Shores, Emerald Isle, and Indian Beach. Quaint fishing communities, such as Harkers Island, Smyrna, Stacy, Davis, Williston, Sealevel, Atlantic, and Cedar Island abound; here residents can trace their ancestry to the earliest Colonial days. The historic port city of Wilmington is the gateway to Wrightsville, Carolina, Wilmington, and Kure beaches. Nearby is Southport, with Caswell, Yaupon, and Long beaches.

Historic Edenton—Retirement with Colonial Charm

Edenton, an historic town that reflects much Colonial charm, is located on Albemarle Sound. It has many well-preserved antebellum houses dotting the waterfront and lining the picturesque streets. Of the 10,000 inhabitants who live in Edenton and Chowan County, about 20 percent are retired.

Climate and Environment. Edenton is located in a highly diversi-fied agricultural and industrial area, with a mild climate that allows for year-round recreation: golf, tennis, swimming, fishing, hunting, boating, and sailing. The average normal temperature ranges from a low of 42° F. in December to a high of 79° F. in summer. The average annual tempera-ture is 60° F. Wettest month, July; driest month, October. The annual rainfall is 48 inches with some light snow. In April, jonquils, tulips, irises, lilies, and climbing roses bloom in masses. Huge elm, pecan, and magnolia trees make green tunnels of residential streets. Most streets are narrow, some only a block or two long, and traffic (both cars and people) moves leisurely. Walkways are painted across the one main street of the three-block business district; pedestrians have the right of way. Some 35 build-ings in town and 20 in the country are considered "historic landmarks."

Medical Facilities. Edenton has a 120-bed hospital, over a dozen doctors, 4 dentists, 2 medical centers, nursing home facilities, and an emergency rescue service.

Housing. Rental housing is scarce, and historic buildings are prohibi-tively high-priced, but two-bedroom retirement homes in and around Eden-ton sell for an average of $40,000.

Cost of Living. Property taxes are relatively low. The city tax is 68 cents and the county tax is 90 cents per $100 valuation.

Recreation and Culture. Edenton sponsors a full-time recreation pro-gram for young and old, and features a public library, visitor center, arts council, craftsman fair, choral society, little theater, and waterside parks.

Special Services to Seniors. Edenton has many fraternal, religious, and social clubs of particular interest to seniors. All recreational programs emphasize senior participation.

For further information: Edenton Chamber of Commerce, Drawer "F," Edenton, NC 27932.

New Bern—Good for Families and Retirees

New Bern, located at the mouth of the Neuse and Trent rivers, is a thriving seaport of some 16,000 people, about 20 percent of whom are re-

tired. Its tree-canopied streets include over 67 major historic points, including more than 3 dozen restored 18th- and 19th-century buildings
(George Washington stayed in one) and Tryon Palace Complex, once home
to royal Colonial governors. Thoughtfully placed chairs allow strollers to
rest. Shops are everywhere, and there is a pleasant bustle of people enjoying themselves working and sightseeing.

Climate and Environment. Lying near the coast, New Bern is warmed
in winter and cooled in summer by Gulf Stream air. The average annual
temperature is 63.3° F.; January is the coldest month, averaging 46.9° F.,
and July is the warmest month, averaging 80.3° F. Average annual precipitation is 55.41 inches including occasional light snowfall.

Medical Facilities. New Bern has a 259-bed hospital and over 80
physicians and surgeons specializing in all branches of medicine.

Housing. The Redevelopment Commission of New Bern is developing
22 acres in a 3-block area along the Trent River, adjoining the present
business district. Proposed development plans call for a blend of residential,
residential-commercial, and commercial buildings, and a motel. First-class
apartments or condominiums are to be placed above small retail stores to
create a waterfront village. Also planned are a major department store, a
governmental office building, an open-air amphitheater for cultural activities, and a 60-store enclosed shopping mall. *Fairfield Harbour* development
offers waterfront building lots, homes, condominiums convenient to sailing,
boating, swimming. *Fairfield Harbour* includes a country club, golf course,
lighted tennis courts, and recreation center. To buy or build a two-bedroom
home costs $40,000 and up. Further inland on the Trent River is *River
Bend Plantation*, where two- to -three bedroom homes located on the river
or near the golf course cost $44,000 to $70,000. *River Bend* offers fishing,
boating, skiing, riding, tennis, and golf. Within New Bern two- and three-
bedroom homes are available from $30,000 to $55,000. An average new home
costs approximately $45,000. Rentals are scarce, especially during the sum-
mer, but off-season—September to May—rentals are available at lower
prices. In October, a typical two-bedroom apartment rents for $190 a month
and a three-bedroom house for $275 a month. Building lots sell for $9,000
and up, and existing two-bedroom houses for about $40,000.

Cost of Living. New Bern's total property tax is slightly lower than
Edenton's: $1.17 per $100 valuation versus $1.58. And, this is still con-
siderably lower than the state average of $1.53 per $100. New Bern city tax
is 45 cents; county tax 62 cents; school and fire district taxes 10 cents each.
Motel rooms and restaurant meals cost less than in many parts of the

state. The Quality Inn is as little as $15 a night, and a complete steak dinner at the Flame restaurant is around $10.

Recreation and Culture. New Bern is the home of the first provincial printing press in the U.S. New Bern maintains a full and active recreational and cultural program, including Craven Community College where many retirees work, teach, and take classes. Fees are approximately $75 per quarter. The town's active retirement program includes such activities as ceramics, arts and crafts, and table tennis, as well as Golden Age and Senior Citizens, Recreation Coin, Deaf, Adult Sports, and Take Off Pounds Sensibly clubs. New Bern also features a civic theater, historical society, garden clubs, and most religious and fraternal orders. An interesting ethnic note: New Bern has a small Lebanese population which has put its stamp on restaurants and cultural activities.

Special Services for Seniors. Besides the several programs mentioned above, the Chamber of Commerce maintains a special committee to help retirees get settled.

For further information:

> New Bern Craven County Chamber of Commerce
> 211 Broad Street
> New Bern, NC 28560

Other Coastal Towns of Interest

Beaufort (pop. 4,000)—still retains the charm of early seaport days. It shares the same mild climate of New Bern, with even more cooling sea breezes in summer and warming Gulf Stream currents in winter. Fishing is particularly good here and many retirees literally "fish for their supper." Beaufort also offers outstanding cultural attractions, including a little theater, symphony, historical and heritage society, and the summer School of Fine Arts (a branch of the University of North Carolina). Retired businessmen have formed an Emeritus Club, and other retirees work as cashiers and clerks in restaurants, motels, and shops. Beaufort has a number of charming two- to four-bedroom homes built in Bahamian style by ship's carpenters. These have been restored and sell for $40,000 and up. Other existing and some new two- to three-bedroom houses are available from $35,000. Rentals are normally available during the winter from $200 a month and up for a one- to two-bedroom unit. Near Beaufort is *Morehead City* (pop. 6,000), also popular with retirees. And just a few miles from the town of *Swansboro* (pop. 2,000) is Hammocks Beach State Park, where you can stroll unspoiled beaches in search of shells.

For further information:

Chamber of Commerce
Beaufort, NC 28516

Chamber of Commerce
Morehead City, NC 28557

Wilmington (pop. 55,000). This historic port city is gateway to Wrightsville Beach, Carolina Beach, Wilmington Beach, Kure Beach, and Fort Fisher. A toll ferry operates between Fort Fisher and Southport on the mainland side of the Cape Fear Peninsula. Wilmington is famous for its Azalea Festival each spring and is a port city rich in history and old homes. Many Northern military, executive, and professional people retire here, because living costs are at least 10 percent lower and building costs 20 percent lower than in most Northern cities. The sun shines 65 percent of the time, the air is clean, and the area has been recommended by doctors for sufferers of sinus, hay fever, and arthritis conditions. There are 50 active clubs—including the Executives Club, which invites visiting lecturers—open to retirees, and the area receives educational TV programs and FM classical music stations. Golfing, fishing, hunting, sailing, and gardening are favorite activities. The mild winters (39° F. to 57° F.) and warm summers (72° F. to 87° F.) permit 3 to 4 annual crops of flowers, grapes, berries, and most vegetables, including strawberries, which some retirees raise for extra money. Retirees have part-time jobs in hotels, motels, restaurants, theaters, real estate offices, and in shipping industries. Wilmington has many new brick homes with central air conditioning; a two-bedroom unit sells for $35,000 and up. Some two-bedroom apartments are available for $200 and up (monthly rental on a year-round lease). A full-range of medical services is available at the 419-bed New Hanover Memorial Hospital in Wilmington and the 99-bed Cape Fears Memorial Hospital.

For further information:

Chamber of Commerce
Wilmington, NC 28401

Southport-Oak Island (combined pop. 5,000). This area lies about 30 miles south of Wilmington, and is situated on a high bluff overlooking picturesque river traffic—yachts and sailing vessels of all descriptions. Southport people are especially proud of the town's historic sites, live-oak trees, and colorful marinas. Oak Island, just across the Intracoastal Waterway, has beautiful beaches and a tranquil environment. The Southport-Oak Island area, which includes Yaupon Beach, Long Beach, and nearby Boiling Springs Lakes, attracts many retirees. Two-three bedroom homes range from $20,000 to $150,000; average price is between $30,000 and $35,000. Taxes average 86 cents per $100 assessed value, including county, town and 4 cent Dosher Hospital tax. Dosher, a full-care facility located in Southport, is 6 to 10 minutes distance from other towns. There is excellent charter and pier fishing, boating, golf, tennis and other sports in the area.

For further information:

Chamber of Commerce
Southport-Oak Island, NC 28461

2. THE PIEDMONT—WHERE THE (PEACEFUL) ACTION IS

Heading from New Bern toward the central part of the state, one notices that the land resembles an eastern West—rural and open but grassy. Many towns classify themselves as "bird sanctuaries." Farmers' roadside stands with an abundance of produce and roadside rest areas—some specially equipped for the handicapped—abound.

The Piedmont area of North Carolina consists of the retirement towns of Winston-Salem, High Point, Greensboro, Chapel Hill, Durham, Raleigh, Southern Pines, Pinehurst, Charlotte, and Gastonia. It starts at the Research Triangle formed by three institutions of higher learning: Duke University (Durham), the University of North Carolina (Chapel Hill), and North Carolina State (Raleigh). The cities of Charlotte, Winston-Salem, Raleigh, Greensboro, Durham, and High Point have both old and new gleaming shopping centers alongside the Colonial charm of older neighborhoods. In the countryside, one can still savor pioneer sights and sounds: rural stores dispensing "Mountain Dew," potters humming along with their wheels, farmers clucking to horses and mules as they plow the fertile tobacco soil.

As one travels south through the Piedmont, the red clay hills soften to great sand dunes covered with long-leafed pines and orchards. This is the area for golfing, riding, hunting, and relaxation.

The Sandhills Area—Leisure with Luxury

The Sandhills area consists of the towns of Aberdeen, Carthage, Pinehurst, Pinebluff, Southern Pines, West End, Foxfire, and Whispering Pines. The "Pines" are the most prominent retirement areas. *Southern Pines* (pop. 8,000) and *Pinehurst* (pop. 1,100) can best be described as the Monterey and Carmel of North Carolina.

Climate and Environment. The Sandhills area is distinguished by its sandy, hilly terrain. It is banana-shaped, about 11 miles wide and 22 miles long, and contains one of the world's finest golfing complexes (68 miles or 333 holes of golf stretch in wide green belts throughout the area). It is protected from severe continental winters by the Appalachian Mountains, and the sandy surface soil provides rapid drainage, leaving the land free of puddles and mud slick. Most summer rainfall occurs as local thunder-showers; snow is infrequent—occurring once or twice per winter month. The coldest month is December, with a mean temperature of 43.9° F., the warmest is July with 78.8° F. The average temperature for summer is 77° F.; fall, 60° F.; winter, 42° F.; and spring, 59° F. Precipitation averages 50 inches per year with an average humidity of 50 percent and an average annual temperature of 61.6° F.

Medical Facilities. Besides the famed Duke University Center for the Study on Aging (Durham), the Sandhills area also has Moore Memorial Hospital, which is staffed and equipped to handle all medical specialties. Moore County has over 62 physicians, 19 dentists, 500 hospital beds, a skilled nursing home, a mental health center, and 11 veterinarians.

Housing. While housing is scarce in the Sandhills area, some single-family two- to three-bedroom homes are available. Costs range from below $40,000 to above $50,000. More moderate comparable housing ($35,000 and up) is available at Pinebluff. In Pinehurst two- to three-bedroom condominiums, including golf membership, are available at $70,000; in Southern Pines, at $60,000. Many fairway lots are for sale at $9,000 to $30,000. Building costs are about $30 per square foot. Some of the more popular developments include *Seven Lakes, Foxfire, Lake Surf, Whispering Pines*—all offering country-club living. Many clubs are "exclusive" but racial and religious barriers are fast disappearing.

Cost of Living. Piedmont cost of living is higher than in the rest of the state, and the Sandhills area is probably the most expensive rural area of all. Retired couples need anywhere from $7,500 to $15,000 annually ($10,000 is about average) to live comfortably. The cost of living, ex-cluding taxes, is about the same as that of Buffalo, N.Y.—about 5 percent above the national average. Moore County has a 4 percent tax (including the state 3 percent tax), and a property tax of 75 cents per $100, based on 100 percent of value. In addition to the county property tax, there are property taxes for the various communities (per $100 valuation): Aber-deen, $1.00; Pinehurst, 66 cents; Southern Pines, $1.00; Whispering Pines, 32 cents. These rates also apply to tangible personal property, but there is an exemption of $7,500 for residents of 65 or older whose spendable in-come does not exceed $9,000.

Recreation and Culture. Golf is king in the Sandhills area, but retirees engage in many other activities from tennis to raising dogs and horses to playing bridge. One of the biggest events of the year, the Stoneybrook Race Meet, attracts some 25,000 spectators. Weymouth Woods, a state nature preserve, is just to the east of Southern Pines. This 400-acre preserve has a museum and visitors' center, and well-marked trails through hilly, stream-laced forests. The Pinehurst Forum brings cultural events (guest lecturers, musicians, and so on) to the area. The community also boasts a little theater group, an arts council, 3 flourishing bookshops, and 4 well-stocked community libraries. Sandhills Community College has a continuing education division offering a variety of courses in aging, health and nutrition, arts and crafts, creative writing, retirement planning, and more. The college will teach any course if a minimum of 12 students sign up. Shopping, especially in Southern Pines and Pinehurst, is a delight.

Special Services for Seniors. As 11 percent of residents are retired or semiretired, activities are geared toward seniors. There are also seniors clubs in most areas.

For further information:

> Sandhills Area Chamber of Commerce
> Post Office Box 458
> Southern Pines, NC 28387

Chapel Hill—"The Southern Part of Heaven"

Chapel Hill (pop. 35,243), with its Colonial beauty, ivy-clad Georgian buildings, and dignified, tree-shaded campus of the University of North Carolina, is the perfect setting for an American Mr. Chips movie. Despite the 35,000 residents (many associated with the university), Chapel Hill looks like an English village. The entire town—including the students— gives a feeling of being neat and tidy. Compared to similar university towns, Chapel Hill is quieter than Ann Arbor, cleaner than Berkeley, and quainter than Princeton.

Climate and Environment. The average temperature in winter is 48.5° F. and in summer 71.7° F.; the average mean temperature is 59.6° F. The average annual rainfall is 45 inches with an average snowfall of 8 inches. The town is rimmed by cool woodlands, with huge trees everywhere. Dominating the town is the 552-acre campus, with over 100 buildings, including the Morehead Planetarium, Coker Arboretum, and the Ackland Art Museum.

Medical Facilities. Chapel Hill has the U.N.C. Medical School, a 750-

bed hospital, 63-bed psychiatry unit, 150-bed chest disease hospital, U.N.C. Dental School and Clinic, and scores of private physicians and dentists. Extensive medical facilities at Durham (Duke University) are only 12 miles away.

Housing. Chapel Hill is home to low-income students and moderately salaried faculty, and housing is reasonably priced and varied. Many two-bedroom condominiums (with tennis courts, swimming pool, clubhouse) sell from $42,000; two- and three-bedroom houses sell for $45,000 and up; two-bedroom apartments rent for $185 a month and up (unfurnished but with complete kitchens, swimming pools, central air conditioning).

Cost of Living. By taking advantage of many low-cost student activities, restaurants, and shops (the Eastgate Shopping Center has a Poor Richard's surplus store offering standard household items at 10 to 20 percent below list price), a retired couple can live in Chapel Hill for under $10,000 a year. But taxes are higher here than in most other parts of North Carolina: the county tax is 84 cents per $100 property value and the city tax is 1.12, bringing the total to $1.96, about 43 cents above the statewide average and in line with taxes in the more expensive Sandhills area (preceding). A retired couple not taking advantage of low-cost student shopping and eating might pay over $10,000 annually just for essentials.

Recreation and Culture. Here's where Chapel Hill excels. Many retirees audit classes at the university for a small fee and attend low-cost or free university concerts, plays, movies, and other cultural events. Chapel Hill has an educational TV station; classical music stations; superb bookstores and libraries; art galleries and antique stores. The Chapel Hill Recreation Department offers a variety of classes from guitar to oil painting to auto mechanics to tennis. It has 2 golf courses, several tennis courts, and a public swimming pool. Private facilities for horseback riding, fishing, and hunting are available.

Special Services for Seniors. Although Chapel Hill has many senior clubs, most retirees are so active and involved in campus and other community activities that they blend into the scene. This is *the* place for intellectual activity as well as physical fitness. Don't come here unless you're prepared to *do* something.

For further information:

> Chamber of Commerce
> Post Office Box 127
> Chapel Hill, NC 27514

Charlotte—Queen City of the Carolinas

Charlotte (pop. 310,000) is the largest city of the Carolinas and it offers the shopping, cultural, and medical facilities of Downtown as well as the comfortable climate and environment of Main Street. It is situated in gently rolling country, and is the textile, financial, distribution, and transportation center of both the Carolinas.

Climate and Environment. Situated at 765 feet and protected by the mountains to the west, Charlotte enjoys a moderate climate that allows outdoor activity about 8 months a year. January is the coldest month with an average temperature of 42° F., and average maximum of 51° F., and an average minimum of 33° F. Summers are warm but not oppressive. Temperature for July averages 79° F. with an average maximum of 88° F. and an average minimum of 69° F. Precipitation is evenly distributed throughout the year, averaging 43.09 inches, including 5.7 inches of snow during winter. Humidity is relatively stable, averaging a not uncomfortable 68 percent annually. About 64 percent of the days are sunny, and the average wind velocity is only 6.9 miles per hour.

Medical Facilities. Charlotte is one of the Southeast's outstanding medical centers with its 3 large general hospitals, 2 specialty hospitals and 1 hospital for long-term patients. Two hospitals have their own nursing programs. The Mecklenburg County Medical Society operates the largest privately owned medical library in the South.

Housing. Because of the recent recession, there is an unusual variety of good homes available in Charlotte. Many two- to three-bedroom houses are priced at approximately $45,000. Charlotte also has many fine condominiums; two-bedroom units sell for around $45,000. Luxury-priced units (2-bedroom) sell from $60,000 to $123,000. The most popular and desirable areas to live seem to be in the eastern, southern, and southeastern sections of the city.

Cost of Living. The county tax rate is 79 cents per $100 valuation; the city tax is 88 cents per $100, for a total of $1.68—2 cents below the state average and lower than Chapel Hill or the Sandhills area. However, *a car is a must* in Charlotte as the public transportation is poor. Once downtown, there are excellent shopping centers concentrated mainly around the Tryon-Trade Streets Square. There are more than 50 shopping centers in the area. Retirees have found jobs in the health field (especially as nurses) and in secretarial, service, construction, auto repair, and other "handyman" capacities.

Recreation and Culture. Charlotte has an opera association, symphony orchestra, oratorio society, art museum, Coliseum Auditorium, and a community college where retirees can take no-cost or low-cost courses. Two major recreational lakes, a nature museum, and Carowinds (an amusement complex) are also nearby. Plans are under way to renovate downtown Charlotte as a cultural center, and to increase nighttime activities.

Special Services for Seniors. The Charlotte Chamber of Commerce is especially helpful in getting newcomers settled, and there is also a Newcomers Club and a New Neighbors League that assists retirees. Retirees make friends through many volunteer opportunities in public schools, hospitals, parks and recreation programs, and so on. Contact the Volunteer Action Center for more information about these opportunities and for a list of clubs and organizations in the Charlotte area. Almost every alumni association, cultural group, civic organization, and other club is represented.

For further information:

> Chamber of Commerce
> 222 South Church Street
> Charlotte, NC 28201

Other Piedmont Towns of Interest

Raleigh (pop. 165,000)—This capital city is located in the geographic center of the state, and is the major governmental, financial, and retail center of eastern North Carolina. However, it has a small-town appearance —the tallest building is the Center Plaza Building, 22 stories high. Raleigh is really urban-suburban, and most buildings look as though they were designed at the turn of the century. The State Capitol would pass as a main library or university annex in many cities, and this low-key appearance adds to its charm. Raleigh has 6 colleges (including North Carolina State University), 3 museums, a state fairgrounds and an arena, memorial auditorium, and civic center. Race relations are easy and cordial. Food and other costs seem relatively low. Two- and three-bedroom homes sell for $30,000 and up.

For further information:

> Chamber of Commerce
> Box 2978
> Raleigh, NC 27602

Mooresville (pop. 9,000)—This town lies 27 miles north of Charlotte and shares the same mild climate. It offers retirees a full recreation program including bowling, tennis, golf, bridge, and other card games. Davidson College (with a superior library) offers excellent cultural activities. Some retirees live here on Social Security benefits alone; others have found jobs with local industries. Good 130-bed hospital; and housing starts at around $35,000 for a two-bedroom retirement home.

For further information:

Chamber of Commerce
Mooresville, NC 28115

Salisbury (pop. 25,270)—This progressive city, 42 miles northeast of Charlotte, has the largest Senior Citizen's Club in North Carolina. It also offers concerts, art museums, little theater (home of the Piedmont Players), and a well-equipped library. Colleges offer seniors night classes and the city recreation department features classes in art, ceramics, interior decorating, and more. Local industry has provided jobs to seniors, especially in restaurants, motels, and other service industries. Two-bedroom brick houses sell for approximately $35,000 to $40,000, and two-bedroom monthly rentals are normally available at $200 to $250 a month.

For further information:

Chamber of Commerce
Salisbury, NC 28144

3. THE APPALACHIAN HIGHLANDS—"LAND OF THE SKY"

As one heads east toward Gastonia, the hills get steeper, the air crisper, and the sky bluer. History and heritage have been preserved in the Highlands. It is a land where uncommon beauty is common. Rhododendrons, mountain laurel, flame azaleas, and wild orchids grow free; bear, whitetail deer, ruffled grouse, fox squirrel, Russian boar, and several other species roam the woods. It is also the home of hundreds of retirees who have settled in such towns as Gastonia, Hickory, Lenoir, Blowing Rock, Boone, Morganton, Black Mountain, Asheville, Brevard, and Tryon.

Highland Farms is a retirement health community outside Black Mountain. The atmosphere here is more like a big family gathering than a health center, and it operates on a "pay as you go; pay for what you get" basis. Efficiency apartments cost about $4,000 with a basic monthly rental (light, heat, water, sewer maintenance, emergency nursing service) of about $200. Fees go to around $7,000 for a two-bedroom apartment, with about $400 monthly rental. There is a fee of around $100 per month for 1 meal daily. Meals are substantial and offer an interesting variety of foods. The Farms has 1 registered nurse for every 6 residents, and the emphasis is on rehabilitation.

Residents come from 33 states and 9 foreign countries. Ninety-five percent are college graduates, including some deans, librarians, teachers, and other professionals. The ratio of men to women is 1:2. The average resident's age is near 80, however residents range in age from their early 60s to over 90.

Residents live here for about $6,000 annually if single; around $9,000 if married. The community has 120 apartments, and a new wing contains indoor shuffleboard, whirlpool baths, arts and crafts areas. A commissary supplies limited food stuffs at supermarket prices so residents can prepare their own meals; a snack bar serves quick meals. Each unit is equipped with a two-way speaker system connected directly to the main nursing station of the Health Care center and emergency care is available day or night.

Many Highlands Farms residents are active in *Black Mountain* (pop. 4,000) civic affairs, because it, too, has many retirees. Black Mountain is only 15 miles from Asheville (see below), one of the most popular retirement centers in North Carolina; however living costs in Black Mountain are 10 percent lower than in Asheville.

Asheville—Center of Unlimited Variety

Asheville, with an altitude of over 2,000 feet and ringed by mountains, retains nostalgic charm while offering big-city amenities. The handsome hotels and civic buildings look as fit and trim as the many retired admirals, generals, and other military leaders it has attracted. Many visitors say *Asheville* (pop. 60,000) reminds them of Colorado Springs, itself a mecca for retired, wealthy military personnel.

Climate and Environment. Asheville enjoys a temperate but invigorating climate. Prevailing winds are from the northwest during all months of the year, and the temperature can vary 20 degrees or more during a summer's day. Temperature extremes have ranged from 7° F. *below* zero to 99° F. However, the average temperature for January is 35.8° F.; for April 55.9° F.; for August 71.5° F. The annual average—54.7° F.

Medical Facilities. Health care facilities are unusually good, with some 215 physicians practicing in the area, including widely recognized specialists. Hospitals, among them a very modern 434-bed unit, rate excellent; there's also a new 640-bed Veterans Administration hospital providing radioisotope and cobalt therapy.

Housing. Two- and three-bedroom retirement houses are available from $30,000 and up; unfurnished one-bedroom apartments rent for under $200 a month; two-bedroom for around $250. The Asheville Chamber of Commerce (see below) publishes a "Housing Apartment Guide" listing available apartments, public housing projects, realtors, banks, and finance companies.

Asheville boasts 5 retirement hotels, offering room and board for approximately $400 monthly per person.

For details write:

The Princess Anne Retirement Hotel
301 East Chestnut Street
Asheville, NC 28801

The Altamont Apartments
76 North Market Street
Asheville, NC 28801

The Manor Retirement Hotel
265 Charlotte Street
Asheville, NC 28804

The Aston Towers Apartments
165 South French Broad Avenue
Asheville, NC 28801

The Vanderbilt Apartments
75 Haywood Street
Asheville, NC 28801

Cost of Living. Most costs, including taxes, are higher here than in other Appalachian cities. Per $100 property valuation, the city tax is 92 cents, county tax 73 cents, city school tax 17 cents. As the school district includes one area outside the incorporated area, and one area within the city is not subject to the school tax, the highest combined Asheville tax is $1.82 per $100 actual value; the lowest combined is $1.65 (state average is $1.53).

Recreation and Culture. Both indoor and outdoor activities are available, including sightseeing at the largest Indian museum of the Cherokee Nation, Great Smoky Mountains National Park, and the Joyce Kilmer Memorial Forest. Asheville has bowling alleys, bridge clubs, dancing clubs, golf, hiking, horseback riding, and so on. The Asheville Community Concert Association gives 5 concerts a year featuring world-renowned artists. The Community Theater Association produces Broadway and Off-Broadway shows with local casts.

Special Services for Seniors. Asheville has 2 fine organizations especially for seniors: Harvest House, 205 East Kenilworth Road, and Senior Opportunity Center, 36 Grove Street. They offer craft rooms, radio, TV, woodworking shops, lending libraries, coffees, teas, card parties, exhibits and picnics, auctions, hobby shows, shuffleboard, horseshoes, table tennis, and classes in ceramics, native crafts, decoupage, handiwork, weaving, holiday decorations, and gifts.

For further information:

Chamber of Commerce
Post Office Box 1011
Asheville, NC 28802

Hendersonville—"The Ideal Retirement Community"

Hendersonville (pop. 8,000) has been described as "the ideal retirement community." About 15 percent of the population is age 65 or over, although all age groups are represented. Distinctive features include an attractive new shopping mall—with serpentine streets to discourage through traffic and lined with top-quality stores—picturesque Victorian dwellings and restaurants, and wooded lanes, perfect for leisurely strolling.

Climate and Environment. At 2,200 feet, Hendersonville enjoys the advantages of a mountain climate, while being protected from severe winter outbreaks by the Great Smoky Mountains. Although the temperature drops below freezing on more than half the winter nights, it rises above freezing in the afternoons. Summer weather is cooler by 5 degrees, both day and night, than most Coastal and Piedmont cities. The mean summer temperature is 71° F., and the winter mean is 41° F.

Medical Facilities. Hendersonville has 65 physicians and 25 dentists; a 234-bed short-term general hospital; a 100-bed fully accredited general hospital; a 15-bed clinic and hospital.

Housing. New two- to three-bedroom homes range from about $50,000 up, although some are available for under $40,000. To build on your own lot (from $3,500) costs about $30 per square foot. One-bedroom apartments rent from $175 a month, and houses from $300 a month. However, during the "season," from May to September, rentals are scarce. See the chamber of commerce's helpful "accommodations directory" listing of available rentals in apartments and motels, and its list of realtors (see below).

Cost of Living. Henderson County levies a sales tax of 1 percent and a county tax rate of 64 cents per $100 assessed value. City tax inside the corporate limits of Hendersonville is 90 cents per $100 value, plus a special school district tax of 30 cents—a total of $1.84 per $100 of true value. Some fire districts add 5 to 7½ cents per $100 valuation.

Recreation and Culture. Hendersonville has many unique cultural and recreational attractions including the Flat Rock Playhouse, the first state theater, which is rated as one of the 10 best summer theater companies in the United States. It also has its own symphony orchestra, flower and antique shows, folk and music festivals, county fairs and horse shows, garden clubs, and street dances. "The County Curb Market," open all year on Tuesdays and Saturdays, features homemade, hand-crafted, and old-fashioned products such as churned butter, country lard, mountain herbs, rugs, quilts, aprons, sunbonnets, bird houses, sun-dried apples, cottage cheese, brown eggs, and gourds. The market is held in an indoor building on one of the main streets, and farmers' wives knit and chat as people browse. Dining in Hendersonville is also a nostalgic experience. At the famous Woodfield Inn, a former stagecoach stop decorated with relics from several Victorian living rooms, you can enjoy homemade biscuits, crispy Southern fried chicken, and home-baked desserts for less than a sandwich lunch in Manhattan.

Special Services for Seniors. Hendersonville is so oriented to the needs and desires of retirees it publishes a special "Retired Residents Directory" listing the state, home town, and former occupation of the residents as well as their phone numbers. *Opportunity House,* a famous cultural center with over 1,800 senior members, is located here as well. Learning (fine arts, crafts, special events like the annual Book-and-Author Dinner and the arts and crafts fair), serving (sewing for the Red Cross and other organizations and making craft items for distribution by the Salvation Army and other worthy groups), and fellowship (weekly lectures, discussions programs, tours, sports and games, photography, and other activities) are stressed. Opportunity House is managed by and for its members and is financed primarily by the sale of handicraft items in its gift shop and a few fund-raising activities. Fees from patron and life memberships supplement dues collected from most participants.

For further information:

Chamber of Commerce
330 North King Street
Hendersonville, NC 28730

Other Places of Considerable Interest

Brevard (pop. 8,000). Although it is only 18 miles away, picturesque roads that meander through dense forests make Brevard a half-hour trip by car from Hendersonville. This town offers as much as many large cities.

The chief attraction is the music festival held each summer, which features some 40 performances: operas, musicals, concerts, and so on. The town also has a theater group and arts council and an active recreation program, which offers square dancing. For the nature-minded, there are miles of trails through the Highlands, complete with cascading waterfalls and tumbling streams. Housing costs are moderate: some condominiums sell for under $40,000; houses for approximately $45,000 and up; and three-bedroom homes rent for only $325 and up per month. County property tax 79 cents per $100 true market value; city tax 82 cents per $100.

For further information:

Chamber of Commerce
Brevard, NC 28712

Tryon (pop. 4,000). Tryon is a retirement gem. At almost every turn there are farmers' stands where you can buy fresh farm and orchard produce. The fascinating kudzu—an Oriental ornamental vine—cloaks the trees and scrubs. (This exotic beauty eventually strangles what it embraces.)

Tryon is sheltered by mountains to the north and east, but is warmed by a relatively free southern exposure. The average annual temperature is 70° F. and it is seldom below freezing. The "worst" climatic feature is the abundant rain, which, combined with the warm weather, makes "almost anything and everything grow" (garden clubs are unusually popular). About 50 percent of Tryon's 4,000 residents are retired. The retired population is diverse—it represents all states and many foreign countries, people from the top of the business world and from the arts. Tryon's spectacular Fine Arts Center is home to theater, crafts, concerts, painting, sculpture, and classic films. Tryon retirees tend to be very independent and private, and while they may participate in some group activities (like church groups), the emphasis is on the individual. "People come here to live—they go to Florida to retire" is how one resident put it. Tryon does have many activities, including an 18-hole championship golf course, horse shows, and "The Meeting Place," an "enrichment center" for retired residents, which provides game rooms, dining areas, craft rooms, gift shops, and so on.

County real estate and tangible personal property taxes are $2.16 per $100, based on property valued at approximately 50½ cents per $100; city taxes are $1.20 per $100, based on property valued at approximately 30 cents per $100. Housing ranges in price from $40,000 to $500,000 for two to three bedrooms, with the average around $75,000. Tryon also has White Oak Terrace, which offers complete retirement living, including long-term care.

For further information:

Chamber of Commerce
401 North Trade Street
Tryon, NC 28782

SUMMARY

North Carolina is a "halfway house" for retirement—near enough to the family still living in the North, yet enjoying the warmth of the South. The charming accents and customs are gentle and not as pronounced as farther South; North Carolina would be one of the easiest states for a Yankee to retire in. It offers diversity and a stimulating environment for both indoor and outdoor activities—plenty to do to nourish the mind and stimulate the body.

A couple of drawbacks: Liquor laws—Until recently, North Carolina state law prohibited hard liquor to be sold in bars or even restaurants except for "private clubs," where you must be a member. Recently, the state approved a local-option measure and some communities allow mixed drinks to be sold. And although some bars and restaurants serve beer and wine, in others you must "brown bag" your own hard liquor or forget about it.

Poor highways and transportation—While roads in North Carolina are adequate, the only really good highway is Interstate 95. Many roads are two-lane, they wind and twist, and if you get stuck behind a truck or a bus, it can be difficult to pass. Also, public transportation is poor or nonexistent in many areas. *A car is a must* if you want to travel in the Tarheel State.

In the chart following this and each state chapter, I've rated the retirement towns discussed according to: (1) climate and environment; (2) medical facilities; (3) housing; (4) cost of living; (5) recreation and culture; (6) special services for seniors. These ratings are based both on the statistical material I gathered and my personal observations. To effectively evaluate any community I urge you to study the checklist in Chapter III. Plan a trip and at least a brief stay to "get the feel" of the place. Before you go, write to the chamber of commerce for additional information.

Here are my ratings for North Carolina's major retirement areas:

Excellent—Chapel Hill, Hendersonville, Tryon, Brevard;

Good—Southern Pines, Asheville, Raleigh, Edenton, New Bern, Pinehurst;

Adequate—Charlotte, Durham.

RATINGS FOR *NORTH CAROLINA* MAJOR RETIREMENT

NEW BERN

Rating	Climate & Envir.	Medical	Housing	Cost of Living	Rec. & Culture	Spec. Senior Svces.
1						
2						
3						
4						
5						

EDENTON

Rating	Climate & Envir.	Medical	Housing	Cost of Living	Rec. & Culture	Spec. Senior Svces.
1						
2						
3						
4						
5						

SOUTHERN PINES

Rating	Climate & Envir.	Medical	Housing	Cost of Living	Rec. & Culture	Spec. Senior Svces.
1						
2						
3						
4						
5						

PINEHURST

Rating	Climate & Envir.	Medical	Housing	Cost of Living	Rec. & Culture	Spec. Senior Svces.
1						
2						
3						
4						
5						

CHARLOTTE

Rating	Climate & Envir.	Medical	Housing	Cost of Living	Rec. & Culture	Spec. Senior Svces.
1						
2						
3						
4						
5						

CHAPEL HILL

Rating	Climate & Envir.	Medical	Housing	Cost of Living	Rec. & Culture	Spec. Senior Svces.
1						
2						
3						
4						
5						

ASHEVILLE

Rating	Climate & Envir.	Medical	Housing	Cost of Living	Rec. & Culture	Spec. Senior Svces.
1						
2						
3						
4						
5						

HENDERSONVILLE

Rating	Climate & Envir.	Medical	Housing	Cost of Living	Rec. & Culture	Spec. Senior Svces.
1						
2						
3						
4						
5						

BREVARD

Rating	Climate & Envir.	Medical	Housing	Cost of Living	Rec. & Culture	Spec. Senior Svces.
1						
2						
3						
4						
5						

TRYON

Rating	Climate & Envir.	Medical	Housing	Cost of Living	Rec. & Culture	Spec. Senior Svces.
1						
2						
3						
4						
5						

1 = Excellent
2 = Good
3 = Fair
4 = Poor
5 = Unacceptable

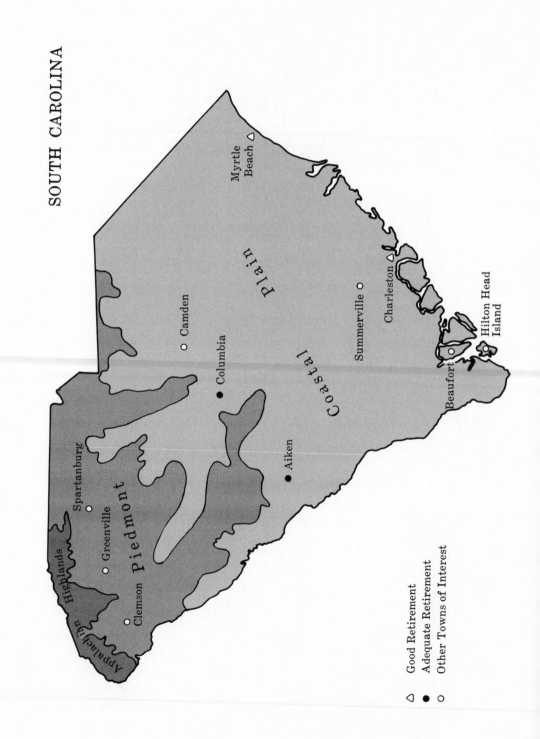

SOUTH CAROLINA

Myrtle
Beach △

Plain

Charleston △

Summerville ○

Coastal

Camden ○

Columbia ●

Beaufort ○
Hilton Head
Island

Spartanburg ○

Greenville ○

Piedmont

Clemson ○

Highlands

Appalachian

Aiken ●

△   Good Retirement
●   Adequate Retirement
○   Other Towns of Interest

V.

SOUTH CAROLINA—

A RURAL "GARDEN OF EDEN"

Descending from North to South Carolina, the land begins to slope more and roll more gently. The highway was one of the best on my trip through the Sunbelt (South Carolina's highways are superior) and the countryside and hamlets reflected more of the Deep South.

South Carolina's topography and geology are like a low-profile North Carolina: mountains in the northwest; a Piedmont section in the center; a Coastal Plain in the southeast. But South Carolina looked more "foreign" to me: white, smooth beaches reminiscent of the Caribbean; Charleston with a West Indian look; luxurious gardens rivaling those of England.

Over 250,000 persons, or 8.7 percent of South Carolina's population of 2,867,000 is age 65 or over. The most popular retirement center in the state is the coastal area—the "Grand Strand" from De Bordieu Beach to North Myrtle Beach; the Charleston area—from Seabrook Island to Isle of Palms; the Hilton Head Island/Beaufort Beach area; the Aiken area; Columbia and the Clemson/Greenville/Spartanburg area.

The "Southern" Climate

In South Carolina winters are short and mild, spring begins in mid-February; summer starts in May and runs through September; fall continues until December. Temperatures may vary 5 to 10 degrees F. from the southern beaches to the northern mountains on any given day, but in the midlands (Columbia) the January average is 53.1° F. and the July average is 73.1° F. The annual humidity averages 75.5 percent with 55.51 inches of rain.

Several factors are responsible for the pleasant, mild, humid climate. South Carolina is located at a relatively low latitude (32 degrees to 35 degrees N.) and most of the state is under 1,000 feet elevation. The warm Gulf Stream flows along most of the coastline, and the mountains to the north and west block or delay many of the cold air masses approaching from these directions. Even the deep cold air masses which cross the mountains rapidly are warmed somewhat as they descend on the southeastern slopes. This allows for an average growing season of 294 days. At least 50 different crops are grown here, the main ones are cotton, tobacco, grains, soybeans, and peaches. Many retirees supplement their income by raising vegetables, flowers, and fruits for sale or for their own use.

A Lower Cost of Living

South Carolina has few metropolitan areas; 52.8 percent of the residents live in rural, semirural, or small-town settings. Many two- and three-bedroom homes in these smaller areas are available for as little as $30,000. The cost of living here is generally lower than in North Carolina, and for a retired couple the cost of living in South Carolina is approximately *one-tenth below the national average*. In other words, if the national average yearly intermediate budget for a retired couple is $9,000, a couple can live reasonably well in South Carolina on about $8,100.

South Carolina's taxes are at least 15 percent lower than North Carolina's. Taxes are structured as follows:

State income tax—2 percent on first $2,000 net income increasing to 7 percent on net income over $10,000. Personal exemptions are $800 per person, but taxpayers over age 65 get an additional $800 exemption. There's also a $1,200 exemption of pension income for retirees age 65 or older and for those with 20 or more years active service with the U.S. Armed Forces.

Property taxes—the state doesn't levy these taxes, but cities and counties do. They average about $100 per $10,000 of actual valuation ($300 on a $30,000 house). Homeowners age 65 or over get a $12,000 homestead tax exemption from both county and municipal taxes. Property tax information is available in the booklet "A Handbook for South Carolina Residents," available at most banks and savings and loan institutions.

Intangibles tax—South Carolina does *not* tax intangibles.

Retail sales tax—a 4 percent sales tax is levied on almost everything except prescription drugs or prosthetic devices. Seniors get half-price admission to state park facilities, free hunting and fishing licenses, and free tuition at state educational institutions.

Independent Housing for Independent Living

Most retirees in South Carolina live in two- or three-bedroom single-family housing (costing about $35,000) in a regular community rather than in retirement villages or communities. In general, rental property is scarce, although South Carolina does have many rental projects exclusively for older people throughout the state. Most are public housing facilities constructed by local housing authorities for low-income residents, and there is usually a waiting list. Rent depends upon income, but varies from $80 to $200 a month. These units are located primarily in Spartanburg, Greenville, Columbia, Laurens, Union, Marion, Aiken, Florence, Lake City, Conway, Sumter, Rock Hill.

These areas also have nursing homes with apartment-type semi-independent living facilities, plus regular nursing home facilities. The state also regulates and licenses many boarding homes for older people.

For further information:

> South Carolina State Housing Authority
> Suite 540
> 2221 Devine St.
> Columbia, SC 29205

Widespread Health Facilities

Although Charleston, Columbia, and Greenville are the main medical centers, each of the 46 county seats contains a health department which offers X-rays, immunization, clinic services, and visiting services by public health nurses, dieticians, physical therapists, and nurses' aides. A Home Health Services Program helps people confined to their homes. Some 110 nursing homes in South Carolina offer intermediate or skilled care to over 7,000 persons and a nursing home ombudsman employed by South Carolina receives complaints or reports from patients and their families and seeks to resolve problems. Community-level services are provided by mental health clinics and centers located throughout the state. Inpatient care for mentally ill persons 55 years of age and older is provided at Crafts-Farrow State Hospital, the S. C. War Veterans Home, and the Long Term Care Center. The state has 88 hospitals with a total of 18,253 beds; 110 nursing homes; 13 personal care homes with 621 beds; 3,489 physicians (1 per 821 residents).

For further information:

"A Directory of Personal Health Services"
S.C. Department of Health and Environment Control
2600 Bull Street
Columbia, SC 29201

A Vigorous and Flourishing Arts Climate

South Carolina has many programs appealing to seniors. Presently the state sponsors some 60 drama organizations, 60 art galleries and museums, over 20 community dance companies, and 5 community symphony orchestras. The South Carolina Open Road Ensemble travels across the state presenting live theater to schools, colleges, community organizations, and seniors' groups. And the South Carolina Arts Commission, as well as many local arts councils and agencies, sponsor arts programs for seniors. The Commission also has a ticket subsidy program under which local organizations may make tickets available to senior citizens at greatly reduced prices.

For further information:

South Carolina Arts Commission
1800 Gervais Street
Columbia, SC 29201

Many Recreational Opportunities for Seniors

Local recreation departments throughout the state offer programs to seniors, ranging from simple checker games to extensive tours. They also use seniors as volunteers or part-time help in operating various programs; retirees serve as umpires, scorekeepers, coaches, instructors, teachers, lecturers, and Santa's helpers. Most recreation departments also set up "Country Stores" where retirees may display and sell items they have made in craft classes—from jewelry to canned vegetables.

All South Carolina state parks reduce rates by 50 percent for seniors for all user charges excluding cabin rentals. Camping programs for seniors are offered at Oconee State Park.

South Carolina is one vast fishing hole with 291 species of fish, ranging from the 250 miles of trout streams in the mountains, 400,000 acres of prime fishing lakes across the midlands, to surf, pier, and Gulf Stream angling in the Atlantic. The Palmetto State also has 115 golf courses— along the "Golf Coast" from the semitropical islands of Hilton Head and Fripp, and the Myrtle Beach golf mecca, to small towns such as Santee, Johnston, and Fort Mill.

With the longest deer season of any state, South Carolina hosts thousands of hunters annually. Rabbits, possum, raccoon, quail, dove, deer, bear, and wild turkey are plentiful.

For further information:

> S. C. Department of Parks, Recreation, and Tourism
> Edgar A. Brown Building
> Columbia, SC 29201

For retirees who want to finish their formal education, the South Carolina Department of Education offers programs in basic and high school education in over 600 adult education centers, located in every school district of the state. Younger retirees who want second careers can get vocational and technical training in all areas of the state. South Carolina features "enrichment" programs (reading, hobbies, new skills) in most areas.

For further information:

> S. C. Department of Education
> Office of Public Information
> Rutledge Building
> 1429 Senate Street
> Columbia, SC 29201

Many Services for Seniors

South Carolina's Commission on Aging is unusually active in providing services for seniors. It works with all schools of higher education to develop courses on gerontology, the social science of aging, for practitioners and for older people themselves. It also serves as an advocate for the state's older citizens and tries to find solutions to their problems. It works with other agencies; administers federal, state, and other funds for appropriate uses; provides 6,000 hot meals daily; conducts pilot programs such as Nursing Home Ombudsman, Home Winterization, Health Screen; stimulates legislation; trains people who work with seniors; promotes special events such as College Week for Seniors at Clemson University, Senior Citizens' Day at the State Fair, Camping, Open House, and various statewide conferences. It also distributes a bi-monthly newsletter to workers in the field of aging and compiles and publishes the comprehensive "Retiring in South Carolina."

For further information:

> South Carolina Commission on Aging
> 915 Main Street
> Columbia, SC 29201

1. COLUMBIA: THE CAPITAL GEM FOR RETIREMENT

At first, Columbia (pop. 112,000 city; 390,000 metropolitan) seems an ordinary small city. There is only 1 flourishing main street and only 1 impressively beautiful building, the State Capitol. But it does have cosmopolitan touches: broad boulevards (some 150 feet wide); hotel rooms decorated in Chinese modern; first-rate Continental restaurants, like the Tivoli in Middleborough Mall. And it has attracted over 10 percent of the retired population of the state, including many retired military.

One reason for its appeal to the military is that during World War II many soldiers were stationed in Fort Jackson, which is within the metropolitan area. They remembered their stay in Columbia fondly, and many returned to retire. Also, the University of South Carolina, in the heart of the city, strives to attract top-caliber students, including retirees who attend classes tuition free. Within the city limits are pleasant residential sections, surrounded by woods and dotted with lakes. A major drawback is the lack of public transportation (the South Carolina Commission on Aging is working to develop minibus transportation for seniors).

Climate and Environment. Columbia is located in the center of the state at an elevation of 275 feet above sea level. North of the city the terrain is rolling, sloping; toward the southern edge it flattens toward the Coastal Plain.

The Appalachian Mountains, some 150 miles to the northwest, protect the city in the winter; people frequently can eat outdoors at Christmas. The mean minimum temperature is 52.1° F., with cold weather lasting only from late November to mid-March. In summers, the Bermuda High blocks any cold air, and the mean maximum temperature is 75.4° F. with the warm weather lasting from May into September. Spring is the most changeable season, with temperatures varying from an occasional cold snap in March to a warm day in May. Fall is delightful with minimum rain and maximum sun. The mean annual temperature is 64° F. and the mean annual precipitation is 45.32 inches (with maximum rain in summer and spring). The humidity averages 71.5 percent, which, on a hot summer day, could be uncomfortable for those suffering from arthritis and sinusitis.

Medical Facilities. Hospital and medical care are among the best in South Carolina and better than average for most Sunbelt localities. Within a 15-mile radius of Columbia are 13 hospitals with a total of 9,252 beds and 522 doctors (1 per 747 persons) and 152 dentists. Richland Memorial Hospital, a nonprofit general hospital located in the city, has a new multimillion dollar facility. It operates in conjunction with the University of South Carolina School of Medicine to assure top-quality medical care.

Housing. Building costs in South Carolina are among the lowest in the nation, and some 70 percent of the housing in the Columbia metropolitan area is owner occupied. Two-bedroom single-family homes sell for $30,000 and up, and some rentals ($300 a month) are available with option to buy. Two-bedroom furnished apartments rent for about $300 a month, with similar unfurnished units renting from $250 a month. Building lots are available from $10,000. Mobile homes sell from $4,000 and rent (some with option to buy) from $150 a month.

Cost of Living. National studies of cost-of-living items indicate that Columbia falls in the middle range of costs (about the same as Durham, N.C.). Based on the intermediate budget of $9,000 annually, a retired couple in Columbia can expect to spend:

Food	Housing	Transportation	Other	Total
$2,532	$2,803	$846	$2,478	$8,659

In Columbia, real property is assessed at 1.258 percent of true market value and personal property at 3.30 percent. This means that the tax on a $25,000 home is $314.50 and the tax on a car valued at $4,000 is $132.

Recreation and Culture. Columbia is the cultural center of South Carolina. Besides being the home of the State Theater of South Carolina, it has a community theater; a Music Festival Association, which sponsors 6 concerts per season and has 6 branch organizations featuring local artists and talent; an Art Museum and Science Museum offering a wide variety of lectures and concerts as well as exhibits; and local drama groups, which provide outstanding performances at the Town Theatre and Workshop Theatre of South Carolina. Columbia also has 12 indoor movie theaters, 2 bowling alleys, 5 public and 4 private golf courses, one public swimming pool, 23 community centers, and numerous parks and playgrounds. Seniors attend spectator sports, concerts, plays, and fine arts exhibitions, and visit museums, historical sites, and many other cultural attractions—sometimes free or at low, discount rates. Lake Murray, 15 miles away, provides facilities for fishing, boating, swimming, skiing, and camping.

Special Services for Seniors. Besides the active South Carolina Commission on Aging, Columbia offers several senior centers, churches, and community and service groups which sponsor senior programs. An active Retired Senior Volunteer Program helps seniors find rewarding and personally satisfying work in the community.

For further information:

Chamber of Commerce
Columbia, SC 29202

2. THE GRAND STRAND—ONLY TWO DEGREES COLDER THAN FLORIDA

On the way to the Grand Strand (named after the 50-mile stretch of beach from North Myrtle Beach to De Bordieu Beach), I passed through *Camden* (pop. 9,000), the oldest inland town in the state. Camden attracts retirees interested in equestrian sports—horseback riding, horse shows, hunt meets, and races. The town annually hosts the Carolina Cup and Colonial Cup steeplechase, and there are 200 miles of bridle paths and 3 racetracks in the area. Although popular as a winter resort, Camden has a year-round recreation program in the N.R. Goodale State Park and Waterlee Lake areas. It boasts a fine arts center, a community center, and a music club. There are some 25 doctors in town. Medical services are available at the 125-bed Kershaw County Hospital, as well as in the hospitals in Columbia, only 30 miles away. It's easy to see why Camden appeals to retirees—the main business area is neat, clean, and efficient; the residential area is quiet and tidy. The local radio station plays religious and other soothing music—a welcome relief from the "country rock" of the rest of the state.

For further information:

Chamber of Commerce
Camden, SC 29020

Leaving Camden, once again I was impressed by the country atmosphere of South Carolina—open, sparsely populated, and rural. I was on the vast Coastal Plain region, which extends from the "Fall Line" (the line of rapids and low falls in the southeastward-flowing rivers at this point) northwest of Columbia. The Coastal Plain is roughly divided at an elevation of about 220 feet (near Orangeburg, Shaw Field, Bishopville, and Bennettsville) by the Orangeburg Scarp, an ancient shoreline. Northeast (toward Columbia) the land is hilly; southeast the plain extends almost featureless to the sea.

I reached the sea at *Myrtle Beach* (pop. 15,000), named for the many myrtle trees (scrubs) in the area. Myrtle Beach is located in the heart of the Grand Strand and is the focal point for these tiny hamlets (most under 1,000 permanent population) that front on the 50 miles of public beaches: Atlantic Beach, Surfside Beach, Garden City, Pawley's Island. Larger towns include *North Myrtle Beach* (pop. 2,000) and historic *Georgetown* (pop. 12,000). Pawley's Island (where Southern aristocracy used to winter) and Litchfield Beach (which "snubs its nose" at Miami Beach) are the most expensive and exclusive. Myrtle Beach has been described as Coney Island, Waikiki, Miami Beach, and the Caribbean rolled into one. Total population of the area, which includes Horry County, is over 80,000.

Here are other vital statistics of the Grand Strand:

Climate and Environment. The area is warmed by the Gulf Stream, making it only 2 degrees cooler than St. Augustine, Fla. The Grand Strand isn't in the hurricane belt, but the area has enough variety in weather to relieve the "hothouse" monotony of most resorts. The mean temperature in January is 54° F.; April, 69° F.; July, 82° F.; October, 71° F. The water temperature is only about 6 degrees cooler, allowing comfortable bathing from April to November. The average annual hours of sunshine (2,900 hours) ranks above Florida areas like St. Augustine and Boca Raton (both with 2,800 hours). The area has 199 clear days; 76 partly cloudy days; an average annual precipitation of 50.4 inches spread through most of the year. Humidity averages 75 percent, which might be uncomfortable in summer, even with ocean breezes to offer relief. Generally, the air and water are clear and clean, and there are no dangerous currents, fish, or red tides to worry bathers.

Medical Facilities. Horry County has Loris Community Hospital with 105 beds and a 40-bed nursing home operated in conjunction with the hospital. The Conway Hospital has 160 beds and the nursing center has 82 beds. The Grand Strand General Hospital, Myrtle Beach, 124 beds, and Georgetown has a large county hospital and modern nursing home. Myrtle

Beach has a 50-bed nursing home in conjunction with the Myrtle Beach Manor retirement complex, and the Sandstorm Nursing Home, a privately owned facility, has 30 beds. The area has some 80 doctors and 25 dentists, averaging about 1 per 1,000 residents (although the ratio is more favorable in Myrtle Beach where some 50 doctors—including specialists—have chosen to retire).

Housing. Nice apartments are difficult to find, but many condominiums are available. Two-bedroom units might rent for only $200 a month in the off-season (September 15 to March 15), but a year-round lease or rental might run $350 a month. House building is picking up, and most two-bedroom units sell for $40,000 to $55,000. Modest beach villas start at $35,000 while high-rise penthouses or oceanfront townhouses might cost $100,000. Off-season many hotels and motels offer low monthly rates ($100 and up) for efficiency units, and two-bedroom homes rent for around $350 a month. While there are no retirement communities as such, developers have plans for cluster-type "retirement villas" to be built sometime in the future.

Cost of Living. It would cost an average couple from $10,000 to $15,000 annually to retire comfortably in this area. In Myrtle Beach, city and county taxes are approximately $10 per $1,000 property valuation, or $300 a year on a $30,000 house and $500 a year on a $50,000 house. Utilities—including electricity and water—average around $75 a month. In addition to the state property tax exemption, Myrtle Beach gives a $250 tax exemption to residents over age 65. There is excellent shopping in the area, and many stores have frequent sales.

Recreation and Culture. Almost everyone plays golf on the 30 courses in the Grand Strand. But you don't have to join a private club to play, and you don't have to be a "golf nut" to retire here. In a survey of why people retired to the Grand Strand, their reasons, in order, were: weather, ocean, people, golf, swimming, fishing, tennis, restaurants, overall atmosphere. Other attractions include retirement clubs, arts and crafts, libraries, community concert series, theater series, a convention center with "name" performers, fishing (for shrimp, clams, oysters, lobster, and even deep-sea fish), and Coastal Carolina College, which attracts retirees both as teachers and students. A popular "hobby" is using metal detectors to beachcomb for coins, rings, and jewelry.

Long ago Canadians discovered that they didn't have to drive all the way to Florida for sunny weather, and they could save 2 days by stopping in Myrtle Beach. So many Canadians enjoyed this area that Myrtle Beach now holds a Canadian-American Festival in mid-March, which attracts 50,000 Canadians annually!

Special Services for Seniors. Most activities are geared to or include seniors, and 2 major organizations, the Grand Strand Retirement Club and the Association of Retired Federal Employees, an affiliate of the National Organization, hold regular meetings and programmed activities. The chamber of commerce has a special Retirement Development Committee to help retirees.

For further information:

> Grand Strand
> Chamber of Commerce
> Post Office Box 2115
> Myrtle Beach, SC 29577

3. CHARLESTON—A BIT OF JAMAICA HERE, A LITTLE BARBADOS THERE

And a lot of charm everywhere. Going to *Charleston* (pop. 65,000) is like embarking on an exotic cruise; every stopping place is an atmospheric port of call. Brookgreen Gardens, billed as a "Garden Museum of American Sculpture," reminded me of Hyde Park in London, with statues. Hundreds of works of art—ranging from "Fighting Stallions" to "Maidenhood"— dwell in this garden setting of what was once a plantation. Magnificent avenues of live oaks, lily ponds, and fountains provide showcases for the sculpture. The overall effect is one of serenity and great beauty.

Near Pawley's Island is the Hammock Shop—an original rope hammock shop built in 1880. The buildings on Pawley's Island have been constructed with old English ballast brick and old timbers and beams, giving an authentic flavor of plantation days. Various shops sell gifts ranging from straw to brass. I had a delightful sandwich lunch in the Waverly Tavern, which serves draught beer in pewter mugs.

There's no place like Charleston, with its pastel houses and tiny gardens behind lacy iron gates—a romantic and historic city that charms the young as well as the old. Downtown, buildings display plaques proclaiming their proud history. In the Battery the breeze is cool and the sights (including Fort Sumter where the first shots of the Civil War were fired) are intriguing. One fascinating aspect: Charleston, as well as most of South Carolina, didn't really recover economically from the Civil War until World War II, and many of the older buildings had to be "preserved" because no one could afford to restore them. Even homes that had suffered in an earthquake some decades ago were braced together with "earthquake rods." Now these dilapitated buildings with their quaint "earthquake rods" are highly prized antiques commanding top prices.

The Charleston area (called the Trident region) consists of Berkeley, Charleston, and Dorchester counties.

Climate and Environment. The Trident region is contiguous and closely allied economically, socially, and politically. Total population of the three counties is about 400,000 with about 275,000 of that urban. About 10 percent of the population is over age 65. The average year-round temperature is 65° F., with the coolest month January (with a maximum 58.9°, minimum 41.5°) and the hottest month July (maximum 86.2° F. and minimum 73.8°). Percentage possible sunshine is 64 percent. The average annual rainfall is 52.1 inches; humidity averages 75.5 percent annually, which could be very uncomfortable on a hot summer day.

Medical Facilities. A new Southern medical center is developing in Charleston. New facilities are constantly being added; at present the medical complex consists of the Medical University Hospital, 500 beds; Roper Hospital, 420 beds; St. Francis Xavier Hospital, 231 beds; Veterans Administration Hospital, 431 beds; Baker Memorial Hospital, 57 beds; Charleston County Hospital, 172 beds; McClennan Banks Memorial Hospital, 31 beds; the Sixth Naval District Hospital of the Charleston Naval Base, 500 beds; and the North Trident Hospital, 100 beds. Three convalescent homes, Dorchester County Hospital, and Berkeley County Hospital are also located in the area. Hospital occupancy rates average 70 percent. Charleston also has 2 nursing homes with a total of 129 beds. There are approximately 2,500 hospital beds in the area and 500 doctors (a patient-doctor ratio of 1 doctor per 800 residents).

Housing. Charleston has many two- and three-bedroom homes on the market, ranging from $30,000 and up. Some two-bedroom rentals are available from $225 a month. Two-bedroom apartments are also available, ranging from about $200 a month. Building lots in outlying areas and on the nearby islands sell for $4,000 and up. Mobile homes sell for $3,000 and up and rent from $150 a month. Housing in the historic areas of Charleston is prohibitively expensive, but there is less expensive housing available (under $30,000 for a two-bedroom house) in some of the outlying areas and islands including Isle of Palms, Sullivan's Island, Edisto Beach, West Ashley, and Peninsula City. Two new resort-residential communities are being completed on Kiawah and Seabrook Islands. These projects feature wide varieties of housing ($35,000 to $55,000 for two-and three-bedroom homes) built around central golf and tennis facilities; they also have boating and access to beaches.

A note of caution: Jack Spauling, editor of the Atlanta *Journal* recently reported: "A flight down to the South Carolina and Georgia coasts is interesting. From the air you can see big buildings right on the tide line (in South Carolina) and the beaches beginning to go. You can see where canals have been dredged and marshes filled by developers—all of which changes currents and eventually shore lines."

Cost of Living. In the Trident area, local property taxes are levied against both real and personal property (but not intangibles). The tax system is very complex. Real property taxes are determined by multiplying the market value by the applicable assessment ratio and then applying the millage rate (1 mill = $1 per $1,000) established for the tax district in which the property is located. For example, to determine the local tax on a $30,000 home located in Charleston County where the millage rate is .180, multiply $30,000 by the 4 percent assessment ratio ($1,200) ; then multiply by the basic rate of .180 mills to obtain the local tax on home and land, $216. As to other costs, recent cost of living indicators provided by the American Chamber of Commerce Researchers Association rate Charleston as follows (100 = NATIONAL AVERAGE) :

All items	Food	Housing	Utilities	Transportation	Health	Miscellaneous
98.1	98.0	89.4	142.5	80.1	84.3	94.7

Applying these indexes to the intermediate budget for a retired couple, where the urban average would total $9,000 annually in 1980, we come up with these figures:

All items	Food	Transportation	Housing	Other (including utilities)
$8,829	$2,609	$643	$2,728	$3,020

Some retirees supplement their income by working part- or full-time as welders, skilled machinists, skilled workers in the shipbuilding and ship repair trades; store managers, secretaries, mechanics, construction workers, and TV repairmen.

Recreation and Culture. In addition to the cultural aspects of Charleston itself—the famous Dock Street Theater, art galleries, ballet, and opera —the seacoast location and the year-round semitropical climate offer the outdoor-minded a wide variety of activities. Water sports are especially popular. But just walking or cycling around this lovely city, and then stopping in one of the many quaint eating establishments, such as Henry's Market Street Restaurant in the old slave market section, where fans still rotate on the ceiling, is fine recreation.

Special Services for Seniors. Senior Citizens Service of Charleston has some 50 chapters and 6,000 members. For $3 a year ($5 for husband and wife) members may use the extensive meeting and recreation facilities at the headquarters building at 259 Meeting Street in Charleston, and get discounts up to 40 percent on various items including drugs, medical and hospital supplies, hearing aids, glasses, electrical supplies, furniture, clothing, jewelry, garden equipment, hobby and craft supplies, gasoline, car washes, dry cleaning, taxi fares, theater tickets, fishing and harbor trips, museum visits, radio and TV repairs, and so on. Federal and state funds enable this organization to serve over 300 hot meals every day. All persons 60 years and over are eligible.

For further information:

Senior Citizens Services
259 Meeting Street
Charleston, SC 29401

and

Chamber of Commerce
P.B. Box 975
Charleston, SC 29402

4. OTHER SOUTH CAROLINA "GARDENS OF EDEN"

From Charleston I drove west to *Summerville* (pop. 5,000), called Flowertown in the Pines. I went there to interview Josie Van Gent Edell, a native of the Netherlands, who has lived in Paris, South Africa, and other exotic parts of the world.

Why did she choose Summerville for retirement? "Lots of land available at reasonable prices" is one answer she gave. And she did buy several acres outside of town because it was "private and had many pine trees." She lives in a rustic mansion on the grounds, and she has built (mainly with her own hands and with salvaged material) a home which she rents to a young couple. She's building another small house, which she hopes to rent or sell to another retiree.

Josie is inspiring in many ways. Although she has lived and worked with the rich and famous in advertising and as a fashion model, and weighs under 100 pounds, she proves that a retiree can still pioneer a way of life and build his or her own housing (she even dug an 80-foot well). She likes Summerville because it has art, book, and music clubs, educational TV and classical FM music, and a temperate climate that allows various outdoor activities including gardening, riding, and golf. "Winters are mild; the only heat I have is a fireplace, and I don't even need air conditioning in the summer."

Summerville has been described as "small but not rural; Southern but not sleepy." It boasts luxurious antebellum homes as well as new developments where modest two- to three-bedroom homes sell for $45,000 and up.

For further information:

Chamber of Commerce
Summerville, SC 29483

Beaufort (pop. 14,000) is the gateway to the Marine Corps station at Parris Island. The town has blocks of pre-Revolutionary and ante bellum homes. There are 26 national landmarks; two university campuses; good hunting, fishing, golf, and tennis facilities; excellent sailing with two major regattas annually. Many retired executives, senior military officers, and former bankers and professional men retire here and are active in an art association, little theater, community center and senior center. Two-bedroom housing is available from $35,000, but rentals are scarce and fairly expensive—$300 to $400 a month. Many retirees have bought land and built their own homes in and around Beaufort and especially on Fripp Island. This area is particularly appealing to seafarers and military retirees.

For further information:

Chamber of Commerce
Beaufort, SC 29902

Hilton Head Island (pop. 9,000) is the largest sea island between New Jersey and Florida, and is often called a "millionaire's playground." However, after crossing the bridge from the mainland to enter the island limits, the first sight I saw was miles of broken-down shacks. The island then becomes more like a semideserted, refined swamp. I finally found the entrance to one of the more fashionable developments and after going through a checkpoint manned by a security guard, I was given a map which pointed out where I was supposed to stay that night. The road was lonely and spooky; I drove for miles without seeing another car or person. Some 10 miles from the checkpoint I encountered "fairway villas"—actually townhouses facing a golf course. My villa had no hot water or phone service, and there was no food (although there was a well-equipped kitchen). The cold water tasted like distilled matches. The thought of finding a restaurant to get something to eat and drink panicked me. (It was Sunday, and because of South Carolina's liquor laws, many restaurants are closed on Sundays. Even the few hamburger or pizza places which do remain open close early.) I finally had to drive all the way to Savannah, Ga. (30 miles) to get food.

Although my experiences on Hilton Head were negative, I did see many attractive accommodations, such as a Hyatt Resort and Holiday Inn. Hilton Head has nice shopping centers and housing developments with homesites from $12,000 and homes from $45,000. There are some less expensive homes (Hilton Head has tried to get away from its "millionaire" image) but most average around $60,000. Some developers here are in financial trouble, and you must be very careful about buying property or housing. I would not choose to retire here, mainly because of Hilton Head's remoteness from other places (Savannah is the nearest large town) and the vast distances within the island itself. I would only feel comfortable retiring here if I could afford to settle in an exclusive "enclave." However, Hilton Head Island does attract some people. Here are additional facts to help you decide:

Climate and Environment. Hilton Head Island is shaped like a boot and it is 12 miles long, up to 5 miles wide, and covers approximately 42 square miles. The highest elevation is about 25 feet above sea level. It has some of the most beautiful sea marshes on the East Coast, and the island is heavily wooded with various subtropical trees: live and water oak, pine, bay, and palmetto trees. The surrounding water moderates the climate, which ranges in the daytime from the mid-40s and 50s in January, to the mid-80s and 90s in July. Nighttime temperatures are usually 20 degrees cooler than daytime temperatures. Rainfall averages 45.66 inches annually and is spread throughout the year—July has the heaviest rains (7.09 inches), followed by September (6.50) and August (6.25).

Medical Facilities. Hilton Head has a new private, nonprofit, fully certified medical facility with personnel and equipment to deliver medical care in over 70 different fields. Specialties include not only family practice, internal medicine, and general surgery, but urology, orthopedic surgery, otolaryngology, ophthalmology, gynecology, dermatology, and dentistry. Twenty-four-hour emergency service and a coronary care unit are available. All patient rooms are private, and the hospital participates in most health insurance programs including Medicare. There are some 25 doctors on the island, assuring better-than-average medical care.

Housing. Homesites are priced from $12,000 (woodland) to over

$70,000 (oceanfront). Two- and three-bedroom houses start at $45,000 and go over $125,000. Higher-priced homes usually face the ocean or waterways or are on fairways. An average two-bedroom house runs $60,000. Some rentals are available, but they are expensive—from $200 per week for a one-bedroom villa ($250 for 2 bedrooms) from March through September to $150 ($200 for 3 bedrooms) from September 8 to March 1. Total building costs per square foot are around $35.

Cost of Living. The tax millage rate on Hilton Head runs as high as .116. This means that a house appraised at $50,000 would be taxed at around $322 (4 percent × $50,000 × .116). This equals $64.40 per $10,000 assessed valuation per home. Nonresidents are taxed at 5 percent of appraised valuation. While the Hilton Head resident tax rate ($64.40) is lower than Charleston's $69.33 per $10,000 valuation, the costs of food, transportation (a car is a must), recreation, and other services are higher. To retire comfortably in Hilton Head requires an income of about $20,000 annually.

Recreation and Culture. The island has 12 miles of beaches, 12 miles of bike paths, 6 marinas, which accommodate up to 100-foot yachts, salt-water fishing, 11 championship golf courses, 2 nature preserves and rookeries, 3 stables, approximately 125 tennis courses, 6 paddle tennis courts, and 260 species of birds, alligators, bobcats, deer, raccoon, and wild turkey. It also has some 75 clubs ranging from the American Association of University Women to the Women's Association of Hilton Head. Clubs of special interest to seniors: an art league, barber shop quartet and chorus, duplicate bridge, Great Books, coin club, League of Women Voters, Rotary Club, polo club, garden club, United Way.

Special Services for Seniors. Although the island is thought of as a retirement center, the average age of the 9,000 inhabitants (the population goes to over 30,000 in summer) is still under 30. Thus, most activities are geared to active outdoor living. However, the clubs listed above appeal to seniors, and there are plenty of public and private golf courses, tennis courts, and boat marinas for senior outdoor activities.

For further information:

> Chamber of Commerce
> P.O. Box 5647
> Hilton Head Island, SC 29928

Aiken (pop. 15,000), the "Polo Capital of the South," is a great place to retire if you're a wealthy horse owner or can afford only low-cost housing. From late October to April, including 3 Saturdays in March, Aiken is the winter training ground for over 300 thoroughbreds and 150 standard-breds. Housing here is plentiful, due especially to the completion of the Savannah River Atomic Construction Project several years ago, after which the government and companies like Du Pont sold $25,000 two-bedroom homes for only $10,000. Many retirees purchased these homes, making Aiken a prime retirement area. Property taxes are low, and many retirees have found jobs in motels, restaurants, and theaters; in clerical and sales jobs; and in professional, technical, and managerial occupations—especially as civil engineers, draftsmen, laboratory technicians, and in the medical and health fields. Education facilities include a branch of the University of South Carolina. Medical services, including about 41 doctors in the area and a 190-bed expanding community hospital, are adequate. Aiken provides a Senior Citizen's Clubhouse and other organizations to help retirees make new contacts. Located only 50 miles from Columbia and 15 miles from Augusta, Ga., Aiken enjoys excellent shopping and recreational opportunities.

For further information:

Chamber of Commerce
Aiken, SC 29801

Greenville-Spartanburg-Clemson (pop. 125,000). This northwestern South Carolina area consists of about 125,000 people: 6,000 in Clemson, 65,000 in Greenville, and 50,000 in Spartanburg. About 10 percent of these are over age 65, so this area has the largest concentration (about 20 percent) of the state's retirees. Some reasons are the abundance of affordable ($30,000 and up) two-bedroom housing; good hospitals with some 2,500 beds and 500 doctors; educational and recreational facilities including Clemson University, Paris Mountain State Park and Table Rock Park, and a County Council on Aging, which provides recreational activities and other services for seniors. Shopping and transportation are unusually good for South Carolina. The Blue Mountains are only an hour's drive away.

For further information:

Chamber of Commerce
Greenville, SC 29601

Chamber of Commerce
Spartanburg, SC 29301

Chamber of Commerce
Clemson, SC 29631

SUMMARY

I liked South Carolina's mild climate, general lack of congestion and overcrowding, pleasant environment, low cost of living, excellent highways, and the "foreign" flavor of some of its cities, especially Charleston.

I didn't like the cockroach I found in my motel room in Myrtle Beach, nor those I saw swarming over the sidewalks in Charleston at night. I was also appalled when I saw fire ant mounds near Summerville. These ants have searing bites that can kill small animals and be extremely painful to humans. Nor do I like the antiquated liquor laws that stipulate drinks must be poured from expensive minibottles (like those sold on airlines) and prohibit drinking on Sunday, causing many restaurants to shut down.

I also felt that most existing retirement developments, which range from exclusive resort/recreation/retirement areas such as Hilton Head Island to subsidized housing for the elderly in larger areas, do not offer enough varied housing for the middle-income retiree (although, as noted, some areas have an abundance of conventional housing suitable for all ages).

Here are my ratings for South Carolina's major retirement areas:
Excellent—none;
Good—Charleston, Myrtle Beach;
Adequate—Columbia, Aiken;
Poor—Beaufort, Greenville-Spartanburg, Hilton Head Island.

RATINGS FOR SOUTH CAROLINA MAJOR RETIREMENT AREAS

COLUMBIA

Rating	Climate & Envir.	Medical	Housing	Cost of Living	Rec. & Culture	Spec. Senior Svces.
1						
2						
3						
4						
5						

MYRTLE BEACH

Rating	Climate & Envir.	Medical	Housing	Cost of Living	Rec. & Culture	Spec. Senior Svces.
1						
2						
3						
4						
5						

CHARLESTON (AREA)

Rating	Climate & Envir.	Medical	Housing	Cost of Living	Rec. & Culture	Spec. Senior Svces.
1						
2						
3						
4						
5						

HILTON HEAD ISLAND

Rating	Climate & Envir.	Medical	Housing	Cost of Living	Rec. & Culture	Spec. Senior Svces.
1						
2						
3						
4						
5						

AIKEN

Rating	Climate & Envir.	Medical	Housing	Cost of Living	Rec. & Culture	Spec. Senior Svces.
1						
2						
3						
4						
5						

GREENVILLE-SPARTANBURG (AREA)

Rating	Climate & Envir.	Medical	Housing	Cost of Living	Rec. & Culture	Spec. Senior Svces.
1						
2						
3						
4						
5						

RATINGS FOR *SOUTH CAROLINA* MAJOR RETIREMENT AREAS

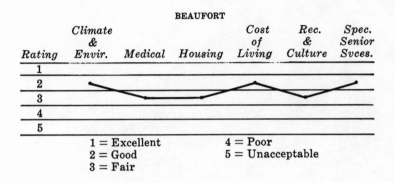

	Climate & Envir.	Medical	Housing	Cost of Living	Rec. & Culture	Spec. Senior Svces.

1 = Excellent   4 = Poor
2 = Good   5 = Unacceptable
3 = Fair

GEORGIA

Piedmont

Appalachian

Highlands

o Dahlonega

o Athens

Washington o

△ Atlanta

Madison o

o Augusta

Piedmont

o Macon

Columbus

Plain

o Helena

Savannah △

Coastal

o Albany

Sea
Island

Brunswick o ✳ St.
Jekyll Island ✳ Simons
Island

Thomasville △   o Valdosta

✳   Excellent Retirement
△   Good Retirement
●   Adequate Retirement
o   Other Towns of Interest

VI.

GEORGIA–LAND OF

PLEASANT EXTREMES

Crossing the Savannah River into Georgia leads not only to a different state, but to a different retirement world. As much as I admired Charleston, I found that Savannah had contrasting charms to offer. And the fact that I had the best omelet of my life in a small Georgia restaurant only whetted my appetite for more of what the state had to offer.

Georgia is a land of some pleasant and extreme surprises. As I drove toward Atlanta, I was on a piney woods plain (69 percent of Georgia land is covered by forests). But nearing Atlanta I saw rolling plateaus, and red clay and pink granite hills, with mountains to the north and coastal flatlands to the south. Georgia is much bigger than I thought—it has the greatest land area of any state east of the Mississippi. And while it probably has more "backwater" rural towns than most states, it has one of the greatest cities of any state—Atlanta.

Although Georgia roads are worse than those in North and South Carolina, people drive faster here (I saw few if any highway patrol cars). I-16 went only to Statesboro than detoured 40 miles or so through rural towns and counties. (I could tell the wet counties from the dry ones by the clusters of liquor stores at the borders.) I-16 picked up again around Dublin and went on into Macon.

As I drove along I passed signs offering senior citizen discounts at Red

Carpet Inns. On the radio Sister Catherine offered to solve ordinary personal problems, while the State Mental Health Department offered to help depression in the elderly.

In Macon I tried to call Ralph Dobbs of the Georgia Department of Industry and Trade. It was then that I learned that my Yankee accent was too much for the Southern drawl, and I had to spell out the name rather than attempt to pronounce it.

While Macon is big enough, it hardly prepares one for space-age Atlanta. Atlanta fully justifies Georgia's claim as the Empire State of the South. It is the symbol and heartbeat of the new South, and Southern economy and transportation (railroads, interstate highways, and air lines) all converge here. Its Hartsfield International Airport is the second busiest in the nation (after O'Hare in Chicago), and offers nonstop air service to Europe. Atlanta is international: It has over 10 foreign consulates and a $35,000,000 Georgia World Congress Center, which attracts international conventions.

Atlanta is the urban extreme; the rest of Georgia is the rural extreme. As one person said: "Atlanta offers a big-city life style; the rest of the state offers good farming." (Peanuts and chickens are the main crops now, replacing peaches.)

That night I dined with Ralph Dobbs and Joel Turner, community education specialist of the Georgia Office on Aging, at the Mansion in the heart of Atlanta. This shingle-style Victorian mansion covers many acres right in the downtown area. The Mansion toasts Atlanta's elegance of the past—each room differs both in design and type of wood used. Several rooms are embellished with tooled leather panels and elaborate gesso embossings, and some have favored Georgian pink marble sideboards.

In this pleasant setting Ralph and Joel identified the major retirement areas in Georgia (zip codes added for those towns not discussed further in this chapter): *Augusta,* a golf center featuring the Bon Aire Retirement Hotel; *Columbus,* near Fort Benning and good for the retired military; *Macon* (31207), also with a military base and active cultural life; *Savannah,* with Southern history and charm; *Valdosta* (31601), home of beautiful lakes and fishing; *Albany* (31701), known for its radium springs; *Thomasville,* with old hotels and culture; *Brunswick* and the "Golden Isles" of *Jekyll, St. Simon,* and *Sea Island; Athens* (30601), housing the University of Georgia and an active Council on Aging; and the smaller towns of *Helena* (31037); *Dahlonega* (30533); *Madison* (30650); *Greensboro* (30642); and *Washington* (30673). For further information on areas not discussed later, write to chambers of commerce (no street address necessary but use zip code).

Four Beautiful Seasons

Because of Georgia's latitude and nearness to the warm waters of the Gulf of Mexico and the Atlantic Ocean, most of the state has warm, humid summers and short, mild winters. In the northern part of the state, summers are cooler and winters colder, but not severely so. All 4 seasons appear —spring is usually short and blustery, and autumn provides long periods of mild, sunny weather.

Mild year-round temperature ranges from a low of 47.5° F. in January to a mid-summer high of 79.8° F. in July. Temperatures seldom rise above the 90s or drop below 0° F. On a typical July day in north Georgia, the temperature ranges from 72° F. in the mid-afternoon to 68° F. at night; in January it is 54° F. to 32° F. On the coast (Savannah), temperatures might be 5° F. warmer on any given day, and the humidity averages 3 percent higher.

Average annual rainfall ranges from more than 75 inches in the extreme northeast corner to about 40 inches in a small area of east central Georgia. From this driest part of the state, rainfall increases toward the south to an average of about 53 inches. The state's heaviest rainfall occurs in winter and early spring, followed by mid-summer. The driest season is autumn, and May is a close second. Snowfall is light and of little significance; only in the extreme mountains does it average as much as 5 inches.

Humidity averages the same in mid-Georgia as in Chicago (70.8 percent), giving the state an advantage over many areas along the eastern seaboard. However, in Savannah and other coastal areas, the humidity averages 73.8 percent annually.

Lowest Cost of Living

Living costs in Georgia are about 10 percent below the national average and they are about the lowest of any Sunbelt state. Even in urban Atlanta, the Bureau of Labor Statistics estimates a retired couple can live on an intermediate budget on approximately $8,330 a year. However, as a general guideline, a retired couple needs about $10,000 income a year to live comfortably in Georgia.

Georgia's taxes are moderate, and the state ranks thirty-second in tax burdens. Taxes break down as follows:

State income tax—based on federal adjusted gross income on a graduated scale from 1 percent on the first $750 for a single person ($1,000 for a married couple) to 6 percent on more than $7,000 for a single person ($10,000 for a married couple). Personal exemptions include deductions of $1,500 for a single person and $3,000 for a married couple. Persons over age 64 get an extra $700 exemption.

Property taxes—the state doesn't impose such taxes, but counties and cities do, ranging down from 75 mills per $1,000 levy, based on 40 percent of value. This works out to an average effective tax rate of about 1.33 percent of market value ($133 per $10,000 valuation). Homeowners over age 61 with incomes less than $4,000 get $10,000 off the fair market value of the home for property tax purposes; those with incomes less than $6,000 get $25,000 off the fair market value of the home when paying school tax.

Intangible tax—10 cents per $1,000 to $1 per $1,000 depending upon classification of intangibles, assessed at full market value.

Retail sales tax—the state imposes a 3 percent sales tax and some localities—Fulton and DeKalb counties for example—impose additional taxes of up to 1 percent, making a 4 percent maximum sales tax.

Georgia does not levy an inheritance tax, and seniors also get free hunting and fishing licenses. State and city taxes combined average around 7.9 percent of income versus 9.7 percent for the U.S. as a whole.

Job opportunities are good in Georgia, especially in Savannah and Atlanta. In Savannah there are jobs available in service industries; for welders, guards, and watch persons; material handlers, secretaries, computer operators, and account recorders; domestic workers, gardeners, and groundkeepers; mechanics and repair people, carpenters and other craftspeople; construction laborers. In Atlanta there are openings for registered nurses, secretaries, cashiers, mail clerks; canvassers and solicitors; automatic-data processing operators and metal processors; computer programmers and related computer technicians; construction workers; light truck drivers; hotel, motel, and restaurant workers; gardeners and groundkeepers.

Abundance of Housing

Generally, both rental and for-sale housing is plentiful in Georgia's retirement areas. Even in Atlanta two-bedroom apartments rent for only $250 a month and up; three-bedroom houses sell for $40,000. Two-bedroom "rustic retreats" sell for as low as $25,000 and two-bedroom condominiums sell for over $100,000. Georgia has plenty of retirement housing available in all price ranges.

To get a directory of retirement housing write:

American Association of Retired Persons
2872 Woodcock Blvd.
Atlanta, GA 30341

For other residential housing write:

Georgia Association of Realtors
3200 Presidential Dr. NE
Atlanta, GA 30340

Good Medical Services for Retirees

Georgia has 221 hospitals with a total of 36,727 beds. It also has 352 nursing homes with a total of 30,667 beds and 21 personal care homes with 1,596 beds. The state has a total of 6,794 medical doctors. A semiprivate hospital room averages $102.30 a day, compared with the U.S. average of over $133.02 a day.

Medical services are good in the Atlanta region and in the more populated retirement centers of Augusta, Columbus, Macon, and Brunswick and the Golden Isles. Rural areas have less adequate facilities. To find out about medical services write:

Medical Association of Georgia
938 Peachtree Street
Atlanta, GA 30309

Georgia Hospital Association
92 Piedmont Avenue
Atlanta, GA 30303

Livability for All Life Styles

Georgia offers everything from the ultrasophistication of Atlanta (with its Space-Age Hyatt Regency and Atlanta Hilton) to the easy pace of relaxed rural living. Georgians have plenty of outdoor activity with 40 state parks and fishing in 1,322 miles of fine trout streams and 84 major lakes, as well as over 100 miles of Atlantic coast. There is also good hunting in

Georgia, especially for quail, deer, wild turkey, rabbit, and squirrel. The mild climate permits golfing at least 300 days a year; Georgia has over 2,500 holes for golfing.

Atlanta, the state capital, offers big-city culture and recreation, including a state museum of science and industry, a memorial arts center, and a historical society; 6 parks featuring miles of walks and roads and offering swimming, golf, tennis, and picnic areas; a world arts and crafts center; state farmer's market; Underground Atlanta (a 4-block restored area featuring exhibit halls, elegant rococo buildings, restaurants, and shops), and 29 colleges and institutions for advanced study (Georgia has 66 institutions of higher learning). Just beyond the Atlanta city limits is Six Flags Over Georgia, a 276-acre family entertainment center presenting Georgia's history under the flags of England, France, Spain, the Confederacy, the U.S. and its own state flag. Sixteen miles east of Atlanta is Stone Mountain Park, a 3,200-acre preserve that surrounds the world's largest granite monolith, rising 825 feet from the plain. The park has 10 miles of nature trails; as well as boat rentals, carillon concerts, museums, and restaurants. Other attractions include the Little White House in Warm Springs, where President Franklin D. Roosevelt died; the 2,500-acre Callaway Gardens; and the restored 1850s town of Westville.

Georgia has a variety of superb small-town restaurants in such towns as Porterdale, Covington, Perry, Dahlonega, Dillard, Jasper, and Hamilton, as well as more sophisticated restaurants in Atlanta and the Golden Isles.

For a list of monthly activities in Georgia, send $1.50 for single copies or $5.00 per year for 6 issues to:

> Brown's Guide to Georgia
> 3765 Main Street
> Suite 202
> College Park, GA 30337

Special Services to Seniors

The active Georgia Office on Aging offers many programs and services for seniors, including nutrition programs in all parts of the state. It also provides tie-line service, in which seniors can call toll free and get advice on any problem.

> Georgia Office of Aging
> 618 Ponce De Leon Avenue N.E.
> Atlanta, GA 30308

The Office on Consumer Affairs at the same address also provides a toll-free line for consumer protection assistance. The number: 1-800-282-4900

And the University of Georgia at Athens sponsors an active Council on Aging with special programs for seniors.

For further information:

> Council on Aging
> University of Georgia
> Athens, GA 30601

1. BRUNSWICK—GATEWAY TO THE "GOLDEN ISLES"

The road from Macon to the fabled Golden Isles narrows to 2 lanes and meanders through piney woods and rolling country. The towns, the people, and the settings look as if they have been preserved for generations. It must have looked the same when Sherman's army marched toward the sea. But today a different army is marching toward coastal Georgia—retirees with hopes for the future.

As one approaches *Brunswick* (pop. 20,000), the land flattens and becomes marshy. This part of the southeastern Coastal Plains is fragmented with numerous islands and embayments extending miles inland. As one crosses the city limits of Brunswick, the peninsula on which the city is located narrows to point the way to three of the Golden Isles—Jekyll, St. Simons, and Sea Island. Lying between these islands and the mainland are the "marvelous marshes of Glynn" described by the poet Sidney Lanier.

Brunswick is a not-unpleasant commercial center with about half the population of the entire metropolitan area. The rest of the population is scattered on the mainland and across the causeways on the Golden Isles.

I paid a 25-cent toll, crossed a mile-long causeway and drove to *St. Simons Island* (pop. 12,000). This is an ancient island with beautiful moss-hung oaks and unspoiled beaches. It is owned by its residents, whose income levels range from about $10,000 to $60,000 annually. A wide selection and variety of housing is available from $35,000 for a two-bedroom cottage. Restaurants, recreation facilities, and cultural events cater to all tastes and pocketbooks. Seafood is a speciality; boats bring in fresh catches daily.The most popular beach areas extend from King and Prince beaches to the Coast Guard site. Massengale Park, a public facility off Ocean Boulevard, is a favorite spot with picnic tables, and clean and wide beaches. A popular recreation is to explore the island on foot or by bike; several bike trails wind through scenic areas. St. Simons Casino near the village offers a wide range of entertainment including bowling, roller skating, table tennis, and a public pool. There are ample facilities for golf, tennis, and fishing. Fishing is permitted from piers, bridges, and riverbanks; you don't need a saltwater fishing license, and surf casting is allowed. For boaters, there are excellent boat ramps, yacht clubs, and boat repair services. There are some 15 doctors on St. Simons, assuring better-than-average medical care. The island has an art center where local exhibits are held.

Sea Island (pop. 1,000) is very expensive, very exclusive, and beyond the reach of the ordinary retiree (houses start at $150,000). About the only way a middle-income retiree could afford to spend time on this island would be to stay at the famous Cloister, a luxurious resort that is a popular spot for honeymooners (daily rates start at $60 per person; monthly rates range from $900 to $4,000). Sea Island is made for luxurious vacationing: the 36-hole Sea Island Golf Course, laid out on the site of an old plantation, is one of the most beautiful in the world. Tennis courts have all-weather surfaces; the Beach Club features ocean-edge dining; riding stables are served by miles of quiet trails. You can also enjoy skeet shooting, lawn sports, and other genteel activities. Sea Island has exceptional medical care, with 1 doctor for every 300 residents.

Jekyll Island (pop. 1,200) is a state-owned island that was once a millionaire's retreat. The Morgans, Goulds, Vanderbilts, and Rockefellers built "cottages" here, and the 25-room cottage of the Rockefellers is now a museum. But the island has been turned into a public park for the ordinary citizen, with 10 miles of pristine beaches, 4 golf courses, several tennis courts, and many facilities for fishing, hiking, biking, and boating. Facing the ocean is an Aquarama—a convention site with a teepee-roofed, glass-walled indoor swimming pool. Aquarama is open all year (air-conditioned in summer and heated in winter). A picturesque amphitheater offers musical and dramatic presentations. To buy housing here, you lease the land rather than own it. But housing is reasonably priced: modern two-bedroom homes are available from $40,000, and some rentals ($300 a month) are available in the off-season. Jekyll has about 10 doctors in the area, for better-than average medical care.

An interesting footnote: About 60 percent of Jekyll residents classify themselves as "retired" compared to 30 percent on St. Simons and 75 percent on Sea Island.

The growing popularity of the Brunswick-Golden Isles area as a retirement center stems from the fact that many people who have vacationed or visited here were so impressed with the area's beauty and easy life style that they chose to retire here.

Here are some other reasons to consider retiring in this area:

Climate and Environment. Marsh and shore land comprise much of the total acreage of Brunswick and the islands, yet there is land available to build on and houses for rent and sale. Weather isn't extreme: The average minimum and maximum temperatures for January are 43.6° F. and 64° F.; for July 73° F. and 91.6° F. Average annual rainfall is 54.7 inches with only a rare snowfall. Residents can often eat Christmas dinner in shirt-sleeves outdoors.

Medical Facilities. Brunswick serves as a regional medical center, with the 303-bed Glynn-Brunswick Memorial Hospital. The hospital staff includes 66 physicians; plans are under way to add a wing and more staff. The Glynn County Health Department serves as district headquarters for a 5-county area. There are speech, hearing, and diabetic clinics. The area has 3 nursing homes with a total of 305 beds; 139 of these are available for skilled nursing care and 134 for intermediate nursing care. Glynn County has 19 dentists.

Housing. Modest two-bedroom retirement homes sell for as little as $28,000 in the Brunswick area. There is a greater variety of housing (single-family homes of brick, wood, and various designs; villas; new and older homes) on St. Simons Island in a wider price range (from $40,000 to $100,000). Jekyll has some modern two- to three-bedroom homes selling for $50,000 to $70,000, but you can only lease the land (on a 99-year lease) and new housing must be approved by the state. Homes in Sea Island are beyond the reach of the ordinary retiree; two-bedroom condominiums cost at least $150,000. In the area some rentals are available at $250 to $350 a month for two- to three-bedroom apartments. But these rates apply to long-term leases; rates drop after Labor Day.

Cost of Living. Retired couples can live here comfortably on around $600 a month if their home is paid for or their mortgages are low. Utilities average about $60 a month. Food costs are about the same as elsewhere, except you can save on local fruits, vegetables, and seafood in season (some people literally fish for their supper). Retirees can supplement their income with part-time jobs in restaurants, motels, hotels, stores, and other service areas.

Brunswick's tax rate is $15 per $1,000 of assessed valuation, based on 40 percent of market value. Glynn County's tax rate is $34.25 to $37 per $1,000 outside Brunswick; total city and county taxes within Brunswick are $45.50. Total taxes per $1,000 for St. Simons are $36.75; $38.50 for Sea Island; $30.50 for Jekyll Island.

Recreation and Culture. Besides the outdoor activities already mentioned, the area provides many educational and cultural activities, including Brunswick Junior College, a unit of the University of Georgia, which offers a continuing education program attended by some 500 retirees. There are also art associations, Audubon societies, bridge clubs, a regional library with 158,00 volumes and a staff of 13; little theater productions; and a "Golden Isles Swingers Square Dance Club."

Special Services for Seniors. The YWCA Activity House has a Senior Citizens Program in which some 1,400 seniors participate. In addition to serving as a referral agency, the Senior Citizens Program offers support by reminding elderly residents of Glynn County that they are entitled to a fair share of the area's resources. Although the Brunswick Chamber of Commerce is seeking more industry and younger families, recreational and educational programs are open to all ages, and retirees blend in with the rest of the community.

For further information:

> Golden Isles
> Chamber of Commerce
> Brunswick, GA 31520
>
> Chamber of Commerce
> St. Simons, GA 31522

2. OTHER RETIREMENT CENTERS IN GEORGIA

Augusta (pop. 60,000 city; 313,390 metropolitan) is as famed for its golf (the Augusta National Golf Course hosts the Masters Golf Tournament during the first week in April) as it is for its Georgia red clay bricks. The short, mild winters and the charm of its broad and flowered parkways, stately homes, and tall pine groves have attracted many retirees. Some have built stately mansions, while others settle contentedly in $30,000 two-bedroom brick retirement homes. The area has 5 major hospitals—including Eisenhower Memorial at Fort Gordon and the Medical College of Georgia—and some 500 doctors, assuring good medical care. Cultural facilities include Augusta College, Paine College; a museum art galley, and an arts council with 25 affiliates. There are 6 golf courses and facilities for hunting, fishing, boating, and camping. Fort Gordon, an army base southwest of the city, is a major contributor to the area's economy.

For further information:

Chamber of Commerce
Augusta, GA 30902

Columbus (pop. 170,000 city; 250,000 metropolitan) is famous for its wide streets (100 to 164 feet) flanked by magnificent trees in grass plots. Dogwood and wisteria add color in the spring. Columbus is home to Fort Benning, the largest infantry post in the U.S., where the U.S. Army Infantry Museum has exhibits from the Revolutionary War to the present. The Columbus Museum of Arts and Crafts houses extensive gun and doll collections and Indian artifacts. Many retired military personnel live here, in modest homes that sell for as low as $30,000 (two- and three-bedroom) and in some of the many rentals in the area ($300 a month for a two-bedroom furnished apartment). There are 5 hospitals in the area, but only about 230 doctors, which doesn't assure the best medical care. However, Columbus does have good cultural facilities including Springer Theater (state theater of Georgia); Three Arts Theater; Bradley Memorial Library; Columbus College and Chattahoochee Valley Community College.

For further information:

Chamber of Commerce
Columbus, GA 31901

Savannah (pop. 120,000) combines the history of Charleston with the charm of New Orleans. Some retirees have bought Regency "Old Town" homes for relatively modest prices ($40,000 to $50,000) and have spent $10,000 to $25,000 to restore them to their former grandeur. They are now valued at $100,000 and up. Others have settled for more conventional ranch-style housing in the suburbs ($45,000 to $65,000). All share the educational and cultural advantages of Savannah, which include a week-long Coastal Empire Arts Festival, the Telfair Art Museum, and the historical sites. Savannah has 3 major hospitals and 300 doctors.

Savannah also features swimming at Savannah Beach.

For further information:

Chamber of Commerce
Savannah, GA 31401

Thomasville (pop. 20,000) is part of the Old South. Antebellum homes line quiet residential streets, and the plantationlike atmosphere evokes nostalgia even in a Northerner. The surrounding countryside extending down into Florida is like a semitropical garden, with azaleas, roses, camellias, and dogwoods adding beauty and color.

Thomasville is large for its remoteness. It offers cultural and educational attractions for retirees, including art and music festivals. Tallahassee (35 miles away) and the Florida beaches are within easy reach. Despite the aristocratic look of Thomasville, costs are reasonable and modest housing is available ($30,000 to $65,000 for two- to three-bedroom houses).

For further information:

Chamber of Commerce
Thomasville, GA 31792

SUMMARY

I liked the vibrance of Atlanta and the relaxed pace of the Golden Isles, but I felt a stranger in Georgia—perhaps because the people and the accents are such a Deep South contrast for a born-and-bred Yankee.

However, I was pleasantly surprised at the fascinating diversity of geography and geology in Georgia (its pink marble is highly prized in interior decorating) and in the rural-urban extremes. Probably no other state offers such contrasts for retirement. But you must be careful to pick the right spot for you. Strangers are often asked about their religious affiliation, and if you don't answer "Baptist," you may find that you're not as acceptable as you thought.

But, again, you can always make friends with other Northerners or Midwesterners who have retired in Georgia, and if you get involved in civic or other community activities, you'll find yourself among acquaintances with similar interests and backgrounds.

Here are my ratings for Georgia's major retirement centers:
Excellent—St. Simons Island, Jekyll Island;
Good—Atlanta, Savannah, Thomasville;
Adequate—Augusta, Columbus;
Poor—Sea Island, Macon, Albany.

RATINGS FOR *GEORGIA* MAJOR RETIREMENT AREAS

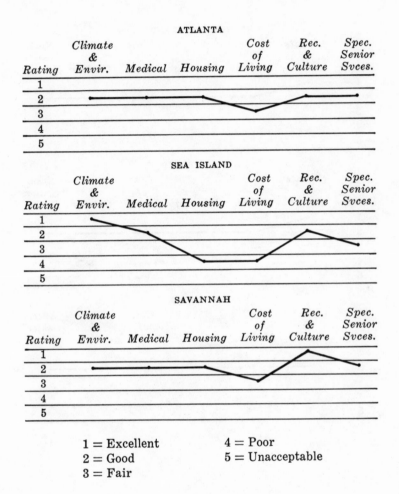

1 = Excellent   4 = Poor
2 = Good   5 = Unacceptable
3 = Fair

RATINGS FOR *GEORGIA* MAJOR RETIREMENT AREAS

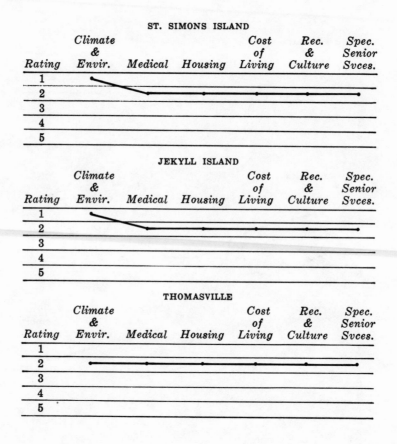

ST. SIMONS ISLAND

Rating	Climate & Envir.	Medical	Housing	Cost of Living	Rec. & Culture	Spec. Senior Svces.
1						
2						
3						
4						
5						

JEKYLL ISLAND

Rating	Climate & Envir.	Medical	Housing	Cost of Living	Rec. & Culture	Spec. Senior Svces.
1						
2						
3						
4						
5						

THOMASVILLE

Rating	Climate & Envir.	Medical	Housing	Cost of Living	Rec. & Culture	Spec. Senior Svces.
1						
2						
3						
4						
5						

RATINGS FOR *GEORGIA* MAJOR RETIREMENT AREAS

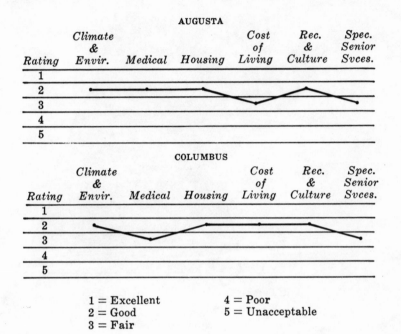

1 = Excellent   4 = Poor
2 = Good   5 = Unacceptable
3 = Fair

FLORIDA

Tallahassee

Northern

Jacksonville

St. Augustine

Gainesville

Ocala   Daytona Beach

Deltona

Tavares
Leesburg   Mount Dora

Brooksville   Orlando

New Port Richey   Central
Tarpon Springs
Dunedin   Tampa
Clearwater

St. Petersburg   Ruskin
Sun City Center   Vero Beach

Bradenton
Sarasota   Eastern

Port Charlotte
Englewood   Punta Gorda   West Palm Beach

Fort Myers   Lake Worth

Western

Naples   Fort Lauderdale

Miami Beach
Miami

Coral Gables

* Excellent Retirement
△ Good Retirement
● Adequate Retirement
○ Other Towns of Interest

Key
Largo

Islamorada

Marathon

Key West

Northern

Pensacola   Panama City

Inset

VII.

FLORIDA—

THE RETIREMENT

SMORGASBORD

Florida is a retirement smorgasbord that I've nibbled at for 15 years. I haven't felt satiated nor have I gotten sick. Even after years of travel and evaluation, my feelings about retiring in Florida are still ambivalent.

One thing I'm sure of: Florida is the number one retirement state. More people are moving to Florida every day (about 1,000) than to any other state. Florida now boasts about 9 million residents, about 17 percent or 1,530,000 of these persons are over age 65. By 1987 the population will soar to over 11,000,000 with an even higher percentage of retirees.

Whatever these newcomers are looking for, they're likely to find it: a high-rise condominium on the Gold Coast (Palm Beach-Fort Lauderdale-Miami) ; a retirement village in the central "highlands;" a cottage on an offshore island. Florida offers everything from the best to the worst; if you're *determined* to retire in the Sunshine State you'll find what you're looking for—if you look hard enough for it.

What draws retirees to Florida? One reason is the healthful climate. Health officials claim that a man of 60 to 70 who retires in Florida can expect to live a year longer than in the nation as a whole, and a woman of the same age can live 13 to 18 months longer. The National Center for Health Statistics adds that the white male life expectancy in Florida at age 65 is 14.2 years; white female life expectancy in Florida at age 65 is 18.2 years. Generally in Florida deaths from the principal diseases of old age—heart disease, tuberculosis, arteriosclerosis, and diabetes—are well below the national average. And the life expectancy for children born in Florida is 18 months longer than the national average.

PEOPLE LIVE LONGER IN FLORIDA

Life expectancy figures for Florida residents are among the highest in the nation. The following table compares the average future lifetime of age groups by sex, starting at age 30.

AGE	WHITE MALE		WHITE FEMALE	
	Florida	*U.S.*	*Florida*	*U.S.*
30	42.0	40.8	48.6	46.6
40	32.8	31.6	39.1	37.1
50	24.5	23.1	30.2	28.0
60	17.5	15.9	21.7	19.7
70	11.7	10.2	14.0	12.4
80	6.9	5.9	7.7	6.8

Source: Florida Department of Commerce

Because you need less food, clothing, heating, and medical care, the cost of living is generally lower in Florida. Personal and property taxes are also lower (see below) and building costs range from 7 to 25 percent lower in Florida than in most Northern states.

The Sunshine State Is Geared Toward Retirees and Retirement Activities

You can always find people of your own age and plenty to do in Florida. Counties with the largest *numbers* of retirees include Pinellas, Broward, Dade, Sarasota, Duval, and Hillsborough. Counties with the biggest *percentages* of retirees include Charlotte (57 percent), Citrus (46 percent), Sarasota (46 percent), Manatee (45 percent), Pinellas (41 percent), and Pasco (40 percent). The most popular retirement cities are Clearwater, New Port Richey, St. Petersburg, Lake Wales, Lake Worth, and Miami Beach. Midwesterners and Gentiles tend to settle mainly on the West Coast; Northeasterners and New Yorkers generally prefer the East Coast, with large concentrations of Jewish elderly in the Miami Beach area. Northerners usually like south Florida while Southerners usually like north Florida. Some towns, such as Tarpon Springs and Lake Worth, draw ethnic blocs (Greeks and Finns, respectively), and several areas of the state have retirement settlements from one of the telephone or oil companies. "Birds of a feather" applies to retirees flocking to Florida; find out if "your group" nests in the same area where you want to settle.

Note that the following areas are expected to grow the most during the next 10 years: Fort Lauderdale, Miami, West Palm Beach, Orlando, St. Petersburg, Tampa, Jacksonville, New Port Richey, Fort Myers, Sarasota, Sanford, Daytona Beach, Lakeland, and Titusville/Melbourne.

1. WHAT FLORIDA HAS TO OFFER

While Florida is somewhat homogeneous geographically—a low, flat peninsula, whose high point is only 345 feet above sea level—the state is divided socially and economically into 4 different regions:

Northern. The region north of a line from Daytona Beach on the East Coast to Ocala to Cedar Key on the West, including the Panhandle (northwestern section). This area is predominantly Southern in people, politics, and practices. It is rolling, piney woods country with several lakes and the highest point of land (345 feet at Lakewood in Walton County). Although it has some large cities—St. Augustine, Jacksonville, Tallahassee (the capital), Panama City, and Pensacola—northern Florida doesn't offer much for retirees, especially Northerners who might feel like strangers here.

Central. The area south of the Daytona Beach-Ocala-Cedar Key line and north of a line from Clearwater on the West Coast to Vero Beach on the East Coast. This includes some of the fastest-growing retirement areas such as Orlando, Ocala, Deltona, Gainesville.

East (Gold) Coast. The area goes from Vero Beach on the north to the Keys on the south and includes Vero Beach, West Palm Beach, Lake Worth, Boca Raton, Pompano Beach, Fort Lauderdale, Hollywood, Miami, Miami Beach, and Coral Gables. It also includes the Florida Keys, which trail off from the Everglades. This is the tinseled Gold Coast of Florida, celebrated in motion pictures and novels.

West Coast. This area starts from Naples in the south and extends to Clearwater-Tampa-St. Petersburg in the north. It contains many popular retirement areas, such as Fort Myers, Punta Gorda, Venice, Sarasota, Bradenton.

Pleasant, Year-Round Moderate Climate

As Florida is surrounded on 3 sides by water, no part of the state is more than 70 miles from saltwater. Fresh sea air circulates throughout much of the inland areas. Florida receives more annual sunshine (average 252 days) than any other state in the entire eastern United States, and the southern part of the state averages 10 percent more sunshine than the northern part.

The *temperature* varies only slightly between coastal and inland areas. The *average annual rainfall* is 53 inches, and about half of that falls between June and August. Next highest rainy months are September to November and March to May; December to May has the least rain. Thunderstorms average 77 days annually, decreasing sharply in the extreme southern part of the state. Hurricane expectancy ranges from 1 in every 7 years in Miami to 1 in every 50 years in Jacksonville. Average temperatures and rainfall:

North- west	North- ern	North Central	South Central	South- west	Lower Eastern	Florida Keys
January Temperatures (degrees Fahrenheit):						
53.9	57.0	60.5	62.4	64.7	66.9	70.2
January Precipitation (inches):						
3.79	2.53	2.10	2.09	1.63	2.16	1.71
July Temperatures:						
81.1	81.4	81.6	81.6	81.7	81.5	83.5
July Precipitation:						
7.96	7.62	8.16	8.14	8.18	6.65	4.54

Sunshine. In the north, sunshine averages 6 hours daily (58 percent of possible amount) and in the south 7½ hours (65 percent of possible amount). Statewide summer sunshine averages 9 hours daily (69 percent of possible amount). Clear days average 120 and cloudy days 100 annually.

Humidity. The most comfortable relative humidity is *below* 72 percent —above that you feel uncomfortable. Unfortunately, Florida's *average* relative humidity is 75 percent, but this ranges from 50 to 60 percent in the afternoons to 85 to 95 percent during the night and early morning. The average humidity is lowest in April and highest in the summer months, July, August, and September. However, the dry soil and sunshine soak up some of the moisture, and cooling breezes offer further relief.

Florida retirees claim that their "blood thins out" and they learn to live with the high heat and humidity. But many advise that *if you can't live through a Florida summer without air conditioning, retire elsewhere.*

Many Floridians escape to the North Carolina hills to avoid the worst of the Florida heat and humidity.

Lower Cost of Living

Day-to-day living costs in Florida average about 10 percent lower than the U.S. average, although not as low as the average in Georgia, Texas, and Louisiana. Compared with most Northern and Midwestern states, you save about 75 percent on winter heating bills; 50 percent on clothing; 25 percent on housing. As you'll eat less, needing less food to supply body heat, you'll save on food costs (which run about the same as the national average). There are often good buys on local produce and seafood.

LIVING COSTS IN FLORIDA

Based on a statewide average of 100, the Division of Budget of the Florida Department of Administration estimates the cost-of-living differentials to be:

Florida Community	Cost of Living Index
Orlando	96.38
Miami	106.96
Ft. Lauderdale	102.00
West Palm Beach	101.40
Naples	101.97
Sarasota	100.14
Tampa	98.65
St. Petersburg	99.16
Lakeland	97.78
Cape Canaveral Area	97.38
Daytona Beach	97.82
Jacksonville	98.13
Tallahassee	95.06
Pensacola	94.37
Gainesville	98.82
Clarksville	94.96

The most expensive area in Florida is Monroe County (Key West); second is Dade County (Miami); Martin County (Stuart). The Orlando area is one of the least expensive sections of Florida.

Florida taxes are among the lowest in the nation. The state has *no* state income tax, state property tax, or inheritance taxes. And Florida offers these *exemptions:*

- $5,000 homestead exemption for those who own real property in the state (as of January 1 in any given year). For those who have been permanent residents of the state for the previous five years as of January 1st of the year of assessment, the homestead exemption is $25,000. If taxes exceed 5 percent of income, they can be deferred.
- Widows, the disabled, and the blind qualify for a $500 exemption. However, the state does levy these taxes:
- a 5 percent sales tax on almost everything except groceries, drugs and health aids, telephone services and utilities, professional services, subscriptions, rentals.
- $5 auto registration fee.
- Florida estate tax is designed to absorb the maximum allowable Federal estate tax credit for state death taxes paid. In the case of an estate of a resident decedent, all of whose property is in Florida, the Florida estate tax is the maximum amount allowable for Federal estate tax purposes as a credit for state death taxes paid.
- There are two classes of intangible personal property tax levied: (1) an annual tax of 1 mill (1-thousandth) of $1 ($1 per $1,000) of shares of stock of incorporated companies; beneficial interest in intangibles held in trust; bonds (but not U.S. Government or Florida state or local); notes; accounts receivable except those secured by realty; (2) $2 per $1,000 of the value of notes, bonds, and other obligations to pay money which are secured by a mortgage, deed of trust, or other lien on real property in Florida. Notes and other obligations, except bonds, which are secured by real property in another state are exempt to the extent secured by such real property out of Florida.

For further information on taxes, write Florida Department of Revenue, Taxpayer Assistance Section, Carlton Building, Tallahassee, FL 32301 (904) 488-6800 or 2574.

AVERAGE BUDGET COSTS FOR A RETIRED COUPLE

	Food at home	Food away from home	Shelter	Home furnish. & maint.	Trans-portation	Clothing	Personal Care	Medical	Misc.*	Income Tax	Total
BOSTON	$1,954	$341	$3,827	$1,499	$1,002	$565	$262	$545	$1,657	$889	$12,541
NEW YORK	1,949	454	3,168	1,510	1,013	558	277	564	1,628	680	11,801
PHILADELPHIA	1,872	393	2,250	1,411	941	533	257	541	1,510	694	10,402
PITTSBURGH	1,789	354	1,920	1,346	1,040	558	267	535	1,478	549	9,836
CHICAGO	1,813	316	2,091	1,365	968	612	274	550	1,474	347	9,810
CINCINNATI	1,761	285	1,605	1,236	1,027	560	246	531	1,394	235	8,880
CLEVELAND	1,735	325	2,176	1,352	1,056	584	297	530	1,494	381	9,930
DETROIT	1,803	315	2,313	1,382	997	598	283	544	1,503	376	10,114
INDIANAPOLIS	1,747	320	2,134	1,336	1,031	556	266	551	1,444	336	9,721
MILWAUKEE	1,672	337	2,230	1,343	1,016	584	256	535	1,450	449	9,872
Average All Non-Florida Cities	1,810	344	2,371	1,378	1,009	571	269	543	1,503	494	10,291
ORLANDO, FLA.	1,571	257	1,565	1,285	996	499	244	549	1,371	127	8,464
DIFFERENCE——— ORLANDO VS. AVERAGE OF OTHER CITIES	−239	−87	−806	−93	−13	−72	−25	+6	−132	−367	−1,827

* Includes average costs for recreation, reading, tobacco products, alcoholic beverages, life insurance, gifts, contributions, etc.

Source: Bureau of Labor Statistics. Based on May 1975 costs. Since then costs have risen an average 6 percent a year.

Average two-bedroom retirement housing costs $35,000 and up, with lower costs on the upper West Coast north of St. Petersburg and higher costs ($45,000 and up) south of Palm Beach. Costs are higher near the beach than inland. Florida cities on the West Coast—from Naples to Bradenton—Richmond Construction Company has built three-bedroom basic homes (stripped-down models) which sell for around $20,000 (not including land). Jim Walter Homes of Tampa sells four-bedroom, two-bath "shell" homes (exterior walls, roof, interior studs, and subfloor) that you can finish yourself for an additional $5,000. And for around $25,000 you can buy a double-wide mobile home that looks like a conventional two-bedroom dwelling. But housing prices are going up.

Generally, Florida housing must withstand brilliant hot sun, insects, termites, heavy rains and flooding, hurricanes (especially in the southern part of the state), long hot summers, and occasional cold spells. To combat these problems, look for housing that has:

■ concrete slab foundations and all-masonry (concrete block stucco) construction. *Avoid* stucco on frame houses, especially older homes;

■ marble chip or ceramic tile roofs with 24-inch overhangs to keep out the sun. The roof should be well insulated to keep out the heat. And windows should have awnings that admit breezes but repel rain;

■ cross-ventilation in rooms and some form of air conditioning. Some homes have heat pumps for cooling and heating, however, air conditioning is more important. Generally, space or wall heaters are adequate for occasional cold days. (Note that Florida Power and Light, the state's largest power company, has had more major power failures than any other utility in the country. High-voltage lines to improve conditions won't be completed until the mid-1980s);

■ floors that are easy to mop—terrazzo preferred;

■ noncorrosive aluminum around windows and doors and copper plumbing fixtures;

■ the highest, driest lot you can find, preferably with a moderate slope for draining. Also ask the builder or real estate agent about a Home Warranty Program and about buying low-cost government-sponsored flood insurance. Because of potential hazards, homeowner's insurance in Florida might cost slightly more than in Northern cities.

Buying retirement acreage or homesites in Florida can be hazardous due to environmental problems and fraudulent sales practices. If you have any doubts, check with the Division of Florida Land Sales, Brock Bldg., Tallahassee, FL 32304. Be especially careful about buying a condominium; many condominium contracts contain legal pitfalls that only a lawyer can spot. Pitfalls include "escalator" clauses for maintenance and services; expensive recreation leases; restrictions on selling and willing property; restrictions on your personal living habits. For a summary of Florida's new condominium laws, send $8 to George E. Mayer, Realtor, 2700 E. Oakland Park Boulevard, Ft. Lauderdale, FL 33306. If you want to build close to the shore, send for "Building Construction on Shoreline Property," available at no cost from Marine Advisory Program, GO22 McCarthy Hall, University of Florida, Gainesville, FL 32611.

Although spraying has eliminated many insects, you may be bothered by mosquitos along coastal and marsh areas; sandflies from Daytona Beach to Miami; fire ants in western and north-central areas.

Unusual Health Facilities

Most Florida medical facilities are centered in major retirement areas. Florida has 247 hospitals with a total of 55,000 beds; 297 nursing homes with 29,304 beds; and 63 personal care homes with 5,652 beds. The state also has 14,604 doctors, which equals 1 doctor for every 604 persons—more than adequate for most health needs. In January 1980, the average cost of a semiprivate hospital room in Florida was $118.51 per day versus the U.S. average of over $133 a day.

Florida also has several *health spas* and *ranches* including:

Safety Harbor Spa
Safety Harbor, FL 33572

Warm Mineral Springs
Venice, FL 33595

Esser's Health Ranch
4005 Lucerne Avenue
Lake Worth, FL 33460

Orange Grove Health Ranch
Route 2
Box 626m
Arcadia, FL 33821

Bay'n Gulf Hygenic Home
18207 Gulf Boulevard
St. Petersburg, FL 33708

Bonita Springs Shangri-La
Bonita Springs, FL 33923

Recreation and Culture—Everything for Everybody?

A recent survey of nationwide recreational interests of retirees totaled 75 different activities. *Florida claims it has all of them!*

Florida is a *fisherman's paradise,* with the largest number of free fishing piers in the world. It has more than 8,000 miles of tidal coastline plus thousands of freshwater lakes and rivers. Among the most popular fish: channel bluefish, red snapper, pompano, sailfish, and marlin.

The Sunshine State is also a *hunter's haven,* especially for turkey, bobcats, red and gray fox, opossum, and raccoon. The main hunting season opens the third week in November and closes the first week in January. You may shoot 2 white-tailed buck deer per season plus liberal bags of squirrel, duck, geese, quail, dove, and at least 1 gobbler. A second turkey season usually opens in March with a limit of 1 per day and no more than 2 for the season. Seasonal limits also exist for dove and duck; actual hunting season dates vary from year to year.

You can play outdoor sports—golf, tennis, shuffleboard—and go cycling and hiking year-round, and enjoy spectator sports: football, baseball, tournament golf, tennis, jai alai, dog and horse racing, rodeos, stock car racing, water skiing, skin diving, and boat racing. Many professional baseball teams hold spring training in Florida. One negative note: Much of Florida's rivers and lakes and much of its coastline is severely polluted. Much swimming is done in pools.

The 3 major *cultural areas* are the Gold Coast between Miami and Palm Beach; the West Coast in the triangle of St. Petersburg-Tampa-Sarasota; Central Florida between Daytona Beach and Orlando-Winter Park. In these areas, especially during the winter, you'll find several good operas, ballets, concerts, plays, musicals, and art exhibitions.

Florida's public school system offers ongoing programs in 64 of the 67 counties, allowing adults to pursue academic, cultural, and liberal arts courses. The Asolo Theater of Sarasota, an official state theater, presents plays in a charming 18th-century theater which was moved from Asolo, Italy, to the Ringling Museum in Sarasota. In addition, Florida features more little theaters per capita than any other state in the country.

Musical activities run a close second to community theater. Florida sponsors several first-rate symphony orchestras, choirs, and community choruses.

For further information write to the Florida Department of Commerce, Tallahassee, FL 32304 for free calendar of events.

Special Services for Seniors

Besides the Florida Division on Aging, Florida has an active Council on Aging that acts as an advocate for older people. There are also many private organizations, such as Clearwater's Senior Citizens' Services, an organization which helps retirees find jobs that aid other retirees (helping the infirm, night companions, chauffeurs, etc.).

Although job opportunities aren't particularly good due to the stiff competition (only 1 percent of persons over 65 find work), the Florida State Employment Services operates an Older Worker Special Program which tries to find jobs for older people. According to the Florida Department of Commerce, between now and 1980 there will be job opportunities for dental hygienists; health records technologists and technicians; other medical and health workers; veterinarians; legal secretaries; industrial technicians; teachers aides; archivists and curators.

The Florida Insurance Commission provides free counseling to seniors on all insurance matters. The Senior Consumer Information Service of the Department of Agriculture and Consumer Services offers literature and provides a toll-free *hot line* to answer consumer complaints (800) 342-2176. Most large cities—Miami, St. Petersburg, etc.—offer counseling to seniors through local Councils on Aging. And in every retirement center there are clubs and organizations for every taste and ethnic group. Popular in many areas are "state clubs" (like Michigan Club, Ohio Club, etc.) where former residents of these states gather for sociability and recreation.

While Florida has many opportunities for recreation, in my opinion the climate—both physically and culturally—is not as stimulating as, for example, North Carolina. But for an easy paced round of fun and games, Florida has it.

For further information:

> Florida Division of Aging & Adult Services
> 1321 Winewood Boulevard
> Tallahassee, FL 32301

2. NORTH FLORIDA—THE SOUTHERN PART OF THE STATE

This is the rolling hills and piney woods section of the state. While more Northern in appearance, it is more Southern in reality; Southern people, politics, and practices dominate the region. Many settlers come from Georgia and Alabama (bordering states) and this is reflected in the culture (some of the strongest radio stations in north Florida come from Thomasville, Ga. and Mobile, Ala.).

While this part of Florida does not have many retirement communities as such, there are some places where retirees settle:

Jacksonville (pop. 570,000). Originally a summer resort, "Jax" has grown into the most industrialized metropolis in the state and the insurance capital of the South. Although it is youth oriented and business minded, it does offer both gracious living and cultural activities: the Jacksonville Symphony Orchestra, Cummer Gallery of Art, Jacksonville Art Museum, Jacksonville University, Ballet Guild, and 4 community theaters. "Jax" has pleasant residential areas, where two-bedroom homes sell for $35,000 and up. Some two-bedroom apartments are available in older, more industrialized sections for under $300 a month. The area has 11 general hospitals and 1 naval hospital with a total of 3,158 beds, and there are some 600 doctors in the area. Health care here is less adequate than in other parts of the state. There are 12,000 business and industries in the area, many serving the major insurance companies and power plant facilities. Some retirees have set up small businesses that cater to these major industries. Jacksonville's combined state and city taxes are among the lowest in the nation: averaging 3 percent of total income versus the U.S. average of 9.7 percent.

For further information:

Chamber of Commerce
Jacksonville, FL 32201

For retirees who want to take advantage of the cultural and recreational facilities of Jacksonville without living in the city, there is less expensive housing ($30,000 for a two-bedroom home) and quieter living in such satellite communities as *Jacksonville Beach* (pop. 15,000), *Neptune Beach* (5,000), *Atlantic Beach* (9,000), *Mayport* (500), and *Ponte Vedra Beach* (1,000). Known as the "Jacksonville Beaches," these communities provide a continuous front of sand and recreation areas. Fishing tournaments, beach events, and a wide variety of festivities are held year-round.

St. Augustine (pop. 15,000 city; 50,000 metropolitan) is the oldest permanent settlement in the United States. Its charming appearance (Spanish towers and steeples, red-capped roofs and low overhanging balconies) and beautifully restored historical areas have long attracted writers and artists. Many retirees are drawn to St. Augustine for some of the finest beaches and best weather in Florida. However, the area is still a tourist magnet, and prices and accommodations are scarce and expensive during the winter. Year-round residents can find ranch-style two-bedroom homes for under $40,000 and some rentals—on a yearly basis—for around $300 a month. There are over 50 doctors in the area, assuring adequate medical care.

For further information:

Chamber of Commerce
St. Augustine, FL 32084

About 20 miles south of St. Augustine is *Palm Coast,* an ambitious project started by International Telephone and Telegraph (ITT). The water-oriented community offers condominiums (two-bedroom) in the $40,000 range. Palm Coast has been faulted for its environmental and consumer practices, but has been working to improve conditions.

For further information:

ITT Development Corp.
A-1-A Bldg.
Palm Coast, FL 32037

Brooksville (pop. 7,000). This retirement town includes *Brookridge,* a modular-mobile home retirement community, that lies between Brooksville and Weeki Wachee Springs. Lots sell from $4,395 and double-wide modular-mobile homes from $20,000. The community offers 24-hour security, championship golf, swimming, sauna, tennis and shuffleboard, an adult recreation complex. Residents own their land and become part of the community.

For further information:

Brookridge
1150 Brookride Central Boulevard
Brooksville, FL 33412

Gainesville (pop. 75,000). This university town, home of the University of Florida, combines the cultural advantages of a small college town with the peace and quiet of a retirement community. Hilly farm and forest country lend a rural air to the community. Gardening, hunting, and fishing are good. The town has over 500 doctors, a 400-bed teaching hospital, and a 500-bed V.A. hospital. Two-bedroom retirement homes are reasonably priced ($30,000 and up) and farmettes and retirement acreage are available for $2,000 an acre and up.

For further information:

> Chamber of Commerce
> Drawer 1187
> Gainesville, FL 32602

Tallahassee (pop. 90,000). This city is predominantly Southern in appearance and traditions. Giant oaks and magnolias line the streets; gracious gardens and quiet residential streets make the city a relaxed, pleasant place to visit, live, and retire. Tallahassee is an excellent retirement location for those who are looking for the advantages of a large town as well as the amenities of a small town. Tallahassee offers good medical facilities (652 hospital beds and 176 physicians), cultural events (Florida State University is here), and modest living—two- and three-bedroom retirement housing priced at $35,000 and up. There are several clubs for retirees.
For further information:

> Chamber of Commerce
> Box 1639
> Tallahassee, FL 32302

Panama City (pop. 40,000). This area with its sandy white beaches and excellent fishing has attracted many retired military as well as Canadians, who have settled in the city and in suburbs like Lynn Haven, Parker, Calloway, West Bay, Springfield, and Southport. Nearby *Destin* and *Fort Walton Beach* also offer attractive retirement areas for military people (much of the area is a military preserve). Besides activities at the military base, retirees attend adult education classes, little theater productions, musical events, and other cultural activities. There are over 50 doctors in the area and three hospitals with over 400 beds.
For further information:

> Chamber of Commerce
> Box 1850
> Panama City, FL 32401

Pensacola (pop. 65,000). This historic, quaint town has intriguing views of Pensacola Bay which can be enjoyed from the cottages and rural estates perched on wooded hills. There is a thriving downtown shopping area, including such establishments as the spacious, Colonial-style San Carlos Hotel which has been converted into modernized retirement apartments. Pensacola offers many advantages to retirees, including an over-50 club, which organizes senior recreation. Although many retirees are from nearby military bases, many are also from Northern and Midwestern states. Many two- to three-bedroom retirement houses are priced at $30,000 and up; land sells for as low as $900 an' acre; county-owned lots at Pensacola Beach are available on a 99-year lease. Pensacola has 3 major hospitals plus a large naval hospital with 1,424 hospital beds and 262 physicians.

For further information:

> Chamber of Commerce
> Box 550
> Pensacola, FL 32593

3. CENTRAL FLORIDA—THE "RETIREMENT BELT"

Central Florida includes that strip of land (I call it the Retirement Belt) between the Ocala-Daytona Beach line on the north and the New Port Richey-Melbourne line on the south. In this area lie many of the developing retirement centers of Florida, such as Deltona, Pine Ridge, Citrus Springs, Marion Oaks, St. Augustine Shores, Leesburg, Mount Dora, Orlando, and Daytona Beach.

Leesburg (pop. 13,500). This city is surrounded by lakes and is known as the "largemouth bass capital." Besides fishing, the town offers golf, shuffleboard, sailing, swimming, little theater, arts and crafts, and adult education classes. Leesburg has two hospitals totaling 300 beds and over 50 doctors. The town's location in the center of the state gives it access to many other Florida attractions. There are many moderately priced homes here, including the mobile home community Hawthorne at Leesburg, recommended by the National Retired Teachers Association and the American Association of Retired Persons. Average 2-bedroom units sell for around $30,000 plus around $125 a month for lot rental. Dr. Earl Kaufman, who developed the continuing education program for retirees at the University of Kentucky and was Director of their Council on Aging, is the full-time director of social and recreational programs at Hawthorne at Leesburg.

For further information:

> Chamber of Commerce
> Box 269
> Leesburg, FL 32748

Mount Dora (pop. 6,600). Nestled among the lakes and hills of central Florida, 25 miles northwest of Orlando, Mount Dora is one of the prettiest towns in Florida. The city rises in terraces from the edge of Lake Dora, reaching a height of 184 feet above sea level—one of the highest elevations in Florida. The unusual terrain, combined with huge oak trees and white frame houses, is reminiscent of a New England college town. Coach lights, shuttered houses, and green gardens add to its "Colonial" charm. The setting attracts many professional and cultured people, and about 50 percent of the residents are retired. The Mount Dora Art League (oldest in Florida), the Ice House Players, concerts by the Florida Symphony Orchestra and a local symphony group, and some 80 other civic and social organizations ranging from the Audubon Society to the Women's Club are key attractions. Outdoor activities enjoyed the year round include golf, tennis, swimming, boating, fishing, shuffleboard, lawn bowling, croquet. The Mount Dora Yacht Club (the state's oldest inland yacht club) sponsors a sailing regatta each year. Average two-bedroom houses sell for $40,000 and up; two-bedroom condominiums for $50,000 and up; two-bedroom apartments from $250 a month. Less expensive housing is available at nearby Dora Pines, where mobile home estates sell for $30,000 including lot, and at Zellwood, where mobile homes sell for about $25,000 and up and lots rent from $100 a month. Residents who live within Mount Dora city limits pay city and county taxes which total about 18.267 mills per $1,000 (after the $5,000 homestead exemption). County taxes vary from 12.117 to 13.627 mills per $1,000. Thus the tax on a $25,000 house is about $258 in the county and slightly more in the city. Mount Dora has some 9 doctors in the city and about 15 in the vicinity. Hospital facilities are available at nearby Waterman Memorial Hospital, a 150-bed unit which serves Mount Dora, Eustis, Tavares, and Umatilla.

For further information:

> Chamber of Commerce at:
> Mount Dora, FL 32757
> Tavares, FL 32778
> Eustis, FL 32726
> Zellwood, FL 32798

Orlando (pop. 120,000). This "gateway" to Disney World offers some of the best and least expensive retirement housing in Florida. Two-bedroom single-family houses and condominiums sell for around $35,000 (while they last) and two-bedroom apartments rent from around $225 a month.

Ranch land sells for $1,000 to $2,000 an acre. Orlando has good medical facilities (3,604 hospital beds and 856 physicians) and is a cultural center with Loch Haven Art Center, the Central Florida Museum, the Florida Symphony, and the Central Florida Civic Theater. In nearby *Winter Park* (pop. 30,000), another popular retirement center, is Rollins College, Florida's oldest institution of higher learning. *Winter Garden* (pop. 8,000) is a leading citrus and resort area, and *Clermont* (pop. 5,000), "the gem of the hills" (because it is situated amid 17 lakes and hills) offers many recreational and retirement facilities. If you write the Orlando Chamber of Commerce, ask for the "Senior Signpost" booklet.

For further information:

Chambers of Commerce at:
Orlando, FL 32802
Winter Park, FL 32789
Winter Garden, FL 32787
Clermont, FL 32711

Deltona (pop. 16,500) is the site of one of the first of the Mackle Brothers retirement communities. The land is dotted with 32 lakes and also includes 2,000 feet of frontage on Lake Monroe. There are 15 houses of worship in Deltona and a 30,000-square-foot Medical Arts complex with about 25 doctors and dentists. The price range of homes in Deltona is from $25,000 to $50,000. Tax rate for Volusia County is $19.551 per $1,000 valuation; with a $5,000 homestead exemption the average annual tax bill is around $400. There is an extensive country club with a championship golf course and comfortable clubhouse. Other Deltona attractions include a modern inn featuring fine food and luxurious rooms at reasonable rates; a community center which holds adult classes in many recreational and cultural subjects; and a federal-and-state-funded Outreach Center. There are some 33,000 homesites in Deltona now; the population is projected to be 45,000 by 1990.

Near Deltona are *De Bary* (pop. 5,000) and *De Land* (pop. 15,000), attractive towns with large retired populations.

For further information:

Chamber of Commerce
De Land, FL 32720

Chamber of Commerce
De Bary, FL 32713

Deltona Area Chamber of Commerce
P.O. Box 152
Deltona, FL 32763

Daytona Beach (pop. 55,000). My uncle Stanley retired here 20 years
ago. He rents a "garage-cottage" in back of a house 5 blocks from the beach
owned by a fellow Michigander, and has made many friends among fellow
Midwesterners. In the last several years Daytona Beach has changed considerably. Once a quiet reserve of family-oriented retirees, it was invaded
by "hippies" and other young swingers, making many seniors afraid to go
out at night. While the "invasion" of young people seemed especially bad
4 years ago, when I visited my uncle last in October 1978, it didn't seem
all that hectic. I would equal Daytona Beach with Union Street in San
Francisco or Peachtree Street in Atlanta. If you're not looking for trouble,
you probably won't get it.

Daytona has most of the good and bad of any town its size, yet it still
retains the attractions that originally drew retirees. Two-bedroom retirement houses sell for as low as $30,000; there are 6 major hospitals with a
total of 939 beds and 195 physicians; a winter arts festival and a summer
music festival; the Halifax Senior Center with free membership and featuring weekly programs including ceramics, card playing, dancing, singing;
a community college, arts and sciences museums; a well-stocked library;
restaurants where retirees aren't expected to tip. Even on a small Social
Security check and company pension, Daytona is one of the very few retirement areas where a retiree can still save money.

Other nearby popular retirement areas include *Ormond Beach* (pop.
16,000), a suburb of Daytona with even lower prices, and *New Smyrna
Beach* (pop. 12,000), with good cultural and sports activities in a Med-
iterranean setting.

For further information:

Chambers of Commerce at:
Daytona Beach, FL 32015
Ormond Beach, FL 32074
New Smyrna Beach, FL 32069

4. FLORIDA'S GOLD COAST—IS ALL THAT
GLITTERS WORTHWHILE?

Leaving the Daytona-Deltona area, I headed south on I-95 for the
glamorous Gold Coast. The road is clear and good, and there are no

congested areas except for Cape Canaveral, somewhat deserted now because of the cutback in the space program.

Vero Beach (pop. 16,000). This is a quiet, elegant place to retire. Although Vero has a relatively small population, it provides housing and shopping centers for far greater, and wealthier, numbers.

Climate and Environment. Vero Beach is situated in Indian River County, located at the northern border of Florida's warmest thermal belt. This belt, resulting primarily from the warm air currents rising from the Gulf Stream, extends southward over West Palm Beach, Miami, and Key West, and is responsible for the subtropical climate, averaging 73.4° F. annually.

Housing. Vero Beach is a relatively expensive area. Two-bedroom houses near the beach sell from $60,000 and two-bedroom homes in the city sell from $40,000. Two-bedroom apartments rent from $250 a month, and some two-bedroom condominiums are available for $350 a month and up. Total city and county tax per $1,000 on nonexempt valuations is about $21 for Vero Beach, $22 for Indian River Shores, $21 for Sebastian, $20.77 for Fellsmere, $18 for Orchid. County tax on nonexempt valuation averages $17.00 per $1,000, varying with locality.

Recreation and Culture. Vero Beach has some 150 clubs ranging from the Arthritis Foundation to women's clubs, and including several senior clubs. The town also features championship shuffleboard courts, golf courses, tennis courts, fishing, and spectator sports (it is winter training headquarters for the Los Angeles Dodgers).

Medical Facilities. Vero Beach has good medical facilities with the 162-bed Indian River Memorial Hospital and a new 216-bed hospital under construction. There are some 70 doctors in the area, assuring good medical care.

For further information:

> Chamber of Commerce
> Box 2947
> Vero Beach, FL 33595

Remember one thing about Florida in general and particularly the Gold Coast—*live on the mainland.* Most towns have "beaches" (Miami-Miami Beach) linked to the mainland by a causeway. The beaches are for tourists; the mainland for cost-conscious residents. Live on the mainland; if you want the glamour of the beaches, you're only a few miles or minutes away. For instance:

Lake Worth (pop. 28,500). This town is only a few minutes from Palm Beach, but it's thousands of dollars cheaper. There is a good supply of homes in the $40,000 to $80,000 range and several condominiums in the $25,000 to $60,000 range, both in large 4-story or single-story complexes. These are mainly to the west of Lake Worth, but there are also smaller 1-building and 8- to 12-unit condominiums scattered throughout the city. Lake Worth features an active program of activities for retirees, ranging from adult education to zoos. It has 2 modern hospitals with 500 beds and 80 physicians, and 6 nursing homes. A publication put out by the chamber of commerce lists 60 separate events and facilities of all kinds, and over 100 social, civic, service, and fraternal organizations catering to just about every ethnic group and social interest.

For further information:

> Chamber of Commerce
> 1702 Lake Worth Rd.
> Lake Worth, FL 33460

West Palm Beach (pop. 70,000). West Palm Beach is just across the causeway from Palm Beach, and dwarfs its parent city. This is where the hired help of Palm Beach used to live. But many other people chose to live here because it is just minutes from the beach and costs are so much less than Palm Beach. Several satellite cities have sprung up around Palm Beach, and some industry (aircraft) has moved in, attracting younger families. But thousands of retirees continue to settle here for the glamour as well as the facilities, which include 23 golf courses and hospitals with a total of 2,048 beds and 655 physicians. In the area, you can buy two- and three-bedroom condominiums and single-family homes from $35,000 to $100,000. Further inland, there are reasonably priced country club-type subdivisions and many two-bedroom condominiums selling for around $35,000.

For further information:

> Chamber of Commerce
> Box 2931
> West Palm Beach, FL 32931

Fort Lauderdale (pop. 156,400). I find the streets and sidewalks of Fort Lauderdale congested, the high-rises on the ocean ridiculously huge, and the air polluted. Yet, Fort Lauderdale has always been a retirement mecca. This is especially true if you own a yacht, because this "tropical

Venice" has 300 miles of palm-lined lagoons, canals, and rivers. If you don't sail, you can at least swim . . . but not in the polluted ocean. Tennis and other outdoor sports abound, and the city's public parks sponsor a year-round program of sports, recreation, and crafts instruction for retirees. While much oceanfront housing is expensive, the area suffered a glut of housing, and you could pick up a good 2-bedroom condominium (while the surplus lasted) for approximately $40,000. Housing is even less expensive west of the city. Broward County (with Fort Lauderdale as the focal point) has 10 major hospitals and numerous smaller private hospitals. There are approximately 500 physicians and surgeons, 100 osteopaths, and 50 chiropractors, as well as other medical specialists in the county.

For further information:

> Chamber of Commerce
> Box 1581
> Fort Lauderdale, FL 33302

The Mecca That Is Miami

Miami (pop. 355,000) and *Miami Beach* (pop. 95,000). I brace myself whenever I drive into Miami. I arrived about rush hour and got caught in the inevitable traffic jam. It was hot and humid, although it was mid-October, and the air was polluted. The clogged traffic was comparable to a Manhattan traffic jam (not surprisingly, many Miamians had lived with New York traffic jams).

The Miami area provides the best and worst in Florida retirement living. Retired executives on fat pensions lounge in beachfront, high-rise condominiums while Social Security pensioners a few miles away on South Beach eat dog food. Cuban refugees have turned downtown Miami into Little Havana, while Orthodox Jews and other ethnic groups have turned South Beach into Little New York. The metropolitan area—containing about 1,500,000 persons and 2,257 square miles—is larger than the states of Delaware or Rhode Island.

Climate and Environment. Miami, county seat of Dade County, is on Biscayne Bay at the mouth of the Miami River. The city is about 3½ miles west of the Atlantic Ocean, separated from it by Miami Beach and Biscayne Bay. The mean average temperature is 75.3° F., with summer averaging 81.4° F. and winter, 65.5° F. Humidity averages 74 percent. Average annual rainfall is 56.3 inches.

Medical Facilities. Miami has outstanding medical facilities. There are 37 private hospitals and 3 operated by the federal government. Combined hospital beds total 11,171. The area has over 3,000 doctors, including specialists in internal diseases that afflict the elderly. Miami also has 38 nursing homes with 5,460 beds. However, hospital costs are high. They average $125 daily for a semiprivate room versus the U.S. average of $133 daily. There are some county and other charitable hospitals that charge only $90 a day for a semiprivate room. But the fact remains that medical care in Miami is among the most expensive in the Sunbelt.

Housing. Besides condominiums, single-family homes, mobile home parks, and so on, Miami has 31 apartment buildings (with some 4,000 units) exclusively for the elderly, and several retirement hotels (usually former resort hotels that have been turned into retirement residences). Many retirement apartments rent from $250 a month and two-bedroom houses sell for $40,000 and up.

Cost of Living. Living in Miami can be as cheap or expensive as you wish. Miami has some of the most luxurious hotels, fanciest restaurants, and most expensive entertainment in the country; it also offers much that is free or low in cost. Like anywhere else you must find your place on the economic scale. One guidepost: The city-county tax on an average retirement home with homestead exemption is about $700.

Recreation and Culture. The Miami area has everything. It offers some 98 art galleries, 18 major auditoriums, 8 colleges and universities, 31 bowling establishments, 45 golf courses, 29 libraries, 57 marinas, 55 nightclubs and theater-restaurants, 4,000 licensed restaurants, 20 FM stations, 10 TV stations.

Miami Beach is one of the main culture centers; almost all Miami operas and concert performances are also presented in Miami Beach's auditorium. The Miami Beach Library ranks second to Miami's, and the art museum houses treasures from various European schools. One advantage of Miami and Miami Beach: *bus and jitney service* is good and you don't need a car to get around this sprawling metropolis.

Miami and Miami Beach also feature some of the best food in the Sunbelt, thanks in part to the international flavor of the city and to the many ethnic restaurants.

Special Services for Seniors. With some 25 percent of the population retired the Miami area provides scores of senior centers and active offices of both the state and area Offices of Aging. Seniors can get help on housing, health, legal matters, nutrition, and other concerns at these offices.

For further information:

> Citizens Information Referral Service
> 955 SW Second Ave.
> Miami, FL 33130

Miami offers some pleasant surrounding areas, especially *Coral Gables* (pop. 50,000), home of the University of Miami. The "ideal" Florida began here in the 1920s when Coral Gables was planned as the "Perfect American City." It is here the Mediterranean-type houses with Moorish arches and palm-shaded patios were first built, and it was here that the first Florida boom started. Coral Gables still retains a colonial charm with its peaceful, quiet, gracious streets. Housing and living costs are relatively expensive here; two- and three-bedroom homes sell for $50,000 and up and two-bedroom unfurnished apartments rent from over $300 a month. But the area offers unusually good medical care, with over 300 doctors, including several specializing in geriatrics.

For further information:

> Chamber of Commerce
> Coral Gables, FL 33134

The Keys (pop. 50,000). This 110-mile coral and limestone chain of islands off the tip of the mainland has attracted few retirees due to the high costs and the distance—Key West, the furthest point, is 100 miles from the mainland. Housing is expensive in the Keys because most of the materials and labor must be shipped in. The average cost of a new two-bedroom, two-bath house is from $60,000. However, retirees do live in inexpensive mobile home parks where spaces rent for an average $100 a month. The Keys have drawbacks: Erosion and land development is slowly killing parts of the northernmost reefs; prevalence of drugs and homosexuality in Key West; higher temperatures in the summer, although ocean breezes moderate the heat. Some of the most popular retirement areas are *Key Largo* (pop. 5,000); *Taverner, Islamorada,* and *Marathon* (pop. 8,000); and *Key West* (pop. 62,000), which is the southernmost city in the U.S. The area (Monroe County) has 241 hospital beds and 46 physicians.

For further information:

> Chambers of Commerce at:
> Key Largo, FL 33047
> Islamorada, FL 33036
> Key West, FL 33040
> Marathon, FL 33050

5. FLORIDA'S WEST COAST—FLORIDA'S MIDWEST

Driving to the West Coast of Florida from Miami is always a pleasure because of the intriguing Everglades. My first stop was *Naples*. Twenty-five years ago, Naples was an "exclusive" tiny village filled with WASP Mid-westerners. Like everywhere else, Naples has changed. Collier County, in which Naples is located, is the seventh-fastest-growing county in the *nation* and one of the fastest-growing counties in Florida. Naples now has a population of some 40,000, which increases 100 percent in the peak of the winter tourist season. There are many new housing developments, shops, and buildings of all kinds—as well as a good deal of traffic congestion. It took me over half an hour just to traverse the main street through town (the state is building a new freeway up the West Coast that will bypass these cities).

In spite of its mushrooming growth, Naples still remains one of my favorite Florida cities. It is clean and has an elegant, country-club look. Good-location two-bedroom houses sell for $40,000 and up, two-bedroom apartments from $37,000, and mobile homes from $25,000 including lots. On a yearly lease you can rent some unfurnished apartments for as low as $250 a month; some furnished at $350 a month. City taxes are 19 mills per $1,000; county taxes about 20 mills per $1,000.

The Naples Community Hospital has a 313-bed capacity and an attending staff of 97. There are over 181 physicians and 47 dentists in the area.

Naples offers many activities, including 100 clubs and organizations; fine municipal beaches and parks; a fishing pier, nature center, dog racing, and fancy shops. Naples, like Southern Pines, N.C., reminds me of an urban Carmel, Cal.

For further information:

Chamber of Commerce
1700 North Tamiami Trail
Naples, FL 33940

South of Naples is *Marco Island* where the Deltona Corporation plans to build a community of at least 1,200 homes.

Fort Myers (pop. 36,000). This is the biggest town north of Naples. Fort Myers calls itself the "City of Seven Happinesses" because it offers everything from great fishing to gourmet food. It also offers amateur theatricals, music and art groups, organized senior activities, and the Pittsburgh Pirates' training games. There are several major hospitals in the area with a total of 1,008 beds and 252 physicians. One-bedroom retirement houses sell for as low as $25,000. And in neighboring Lehigh Acres you can enjoy country-club living in homes ranging from $25,000 to over $100,000. Charming living is also available on nearby *Sanibel* and *Captiva* islands.

For further information:

Chambers of Commerce at:
Fort Myers, FL 33902
Lehigh Acres, FL 33936
Sanibel, FL 33957
Captiva, FL 33924

Punta Gorda (pop. 9,000) ; *Port Charlotte* (pop. 35,000). A few miles north of Fort Myers is Punta Gorda, the commercial as well as governmental seat of Charlotte County. This is one of the fastest-growing areas in the state, and the focal point for many retirement communities, the biggest of which is Port Charlotte. I first saw this area in 1963; it's grown so that on a recent visit I didn't recognize a single landmark. Port Charlotte's residents live in more than 13,000 homes which average at (for a two-bedroom unit) $35,000. The area has 3 hospitals and some 100 doctors, yacht clubs, 5 recreation centers, 3 country clubs with 18-hole championship golf courses, and a $3 million cultural center with a nationally recognized adult education school. Half the residents are retired or semiretired.

Other nearby developments include *Emerald Pointe, Deep Creek,* and *Punta Gorda Isles.*

For further information:

Chamber of Commerce
98 Tamiami Trail
Punta Gorda, FL 33950

Englewood (pop. 20,000). Across Lemon Bay from Punta Gorda lies Englewood, linked by bridge and causeway to a 9-mile long stretch of some of the finest beaches on Florida's West Coast. About half of the residents are retired and they live in a variety of moderately priced housing including mobile homes, which sell for around $25,000 up. As the community lies in both Charlotte and Sarasota counties, it enjoys facilities of both. Located within a 35-mile radius are 5 excellent hospitals with a total of 1,300 beds. The Englewood Recreation Council, an organization of volunteers guiding the activities of the recreation center, organizes activities for adults. Englewood also sponsors numerous clubs and has program luncheons, variety shows, and tours to nearby attractions.

For further information:

> Chamber of Commerce
> 601 South Indiana Ave.
> Englewood, FL 32032

Sarasota (pop. 58,800). Sarasota is reputed to be a cultural oasis on Florida's West Coast.

Climate and Environment. I was impressed with the broad boulevards and the neat, clean buildings, and grateful that it is cooler in Sarasota than in either Miami or in West Coast areas to the south. When a hot or humid front comes into Florida, it often affects Miami and the central part of the state but spares Sarasota. This is partly because the Barrier Islands or Keys separate Sarasota's principal bays and the Intracoastal Waterway from the Gulf of Mexico. The temperature drops in the evening, making sleeping comfortable even in summer. Winter temperatures average in the 60s; summer temperatures rarely reach 95° F.

Medical Facilities. Sarasota has several hospitals and nursing homes specializing in geriatric care, with 1,301 hospital beds and 330 physicians in the area.

Housing. Sarasota is satisfactory for retirement in many ways. Good two-bedroom houses are available from $40,000; some two-bedroom apartments rent from $300 a month. At Mt. Vernon (80 waterfront acres on Sarasota Bay) two-bedroom homes sell from $35,000, and at Village Brooks, two-bedroom townhouses start at $25,000. Even lower-priced housing is available at 7 "retirement residences or centers" approved by the Better Business Department of the Sarasota Chamber of Commerce. Combined city and county property taxes are about 14.5 mills per $1,000; school taxes about 8.4 mills per $1,000.

Cost of Living. Shopping is a special treat, especially at St. Armand's Circle and on the Keys (connected by a causeway). There are job opportunities for retirees here in hotels, motels, restaurants, theaters, travel agencies, real estate, and in clerical and sales occupations.

Recreation and Culture. Cultural activities include facilities for the performing arts at the Asolo State Theater and Van Wezel Performing Arts Hall, and the Players Theatre. Sarasota hosts both professional and amateur theater companies. The Florida West Coast Symphony Orchestra, the Sarasota Concert Band, and other groups offer music, while the Sarasota Exhibition Hall and many galleries feature art. There are also the

Ringling Museum Complex, antique car and glass blowers' exhibits, and the Sarasota campus of the University of South Florida.

There are 16 city parks and 22 county parks including 7 beach areas (35 miles of beaches) for bathing. You can fish and boat from the $1 million municipal marina, and golf on the 36-hole municipal course.

Special Services for Seniors. Sarasota has many Senior Friendship Centers and other places of hospitality for older adults.

For further information:

> Chamber of Commerce
> Box 308
> Sarasota, FL 33578

Bradenton (pop. 30,000). Bradenton is a few miles to the north, and is the "mobile home capital" of Florida's West Coast. It includes the extensive development of Colony Cove (across the Manatee River at Ellenton) where lots rent for $90 a month and two-bedroom mobile homes sell for around $26,000. Despite the profusion of mobile homes and other small retirement housing, Bradenton seems to be a stable community. It offers a well-organized program of social activities and recreation; arts and music; golf and tennis. It also provides senior centers and other retiree clubs. West of the city, over a toll-free bridge, are 3 satellite communities: *Anna Maria, Bradenton Beach,* and *Holmes Beach.* Bradenton Beach has small homes and a relaxed pace; Anna Maria has more elegant waterfront housing; Holmes Beach has more modern dwellings.

For further information:

> Chamber of Commerce
> Bradenton-Mantee County
> Box 321
> Bradenton, FL 33506

6. THE GULF COAST RETIREMENT KINGDOM

St. Petersburg (pop. 250,000). Although when I arrived the highway was clogged with traffic, the pace was a lot slower than in Miami. About one-third of St. Petersburg residents are retired, and my impression of St. Petersburg has been that it's a place for *older* people—perhaps in their 70s and 80s—rather than those in their 50s and 60s. But I was pleasantly surprised to see so many young (20s and 30s) faces on the street and to learn that the younger population has soared in recent years, injecting new life into the community. St. Petersburg still is paradise for older folks, mainly because of the tremendous number of facilities and advantages it offers to the senior age group.

Climate and Environment. The weather stays about the same year-round with the mean temperature in January 63.3° F.; April 73.1° F.; July 73.1° F.; October 73.1° F. Rain falls in each of these months, averaging about 3 inches each month. St. Pete guarantees 361 days of sunshine, and the St. Petersburg *Evening Independent* gives away its newspaper free every day the sun fails to shine. Humidity averages 75.25 percent, which is uncomfortable on hot days.

Medical Facilities. The area has 22 hospitals and numerous convalescent and nursing homes with a total of 5,602 beds and 619 physicians (400 of whom are in St. Petersburg itself). Although the area claims it is one of the most "hospital overbedded areas in the nation," there is only 1 doctor for every 719 people in Pinellas County as a whole. This is not adequate for the county's older population, although St. Petersburg itself has 1 doctor for every 436 residents, which is adequate. Hospital rooms in St. Pete average $125 daily for a semiprivate room. This is about $5 above the Florida average, but $8 less than the U.S. average. St. Petersburg also boasts its Bayfront Medical Center—classified as a "tertiary facility." This means that it has expensive, sophisticated equipment needed by only a few people and intended to serve an entire region; offers a comprehensive array of services; serves as a teaching facility; is a research center. St. Pete must be healthy; I've visited the main senior center several times and have seen ardent swains of 75 wooing fair maids of 70. And I've watched the "Kids and Kubs" (men over 75) play spirited softball. There's a saying that you're not considered old in St. Petersburg until you reach 90.

Housing. Two-bedroom retirement homes range from $25,000 to $125,000; the average is between $35,000 and $45,000. Mobile home parks are popular; the average mobile home with extras costs about $25,000. Initial hook-up charges may run $75 to $90 and rentals average $90 a month. Two-bedroom apartments range from $200 a month for an efficiency to $1,000 a month for completely furnished luxury condominiums on the water. Property taxes are the sum of the city, county, and school taxes based on 100 percent of the appraised value of property. Millage ranges from 15.592 to 21.492 depending upon location.

Cost of Living. In a recent American Chamber of Commerce Researchers Association survey of 174 American cities, St. Petersburg ranked sixth lowest in prices for basic goods and services. Liquor and movie theater tickets are particularly low. Many retired couples live in St. Pete for around $8,400 annually thanks to convenient, low-cost shopping facilities such as Webb's City, "The Bargain Capital of the Suncoast," which offers bargains on everything. It has the largest flea market in Florida and an all-you-can-eat cafeteria ($3, tax included). Many retirees raise vegetables (2 crops a year) and fish for their supper.

Recreation and Culture. From museums to the symphony to theater, St. Petersburg has whatever form of entertainment you want. Major museums include the Museum of Fine Arts, the St. Petersburg Historical Museum, the new and growing Pinellas County Historical Park and County Historical Museum. St. Petersburg's Bayfront Center offers a year-round entertainment program including Broadway plays, major sports events, and the Florida Gulf Coast Symphony. There are 10 existing and 3 developing parks in the area, offering some 2,300 recreational acres. Many retirees enroll in educational programs available through St. Petersburg Junior College, the University of South Florida, Eckerd College, and Stetson University College of Law. After Miami, St. Petersburg offers the finest array of cultural activities in Florida.

Special Services for Seniors. St. Pete has over 300 organizations offering services and recreation for all age groups, especially seniors. At the Mirror Lake, Sunshine, and Bartlett community recreation centers there are year-round programs of shuffleboard, and lawn bowling, tennis, archery, trap and skeet shooting, and so on. There are 31 golf courses in the area, 15 of which are public and semiprivate, and 45 tennis courts. Dog and horse racing, jai alai, and professional sports are popular here. Many beautiful and exotic gardens—Sunken Gardens, Busch Gardens, Tiki Gardens—offer entertainment and recreation. Each Sunday the St. Petersburg *Times* prints a full calendar of events and gives information on joining clubs.

For further information:

> Chamber of Commerce
> Box 1371
> St. Petersburg, FL 33731

Dunedin. Just north of St. Petersburg, Dunedin, founded in 1860, claims to be the oldest settlement on the West Coast of Florida. Dunedin is a small town—population 32,000—and half of its residents are retired. As a "wee bit of Scotland" in Florida, it is host to an annual Highland Festival and Games, and its bagpipe band is nationally recognized. Dunedin is a city of parks, culture, and recreation. The community center offers all-day activities and adult education classes. Two-bedroom homes sell for $30,000 and up; building lots for $5,000 and up. Mease Hospital and Clinic has 202 beds, with plans to expand to 500 beds by 1980. Dunedin also has 2 nursing homes, 50 doctors, and a visiting nurse service.

For further information:

Chamber of Commerce
Dunedin, FL 33528

Tampa (pop. 500,000) is Florida's third largest city, and the industrial neighbor of St. Petersburg. It offers retirees the recreation facilities and proximity of St. Petersburg, but it has some of the industrial congestion and pollution problems of Miami. Tampa has a large Hispanic population, centered in Ybor City, a 2-square-mile section within the city which also houses the cigar industry. Many Spanish restaurants, coffeehouses, and cigar factories are here.

Cost of living and housing costs are much the same as in St. Pete. Two-bedroom homes sell for $30,000 and up and two-bedroom apartments rent from $250 a month and up. All-State homes will build three-bedroom homes on your own lot (lots average $17,000). There are 16 major hospitals in the area and 876 doctors; hospital rooms average $106 daily for a semiprivate room. Seniors age 60 and over get special discounts at over 300 businesses in Hillsborough County.

Cultural facilities include the Florida Gulf Coast Symphony, 2 museums, a $2.4 million library, 5 local community theaters, and convention hall. Educational opportunities include Hillsborough Community College with 2 campuses, and the universities of Tampa and South Florida. The noted Dr. Max Kaplan conducts a Leisure Studies Program at the University of South Florida. Dr. Kaplan's studies have set the pace of senior leisure activities throughout the nation. Tampa's parks provide well-organized adult recreation programs and Golden Age Clubs with accents on bridge, arts and crafts, square dancing, and physical fitness. Tampa is a sports-minded area featuring jai alai; horse, auto, and greyhound racing; and professional baseball, soccer, and football.

Because Tampa is not as crowded with retirees as surrounding areas, lower-cost housing is available in some of the older sections, and there are part-time and full-time jobs in shops, restaurants, and theaters as well as in sales and clerical fields. However, because of Tampa's industrial environment, most retirees still prefer St. Petersburg, Clearwater, or Sun City Center.

For further information:

Chamber of Commerce
Box 420
Tampa, FL 33601

Sun City Center (pop. 6,000). This area, about 15 miles southeast of Tampa, is good retirement country. Sun City Center, with counterparts in Arizona and California, lies just east of Ruskin. It is a thriving community with hundreds of homes (around $35,000 and up), fronting on bass-filled lakes or on championship golf courses, and it offers activities from golf to lawn bowling, shuffleboard, swimming, tennis, square dancing, arts and crafts, cards, fishing, sailing, and cycling. Sun City is a self-contained community with shopping facilities and a medical center. It appeals mainly to middle-income retirees who want an active social life.
For further information:

Sun City
Chamber of Commerce
P.O. Box 5698
Sun City Center, FL 33570

Clearwater (pop. 90,000). This is the vast area just north of St. Petersburg. In contrast to the congestion and "oldness" of St. Petersburg, Clearwater is expansive and new, and is one of the fastest-growing areas of Florida. It probably offers a greater variety of housing at a wider range of prices than any other Florida city. One-bedroom homes sell for as low as $15,000; two-bedroom homes and condominiums start under $40,000; two-bedroom apartments rent for under $300 a month; and many mobile home parks either sell units (around $25,000) or rent space (average $90 a month). Clearwater has 3 hospitals of its own and shares medical facilities with St. Petersburg. In addition, Clearwater has installed a $350,000 brain scanner in its Morton Plant Hospital that can help diagnose mental disorders. Clearwater has over 340 doctors in the area, about 1 doctor per 252 residents, which assures better-than-average medical care. Its Fine Arts Center features little theater productions and arts and crafts exhibits. Clearwater caters mainly to middle-income families seeking a place in the sun.
For further information:

Chamber of Commerce
Clearwater, FL 33515

On the coast to the north of Clearwater lies *Tarpon Springs* (pop. 15,000), a picturesque Greek fishing village. Greek culture, names, food, and entertainment have put their stamp on this area, and it is mainly a tourist attraction and a sponge-fishing center. You don't have to be Greek to settle here, but you should at least know the Greek language and like Greek atmosphere.

For further information:

Chamber of Commerce
Tarpon Springs, FL 33489

New Port Richey (pop. 10,000). New Port Richey probably has the best buys in housing on Florida's West Coast. It has several retirement developments in the area. *Highland Lakes* in the Palm Harbor area is a U.S. Home development consisting of some 6,000 units on over 800 acres of rolling ground that was formerly an orange grove. It features four-plex villas that sell for about $40,000 (with monthly maintenance fees of under $100) and appeal to white-color retirees looking for country-club status. Homes are attractive and extremely well built; owners get clubhouse privileges that include swimming pool, shuffleboard, billiard rooms, card room, auditoriums, and lounges. *Timber Oaks,* nearer New Port Richey, caters to blue-collar families. Fairway villas sell from $25,000 to $35,000, with a monthly maintenance fee about $75. The trees, fields, and woods provide a lovely setting. Social activities include bowling, dancing classes, arts, and crafts, games, and so on.

This area also has a number of mobile home developments of Boyce Enterprises. These consist of parks or "villages" where mobile homes sell for as little as $25,000 including the lot. A bit further north at Hudson is Club Wildwood, another attractive mobile home village that has a low rental of $90 a month. Homes sell for $20,000 to $40,000.

Highland Lakes, Timber Oaks, and other retirement communities use medical facilities in nearby Clearwater and St. Petersburg. New Port Richey has some 30 doctors and 2 hospitals in the area, equaling 1 doctor per 333 residents, more than enough for adequate medical care.

For further information:

Chamber of Commerce
407 West Main Street
New Port Richey, FL 33551

For information on Timber Oaks and Highland Lakes:

> U.S. Home of Florida, Inc.
> One Countryside Office Park
> Clearwater, FL 33518

For information on Boyce Homes:

> Boyce Homes
> Post Office Box 608
> New Port Richey, FL 33552

For information on Club Wildwood:

> Club Wildwood
> 169 Club Wildwood
> Hudson, FL 33568

SUMMARY

I *liked* the fact that whatever you're looking for in retirement living you can probably find—at more reasonable cost—in Florida than in any other Sunbelt state.

What I *didn't* like about Florida is the congestion—especially in the Palm Beach to Miami area on the East Coast, and the Naples to St. Petersburg area on the West Coast; the flatness of the land (I prefer hills and mountains); the monotony of the weather (I prefer a more invigorating, seasonal climate); and the "fun and games" atmosphere of many areas (I like more cultural events). Unfortunately, part of the problem lies in the warm, humid weather, which doesn't seem to be conducive to much intellectual activity.

Here are my personal ratings for Florida's major retirement areas:

Excellent—Mount Dora, Vero Beach, Naples, Sarasota;

Good—St. Augustine, Gainesville, Tallahassee, Miami/Miami Beach, Pensacola, Lake Worth, West Palm Beach, Dunedin, Clearwater, New Port Richey, Tarpon Springs, Sun City Center, St. Petersburg, Orlando, Daytona Beach, Port Charlotte;

Adequate—Brooksville, Tampa, Panama City, Leesburg, Tavares, Ocala, Punta Gorda, Fort Lauderdale, Fort Myers, Englewood, Bradenton, Jacksonville;

Poor—The Keys.

RATINGS FOR *FLORIDA* MAJOR RETIREMENT AREAS

TALLAHASSEE

Rating	Climate & Envir.	Medical	Housing	Cost of Living	Rec. & Culture	Spec. Senior Svces.
1						
2	●	●	●		●	●
3				●		
4						
5						

MARION OAKS-OCALA

Rating	Climate & Envir.	Medical	Housing	Cost of Living	Rec. & Culture	Spec. Senior Svces.
1						
2	●		●	●	●	●
3		●				
4						
5						

ORLANDO

Rating	Climate & Envir.	Medical	Housing	Cost of Living	Rec. & Culture	Spec. Senior Svces.
1						●
2	●	●	●	●	●	
3						
4						
5						

PENSACOLA

Rating	Climate & Envir.	Medical	Housing	Cost of Living	Rec. & Culture	Spec. Senior Svces.
1						
2	●	●	●	●	●	●
3						
4						
5						

RATINGS FOR *FLORIDA* MAJOR RETIREMENT AREAS

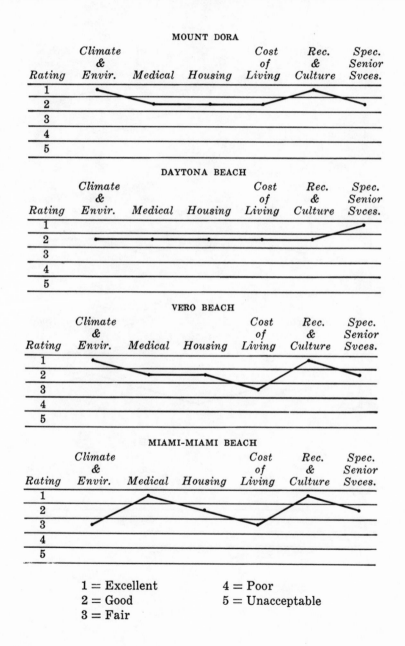

1 = Excellent   4 = Poor
2 = Good   5 = Unacceptable
3 = Fair

RATINGS FOR *FLORIDA* MAJOR RETIREMENT AREAS

NAPLES

Rating	Climate & Envir.	Medical	Housing	Cost of Living	Rec. & Culture	Spec. Senior Svces.
1	●				●	
2		●	●			●
3				●		
4						
5						

FORT LAUDERDALE

Rating	Climate & Envir.	Medical	Housing	Cost of Living	Rec. & Culture	Spec. Senior Svces.
1						
2		●	●		●	●
3	●			●		
4						
5						

THE KEYS

Rating	Climate & Envir.	Medical	Housing	Cost of Living	Rec. & Culture	Spec. Senior Svces.
1						
2					●	
3	●	●		●		●
4			●			
5						

PORT CHARLOTTE (AREA)

Rating	Climate & Envir.	Medical	Housing	Cost of Living	Rec. & Culture	Spec. Senior Svces.
1						
2	●	●	●	●	●	●
3						
4						
5						

RATINGS FOR *FLORIDA* MAJOR RETIREMENT AREAS

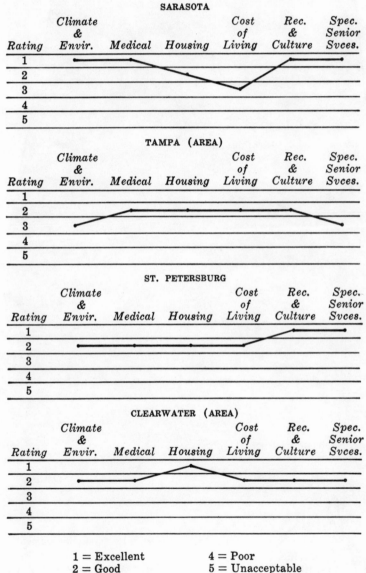

1 = Excellent   4 = Poor
2 = Good   5 = Unacceptable
3 = Fair

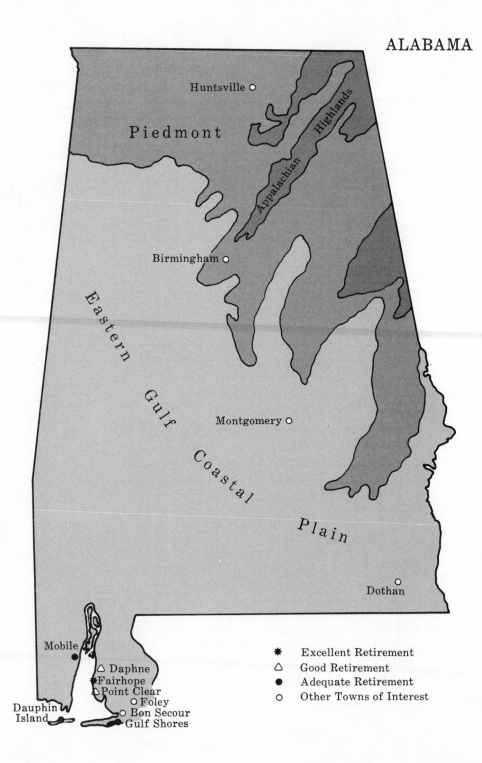

ALABAMA

Huntsville ○

Piedmont

Appalachian Highlands

Birmingham ○

Eastern Gulf Coastal Plain

Montgomery ○

Dothan ○

Mobile ●

△ Daphne
✳ Fairhope
△ Point Clear
○ Foley
● Bon Secour
Gulf Shores

Dauphin
Island

✳   Excellent Retirement
△   Good Retirement
●   Adequate Retirement
○   Other Towns of Interest

VIII.

ALABAMA—

RETIREMENT IN THE

HEART OF DIXIE

Alabama's main retirement areas are located along the Eastern Shore of Mobile Bay, and in the Mobile area.

Alabama has other cities suitable for retirement, including *Huntsville* (pop. 150,000), which is set on the side of a sharply curving valley with a jagged horizon of mountains to the east. This is a rocket center, and the city has a cosmopolitan atmosphere, with residents from all over the world.

Dothan (pop. 45,000), just above the Florida border in the southeast part of Alabama, also offers attractive retirement. It is a marketing center for local farms and has attracted new industries including those involved in the manufacturing and processing of peanuts, corn, cotton, and cattle. Dothan sponsors a flourishing civic ballet, concert association, and a little theater group.

As a whole, Alabama offers a number of advantages to retirees including:

Good Outdoor Weather

The temperature averages 65.8° F. (close to the ideal) with a range of about 44° to 62° F. in January and 73° to 92° F. in July. Average annual rainfall is 53.3 inches; humidity averages 69 percent. This climate permits people to enjoy the beaches almost year-round, including boating, swimming, and fishing. The state is rich in timber, coal, iron, clay, and stone—two of every three acres in Alabama is covered with "green gold"—trees, both hard and soft woods—mainly oak and pine. And Alabama leads the nation in navigable waterways with 2,092 miles.

Moderate Cost of Living

Living costs in Alabama's larger cities and coastal resort areas are near the national average. Costs in Birmingham are slightly (1.1 percent) above the national average, while costs in Huntsville drop to 98 percent and in Mobile to 94.6 percent of the U.S. average. Further inland, costs drop to as low as 86 percent of the national rate. Retired couples can live adequately on $8,500 a year. Among special tax advantages for Alabama retirees are a $5,000 assessed value property-tax exemption and *complete property-tax exemption* for anyone 65 or older who has an annual reportable income of not more than $7,500, resides on the property and owns not over 160 acres. Taxes average about $75 per $10,000 valuation.

The *income tax* ranges from 1.5 percent of the first $1,000 of income to 5 percent over $5,000. A single person gets a $1,500 exemption; married couples $3,000; dependents $300.

The *sales tax* rate is 4 percent, with additional taxes imposed by some counties and/or municipalities. *Prescription drugs are exempt for persons age 65 or over.*

Unusually Attractive Homes

Alabama has unusually attractive homes in retirement areas like Point Clear, Fairhope, Daphne, and Montrose, as well as outstanding senior citizen rental apartments in Mobile. Two-bedroom retirement homes are moderately priced (around $35,000 and up) throughout the state, especially considering the style and quality of construction.

Low-Cost Hospital Facilities

Medical facilities are generally adequate in the larger cities—especially Birmingham, which has the University of Alabama Medical Center—and in some rural areas, such as Fairhope, they are more than adequate. However, if you plan to move to Alabama, be sure that your area has the desired medical facilities and available doctors. Alabama has a total of 138 hospitals with 19,896 beds. Alabama also has 210 nursing homes with 20,090 beds. A semiprivate hospital room averages $94.67 daily versus the U.S. average of over $133 a day. There are 4,071 doctors in the state, which equals only 1 doctor for every 906 residents—less than adequate.

Recreation and Culture

Most of Alabama's retirement areas have better-than-average recreational and cultural advantages for retirees. These range from outstanding libraries to little theater groups to interesting restaurants. The arts and crafts centers are outstanding in some rural areas, such as Fairhope.

Birmingham has a music hall, theater, large exhibition hall, and coliseum in the 6-square-block civic center. Mobile has 4 picturesque historic districts, which protect some 250 prominent architectural landmarks dating to the early 19th century. Imposing Mobile landmarks include Oakleigh Mansion, City Hall-City Market, Barton Academy, the Fort Conde-Charlotte House, Admiral Raphael Semmes Home, the Cathedral of the Immaculate Conception, and the Battleship *Alabama*. Mobile also boasts the Old World Spanish Plaza, decorated with fountains and tiles from cities in Spain.

Special Services for Seniors

Alabama has a nutrition project for the elderly in each of its 67 counties. Fifty-eight counties are served by Area Agencies on Aging and 2 counties are served by Community Service Projects. Another 5 counties are initiating special transportation programs for elderly and handicapped persons. The University of Alabama's Center for the Study of Aging has organized a Consortium of Educators in Gerontology, which coordinates the sharing of information, resources, and expertise in the field of aging in Alabama.

For further information:

> Commission on Aging
> State of Alabama
> 2853 Fairlane Drive
> Building "G" Suite 63
> Montgomery, AL 36130

> Center for the Study of Aging
> University of Alabama
> Post Office Box 1935
> University, AL 35486

1. BALDWIN COUNTY—GRACIOUS LIVING IN A
GARDEN SETTING

I entered Alabama in Baldwin County, crossing on a bridge from Florida a few miles west of Pensacola.

As soon as I saw the "Welcome to Alabama" sign, I felt I had stepped into a vast agricultural preserve or a garden. Green fields of corn, pecan orchards, and trees heavily laden with brown nuts were everywhere; sleek black-and-white cattle grazed in rolling meadows. I passed tall stands of evergreens, enormous green oaks with tendrils of gray Spanish moss, and dogwood trees promising delicate white blossoms.

South of here are snowy white beaches with surging green breakers and bays. This is the home of such quaint towns as *Bon Secour* (pop. 750), settled by Germans, French Creole, Spanish, and Danes, who fish, gather shrimp, and farm for a living. It's also the locale of the retirement/resort community of *Gulf Shores* (pop. 2,000), where Gulf lots sell for $23,000 and three-bedroom, two-bath homes cost about $50,000. Gulf Shores features 2 fine golf courses, surf fishing, and a fishing pier.

To the west lies *Dauphin Island* (pop. 1,000), reached by a toll-free, 4-mile-long bridge and causeway from Mobile. This popular recreation/ retirement area is expected to triple in population in the next 6 years. Two-bedroom beach homes sell from $30,000, but there is a shortage of rentals during the resort season.

Medical facilities in Baldwin County center mainly in Fairhope (see below) and in *Foley* (pop. 5,000), an agricultural center, which has the 59-bed Hill-Burton Hospital and a 124-bed nursing home. Nearby is the South Baldwin Hospital, Baldwin County's largest, with 82 beds and a staff of 159.

The area also boasts the South Baldwin Chamber Theatre, the largest and most active drama group in the county.

The Eastern Shore Retirement Region

Many retirees have been drawn to Baldwin County's Eastern Shore, where the towns of *Fairhope* (the main center), *Point Clear*, and *Daphne* sit side by side on high bluffs overlooking Mobile Bay. This is probably the southernmost point in the U.S. where you can still enjoy four distinct seasons. The mean temperature is about 68° F.; January temperatures average 53.9° F. and July 82.2° F. Being coastal, the towns have high humidity (average is 70 percent) and 62 inches of rainfall annually, which keep "gardens green and complexions soft and glowing." Winds are southerly, and the air is washed, fresh, and wholesome after its 600-mile trip across the Gulf of Mexico.

The Eastern Shore offers cultural attractions including the Dogwood Theatre Festival, which schedules summer stock plays, and the Earth Drama Club, which presents shows at the Grand Hotel in Point Clear. The Eastern Shore Academy of Fine Arts features fine arts education.

The Eastern Shore also features "jubilees" 6 times a year, when the shrimp and crabs struggle to get out of the bay onto dry land. When residents spot the signs of the migration, they cry "Jubilee" and get to work with galvanized tubs, croaker sacks, gigs, and rowboats. Jubilees usually last 4 or 5 hours; it's not exceptional for an ardent resident to gig 100 flounders, scoop up a barrel of shrimp and another of crabs, and get a cask full of soft-shell crabs. This provides enough fish for meals far into the year.

Fairhope (pop. 7,200), with its magnificent waterfront, stately municipal pier, breathtaking views, and notable artists' colony, is the crown jewel of the Eastern Shore.

Medical Facilities. Fairhope also has unusually good medical facilities. The cardiac care unit at Thomas Hospital ranks with the best in the country. It can transmit cardiograms to physicians as far away as Boston and New York for analysis. A semiprivate room here averages $80.00 daily. Fairhope also has the excellent Bay Medical Clinic, with a pathologist, radiologist, psychiatrists, and other specialists. Some 12 physicians live in town, assuring more than adequate medical care.

Housing. Fairhope has lovely, well-built housing. Generally, three-bedroom, two-bath houses on a 100-by-100-foot lot sell for about $45,000. To build on your own lot (lots cost from $7,500 to $12,000) costs from $40,000 to $50,000. To park a mobile home in a 400-square-foot lot costs $50 to $75 a month. There are 250 condominium units in the Fairhope area at 3 different locations, costing from $25,000 for a studio to $75,000 for two bedrooms. There are few rental apartments or houses, but vacancies rent from $200 a month. One planned community, Lake Forest, offers country-club living in two- and three-bedroom homes for around $40,000. Property taxes average 1 percent of market value: $500 on a $50,000 house (house assessments are going up).

Fairhope has a unique housing situation. The town was established by settlers from Des Moines, Iowa, who were followers of Henry George, advocate of the "single tax." Much of the land (about 15 percent in the city; 25 percent in the surrounding area) is in the Single Tax Corporation, which leases to homeowners for 99 years. This arrangement makes land less susceptible to inflation, so values remain stable. Fairhope also offers a unique apartment complex that is located on a quiet street just off the main thoroughfare. The complex includes a greenhouse, private patios, wood-burning fireplaces, and complete security.

Cost of Living. While living costs are about the same as elsewhere in Alabama, the casual way of life, proximity to goods and services, and bountiful climate (less clothing and lower heating costs) reduce expenses. Some retirees save even more money by raising tomatoes, beans, carrots, and other vegetables in the fertile soil, and many fish for their supper. Farmers' markets in the area offer home-grown produce at low costs. To live comfortably here, a retired couple should have an annual income of at least $10,000.

Recreation and Culture. Fairhope is the area's cultural center. It has a modern, pleasant library with over 40,000 volumes, and a 500-member Art Association which sponsors an academy where successful and dedicated artists conduct classes in watercolors and oil, portraiture, still life, and landscape painting. A men's coffee club meets weekly at the Art Academy. During the annual Arts and Crafts Week in mid-March, thousands of visitors flock to Fairhope to see the dogwood and azaleas in bloom.

Fairhope's Adult Recreation Center features a daily program of activities including art and handicrafts, bridge and other games, field trips and related events. Fairhope is home to some 68 clubs and organizations—all with senior participation.

With Fairhope as the geographical center, these two other towns form a continuous community:

Point Clear (pop. 1,000) is the most luxurious part of the community. Its magnificent Grand Hotel, a resort hotel where rates start at $50 daily, draws distinguished guests from all parts of the world. The adjacent elegant Lakewood Club features championship golf. Other facilities nearby offer horseback riding, skeet shooting, freshwater and deep-sea fishing. Many large, comfortable houses (prices range from $70,000 to $300,000) line the water's edge.

Daphne (pop. 3,800) is the "farming" section of the community and many residents grow potatoes and other vegetables in the rich soil. The area was named for the laurel tree that grows profusely along the wooded roads and trails. Between Daphne and Fairhope lies the unincorporated village of *Montrose* (pop. 400). Many prosperous farms start in the countryside to the east.

Point Clear, Daphne, and Montrose use the medical, cultural, recreational, and shopping services of Fairhope.

For further information:

Eastern Shore Chamber of Commerce
P.O. Box 507
Fairhope, AL 36532

2. MOBILE—FRENCH AND SPANISH INFLUENCES

I entered *Mobile* (pop. 200,000) through the George Wallace Tunnel, connecting the Eastern Shore of Mobile Bay with the city. Some Alabamans view Mobile as a state in itself. It is probably one of the most conservative areas in the country, and the Catholic influence remains strong here. Mobile was the site of the first Mardi Gras festival in the United States. Like New Orleans, Mobile has "mystic societies," which hold annual balls climaxing just before Ash Wednesday. Mobile rivals New Orleans with its lacy iron railings and French and Spanish influences. It seems a cross between Smalltown, USA, and a large city.

Climate and Environment. Mobile is approximately 30 miles from the Gulf of Mexico, and its weather is influenced considerably by the Gulf. Summers are consistently warm; temperatures on a normal summer day range from the low 70s to the high 80s or low 90s. Fortunately, extreme temperatures are checked somewhat by sea breezes. Eighty-one days a year have temperatures over 90° F., and on some rare days the temperature may exceed 100° F. Winter weather is usually mild except for occasional invasions of cold air. January is the coldest month of the year, with an average minimum temperature of 43.2° F. An average winter has fewer than 20 days below freezing and a low reading of about 23° F. Residents can generally eat outdoors on Christmas day. Average annual temperature: 67.5° F.; average annual rainfall: 62.9 inches; average annual humidity: 71 percent. Industrial smog may be a problem in the morning.

Medical Facilities. The Mobile area has 6 general hospitals, a private mental health hospital, a public mental health center, and a diagnostic clinic and rehabilitation center. Total number of beds: 1,711. The 3 general hospitals maintain nursing schools. The University of South Alabama Medical Center is part of that university's medical school. Hospital rooms average $81.82 daily for a semiprivate room—even lower than the state average of $94.67 daily. Some 270 doctors reside in the area, providing adequate medical care.

Housing. Many retirement homes sell from about $35,000, and condominiums sell for $40,000 to $75,000. Three-bedroom houses sell for approximately $45,000 to $65,000. Mobile has more homes available for sale than most of Alabama's other coastal areas.

Cost of Living. Mobile's cost of living is lower than in most other Alabama cities as well as most cities in the Southeast and the nation. Salaries, however, are low, which mitigates the effect of the lower living costs. *There is a 6 percent sales tax* on everything except persons over age 65 are exempted from the 2 percent city tax on prescription drugs. *Property tax* per $1,000 assessed valuation is $7.00 for the city; $17.00 county; $6.50 state; and $17.50 school. Assessment rates of true market value are 15 percent residential; 25 percent commercial; and 30 percent utilities. Average property taxes are about $200 a year. Utilities cost an average $85 a month, with a high of $140 a month in summer because of air conditioning.

Recreation and Culture. The Mobile Chamber of Commerce lists some 200 clubs, ranging from ABBA Temple Shrine to the Zonta Club. The areas outstanding country club, Cypress Creek, has an 18-hole championship golf course that is designed to reflect the southern Alabama landscape with its elegant backdrop of moss-draped oaks, airy cypresses, and majestic magnolias. The course remains open year-round; the club restaurant offers a gourmet menu. Mobile has unusually fine restaurants, which feature French, Spanish, continental, and seafood cuisines.

Mobile's first citizens were French, and the French verve for living remains. The fine arts program compares well with those in larger cities; there is first-class symphony, opera, ballet, choral groups, paintings, and sculpture, as well as ceramics, handicrafts, and adult education classes. For a listing of all forthcoming events write to the Allied Arts Council, 401 Auditorium Drive, Mobile, AL 36602.

Special Services for Seniors. Mobile's outstanding Area Agency on Aging provides transportation, home health care, a home repair program, multipurpose centers, legal services, gerontology workshops, daily hot meal programs at 11 sites in Mobile, Baldwin, and Escambia counties, information and referral services, day care for elderly, telephone reassurance, workshops, and so on. It functions as an umbrella agency for services; its primary functions are to assess available resources, plan comprehensive service systems, pool resources, and coordinate programs.

Senior Citizens Services is a private, voluntary, nonprofit charitable organization serving seniors. Programs include transportation, information, outreach services, escort service, and seminars on estate planning, income maintenance, and other activities. This organization is currently

working to increase employment opportunities through a Foster Grand-parent Program and a drive to get seniors jobs in large department stores.
For further information:

> Area Agency on Aging
> 250 Water Street
> Post Office Box 1665
> Mobile, AL 36601

> Senior Citizens Services
> Post Office Box 7191
> Mobile, AL 36607

SUMMARY

I was pleasantly surprised at the towns on Alabama's Eastern Shore. Fairhope, in particular, is one of the outstanding retirement areas of the country. I was also impressed with the culture and charm of Mobile—especially the French, Spanish, and cosmopolitan flavor of its hotels and restaurants—and with the city's historical areas.

To really feel at home in Alabama, however, one's views should be conservative and perhaps even provincial. More sophisticated retirees from liberal areas of the Northeast or Midwest may find Alabama politically hostile and culturally sterile.

Here are my ratings for Alabama's major retirement areas:
Excellent—Fairhope;
Good—Daphne, Point Clear;
Adequate—Mobile, Gulf Shores, Dauphin Island.

RATINGS FOR *ALABAMA* MAJOR RETIREMENT AREAS

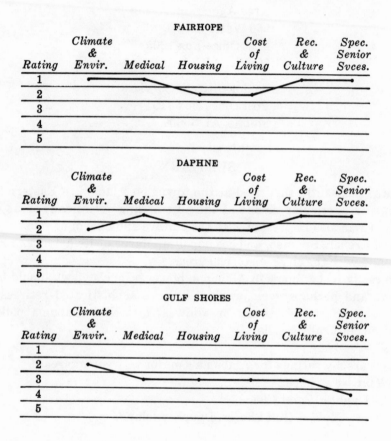

RATINGS FOR *ALABAMA* MAJOR RETIREMENT AREAS

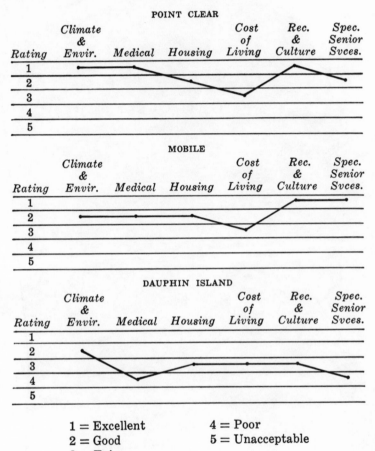

POINT CLEAR

Rating	Climate & Envir.	Medical	Housing	Cost of Living	Rec. & Culture	Spec. Senior Svces.
1						
2						
3						
4						
5						

MOBILE

Rating	Climate & Envir.	Medical	Housing	Cost of Living	Rec. & Culture	Spec. Senior Svces.
1						
2						
3						
4						
5						

DAUPHIN ISLAND

Rating	Climate & Envir.	Medical	Housing	Cost of Living	Rec. & Culture	Spec. Senior Svces.
1						
2						
3						
4						
5						

1 = Excellent   4 = Poor
2 = Good   5 = Unacceptable
3 = Fair

MISSISSIPPI

Piedmont

Eastern Gulf Coastal Plain

○ Greenville

○ Vicksburg   ○ Jackson   Meridian ○

Natchez Trace Parkway

○ Natchez   ○ Hattiesburg

△ Good Retirement
● Adequate Retirement
○ Other Towns of Interest

                                    Ocean
                                    Springs
          Gulfport   △
                      ● Biloxi   ○
               Pass Christian   Pascagoula

IX.

MISSISSIPPI–

A STATE OF LOVELY

SURPRISES

I wasn't prepared for Mississippi's beauty. I'd always thought it had a swampy coast and a dusty interior. But I found that Mississippi offers some lovely retirement areas and retirement advantages that might be overlooked by someone seeking a place in the Sunbelt.

The state has a total population of 2,389,000, of whom about 360,000 are age 60 or over. About 35 percent of Mississippians are nonwhite. Most retirees who settle here from other states concentrate in the coastal areas (Pascagoula to Pass Christian) or in the larger cities of Hattiesburg, Vicksburg, Jackson, Greenville, Meridian, and Natchez. Until the 1930s Mississippi was like one great cotton plantation, but in 1936 the state launched its first industrial recruitment program entitled "Balance Agriculture with Industry." The program was a resounding success; unfortunately, the increased industry has caused air pollution in formerly lovely cities such as Natchez.

The federal government strongly affects Mississippi's economy: it provides some 45 percent of state and local government revenues. When federal revenue sharing went into effect, Mississippi received more per capita than any other state. Mississippi's economy depends as much upon computers as it does on cotton; lumbering, shipbuilding, fishing, and dairying are also important.

A Subtropical Climate

Winters are brief and mild; summers long and warm. The average annual temperature is around 66° F., with January temperatures ranging from 35° to 60° F. and July temperatures ranging from 70° to 93° F. Rainfall averages around 55 inches a year. Coastal areas are the wettest; the Delta areas have the least precipitation. Humidity averages 76 percent annually in Jackson and 69.3 percent annually in Meridian.

A Lower Cost of Living?

While overall living costs in Mississippi might be 5 to 10 percent below the national average, Mississippi's 5 percent retail sales tax is the most all-inclusive in the nation, extending to medicine, groceries, and even food stamps. About 56 percent of Mississippi's tax revenues come from general and selective sales taxes, the highest of any Southern state except Florida.

The *state income tax* is 3 percent on the first $5,000 or part, and 4 percent on all amounts over $5,000. Personal exemptions are $4,500 for single persons and $6,500 for married couples, and $5,000 of some retirement pay is exempted. A deduction of medical expenses over $2,000 is allowed; if the taxpayer is over age 65, there is an additional exemption.

If over age 65 there is no property tax if the final assessment is under $5,000. The average county property tax on rural property is 62 mills, with an average percentage of assessed valuation of 20 percent. The average total municipal (county and city) millage rate is 80 mills, with an average percentage of assessed valuation of 25 percent.

Low-Cost Housing

Single-family two-bedroom homes range from about $30,000 to $45,000 with prices 15 percent higher in the Gulf Coast and Jackson areas. Down payments are generally 5 percent of sale price or evaluation, whichever is less.

Two-bedroom houses in Jackson and Gulf Coast areas rent for approximately $250 to $400 per month. Rentals in smaller towns and rural areas are slightly less.

Mobile homes sell for around $10,000 to $20,000; lots rent for about $75 a month, including water, garbage pickup, and sewer fees.

Mississippi has no "retirement communities"; however, there are apartments designed exclusively for the elderly (62 and over) and their spouses whose incomes fall within specified limits. Write:

> Madonna Manor Apartments
> 550 Houston Avenue
> Jackson, MS 39309

> Santa Maria del Mar Apartments
> 300 East Beach Boulevard
> Biloxi, MS 39606

> Villa Maria Apartments
> 921 Porter Street
> Ocean Springs, MS 39564

Monthly rental fees are approximately $150 for efficiencies and $190 for one-bedroom apartments.

Some retirement homes are owned and operated by the Methodist Church. Write:

> Seashore Manor
> West Beach
> Biloxi, MS 39530

> Traceway Manor
> Highway 6 West
> Tupelo, MS 38801

Better Than Average Health?

Eighty percent of older Mississippians say they have "average or better-than-average" health; 75 percent say their health is better than other people's their age; only 22 percent say bad health prevents them from leading active lives.

Mississippi has several day care centers which include social, health, transportation, recreation, and nutritional services. The state provides a nursing home ombudsman to receive complaints and inform all parties concerning the findings.

Medical facilities—doctors and hospitals—are generally good in populated areas, but you should check on facilities in rural communities. Mississippi has 115 hospitals with a total of 17,423 beds, and 149 nursing homes with 12,842 beds. There are 2,424 doctors in Mississippi. Hospital rates average a low $71.90 daily for a semiprivate room, about *half* the national average.

Prime Outdoor Recreation

Mississippi is an outdoorsman's paradise. It has 17 state parks, which offer boating, camping, fishing, nature trails, and refreshment facilities. It also features 4 historical sites and the pastoral Natchez Trace Parkway.

The Magnolia State is a freshwater fisherman's dream. There are thousands of miles of clean streams and rivers and small farm ponds which yield largemouth bass, bream, and catfish. The Mississippi Game and Fish Commission owns or has under lease 20 prime fishing lakes offering bass, bluegill, crappie, and channel catfish. Bass fishermen come from all over the nation to fish Ross Barnett Reservoir near Jackson and Okatibbee Reservoir near Meridian. Crappie fishermen make the same journeys to "Great Lake Country" in north-central Mississippi. Within short drives of each other are giant impoundments such as Grenada, Sardis, and Enid reservoirs. The world-record white crappie, 5 lbs., 3 ozs., was pulled from Enid Reservoir.

The state also boasts more than 1½ million acres of prime game land in 15 State Wildlife Management Areas and 2 National Wildlife Refuges open for public hunting. Hunters may choose from all types of game habitats—from marshy waterfowl havens or broad fowl-filled lakes to huge tracks of pine and hardwoods where deer and turkey are fair game. *No license is required for residents 65 and older.*

For further information:

> Mississippi Game and Fish Commission
> Post Office Box 451
> Jackson, MS 39205

Many Services for Seniors

Mississippi has a Council on Aging and is divided into 10 Area of Aging service areas that blanket the state. The more developed programs are in the Central area (which includes Jackson) and the Southern area, which takes in all the popular coastal towns (see below).

Services provided through contractual agreements or other agreements include: nutrition, transportation, information and referral, multipurpose senior centers, advocacy (legal services and friendly visitors-nursing home ombudsman), in-home services and telephone reassurance.

Area Aging Agencies also cooperate/coordinate with Retired Senior Volunteer (RSVP) grantees and meals-on-wheels operators.

For further information:

> Mississippi Council on Aging
> 802 N. State St.
> Room 301
> Jackson, MS 39201

1. THE GULF COAST—AMERICA'S RIVIERA

I entered Mississippi northeast of Pascagoula, but instead of staying on I-10, I opted for the "scenic route"—U.S. 90. Just outside of Pascagoula are 26 miles of golden sand beaches known as "America's Riviera." The sun, sand, and sea combine to make this one of the most picturesque spots on the Gulf Coast. However, the feeling of tranquility and beauty is somewhat marred by the fact that the water is polluted and hardly anyone swims in the ocean. But the beaches are free and clear and the sights— ancient oaks, semitropical gardens, historic buildings, luxurious resorts— intriguing.

Pascagoula (pop. 35,000) is the industrial center of this area. It makes destroyers, assault craft, and submarines for the Navy; shrimp boats and barges; building and industrial products. There are job opportunities here for auto mechanics, air conditioning and refrigeration mechanics, marine electricians, electronic technicians, pipefitters, welders, machinists, sheet-metal workers, shipfitters, secretaries, and insurance agents.

The area boasts some 30 golf courses from Pascagoula to Gulfport. There are wide, green fairways lined with towering pines and moss-hung oaks, and some greens overlook the Gulf of Mexico. Fishermen go out for marlin and other deep-sea fish, while others fish from piers and bridges for crab, mullet, surf fish, or flounder. There are many historic landmarks, such as Beauvoir, last home of Jefferson Davis, which is open year-round to visitors. The most famous landmark is the Biloxi lighthouse, built in 1848.

This "Riviera" is a land of tropical sunshine and cooling breezes where there are no defined seasons. Temperatures range from a July high of 89.7° F. to a December low of 63.1° F. Nighttime temperatures sink 15 to 18 degrees. Humidity is highest (96 percent) in July and lowest (52 percent) in May. Spring blends into summer, summer mingles with fall, and both spring and fall overlap into so-called winter. Rain usually falls at night (average 62 inches annually) ; the daytime showers of spring and fall don't usually hamper outdoor activity. Hurricanes do strike here; the last was Camille in 1969, which destroyed much of Pass Christian (see below). The area has three hospitals with approximately 1,040 hospital beds and 200 doctors.

The "Riviera" offers many good retirement communities including:

Ocean Springs (pop. 17,000). This town started as a health resort in the 1800s and was frequented for its health-giving springs. Its high location spares it from most hurricanes (including Camille). Pecans and moss-draped oaks canopy the streets; century-old houses mingle with new ones of brick veneer construction. There is a good supply of housing and lots available; lots (90 by 145 feet) sell from $7,500 and construction costs range from $20 to $30 a square foot. Rental housing is also plentiful; two-bedroom apartments rent for $250 a month and two-bedroom houses sell from about $30,000. Effective tax rate: $21.46 per $1,000 valuation.

Ocean Springs is also home to Villa Maria Apartments (921 Porter Street), built by the Catholic Charities Housing Association of Biloxi. Monthly rates are from $162 for efficiencies to from $179 for one-bedroom apartments. To qualify you must be age 62 or over with a gross annual income of not more than $8,400 for a single person or $9,216 for a couple.

For further information:

Chamber of Commerce
Ocean Springs, MS 39564

Biloxi (pop. 55,000) is the largest city on the Gulf Coast. It is also the cultural center of the area, housing a fine arts coliseum. Biloxi has a $1 million boat marina, 6 major, and many resort hotels. Keesler Air Force Base, the electronic training center of the Air Force, is within the city limits, and its payroll adds to Biloxi's economy. Biloxi also has a "strip" where the military and tourists find "rest and relaxation."

There are four major hospitals in Biloxi including the VA Center and Keesler AFB Hospital, the second largest Air Force medical complex in the world.

The Santa Maria del Mar Apartments (300 East Beach Boulevard), designed to meet the needs of retirees, are 13 stories high and stand on a promontory commanding a view of the Gulf of Mexico. They provide security around the clock and feature a social program of recitals, lectures, and films, as well as transportation to Dukate Senior Center where residents participate in arts and crafts. Residents must be 62 years of age or older; federal subsidies are available so that no resident will pay more than 25 percent of his income if it is below $8,016 for 1 person and $8,784 for 2 persons. Depending upon income, efficiency apartments rent for from $117 to $195 a month and one-bedroom apartments for from $133 to $221 a month. Because Biloxi is a resort area there are plenty of activities and recreations; however, costs are probably higher here than in other coastal towns.

For further information:

Chamber of Commerce
Biloxi, MS 39533

Gulfport (pop. 46,400). This city was rated with the "highest quality of life" in Mississippi by the Institute of Urban Research at the University of Mississippi. The municipal airport, one of the busiest in the state, also serves as an Air National Guard training center. A $25 million coliseum and convention center opened recently, and a fine arts center is planned. The modern library houses 85,000 volumes plus microfilm facilities. Gulfport offers quality downtown shopping; the mammoth Edgewater Plaza Shopping Center, with Sears and other chain stores, lies between Biloxi and Gulfport.

Living costs are moderate. A semiprivate room in Gulfport's hospital averages $85 daily, and the municipal property tax totals 59 mills on 25 percent of appraised value. Housing is plentiful at most price ranges, and costs are less than in Biloxi. Two-bedroom houses sell for $30,000 and up.

For further information:

Chamber of Commerce
Gulfport, MS 39501

Pass Christian (pop. 5,000). Hurricane Camille destroyed much of this town in 1969, however, it has been rebuilt and is clean, bright, and modern. For a town its size it offers unusually good cultural and recreational facilities: a city library, art league, fishing pier, small craft harbor, picnic park, yacht club, oyster reef. Land is available. Lots of 100 by 150 feet sell for from $4,000 to $14,000; building costs are from $20 to $30 a square foot. Many brick veneer houses sell from $30,000, and two-bedroom apartments rent from $250 a month, furnished. The tax levy is 47 mills plus 29 mills for the school district.

For further information:

Chamber of Commerce
Pass Christian, MS 39571

2. INTERIOR MISSISSIPPI—ROLLING, PRETTY, AND GREEN

As much as I admired tropical, coastal Mississippi, I enjoyed even more the rolling, green, tree-sprinkled hills of the interior. I entered Mississippi's interior on I-55 south of McComb, driving up through Louisiana (see next chapter). The farther north (toward Jackson), the more pastoral the scenery. To me, Mississippi is one of the prettiest states in the Union.

Jackson (the capital, with about 200,000 population) was even more of a surprise. It's green, open, and pleasant—prettier than Baton Rouge or Montgomery, the capitals of Mississippi's neighbors Louisiana and Alabama, respectively. It has been called Little Atlanta because of its growing facilities, jet airport, and new light industry. Jackson is the heart of Mississippi's business-media power structure, and many printing plants throb through the night. The downtown area is "button-down and neat." I ate at one of the leading downtown restaurants (which serve only beer) and was disappointed at the quality of food, service, and atmosphere. It wouldn't have qualified as an automat in New York. The best restaurants are located out of the city limits.

Jackson has some 2,718 hospital beds in the area and almost 350 physicians, providing about the best medical and hospital care in the state. A semiprivate room averages $70.82 daily, a bit below the state average of $71.90 daily.

Jackson just annexed a large surrounding area and is one of the fastest-growing areas in the state. Unfortunately there's a shortage of low-cost housing in Jackson, although a fine senior citizens complex—Albermarle Center Apartments with 152 one-bedroom units and rents based on income—is in the heart of the city. The "Jackson Apartment Hunter's Guide" ($1 from Post Office Box 1073, Jackson, MS 39205) pinpoints available apartments.

Jackson is also the culture center of the state, with its own symphony orchestra and special programs. However, for those accustomed to a more sophisticated urban area, Jackson can seem rather dull and quiet.

Meandering Along the Historic Natchez Trace

I headed for Natchez and took the scenic, historic Natchez Trace. Once an Indian path, then a wilderness road between Natchez and Nashville, and from 1800 to 1830 a highway binding the old Southwest to the Union, the Natchez Trace has been a vital link in the growth of the nation. Now it is a scenic parkway where a 50-mile-per-hour speed limit, winding roads, sylvan glades, cotton fields, and green forests soothe the mind and body. Markers, exhibits, and trails explain why this frontier road has been remembered.

Natchez (pop. 25,000) is lovely with many fine antebellum houses. And the Natchez Pilgrimage Association and Natchez Garden Club present fine programs and offer nostalgic tours. But Natchez suffers from air pollution and congestion. You should investigate further before deciding to retire here.

SUMMARY

I liked the tropical resortlike atmosphere of Mississippi's Gulf Coast area and the rolling, pretty, green interior. But I didn't like the provincialism of the interior, including Jackson. Mississippi might appeal to those looking for a "tidy and neat" retirement existence, but those who want a more stimulating physical and psychological life style should probably search elsewhere.

Here are my ratings for Mississippi's major retirement areas:
Excellent—none;
Good—Ocean Springs, Gulfport;
Adequate—Biloxi, Pass Christian, Jackson.

RATINGS FOR *MISSISSIPPI* MAJOR RETIREMENT AREAS

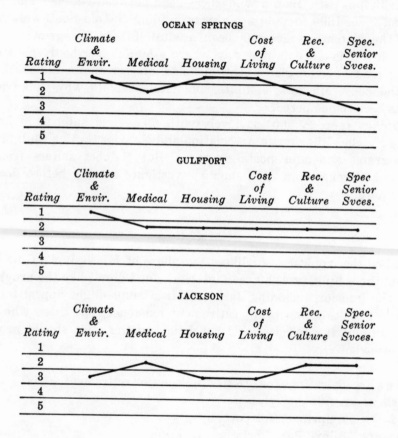

RATINGS FOR *MISSISSIPPI* MAJOR RETIREMENT AREAS

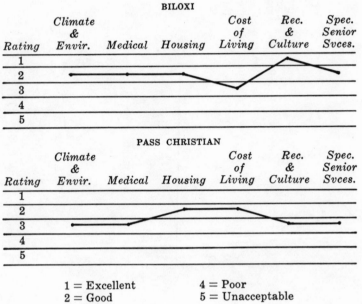

1 = Excellent   4 = Poor
2 = Good   5 = Unacceptable
3 = Fair

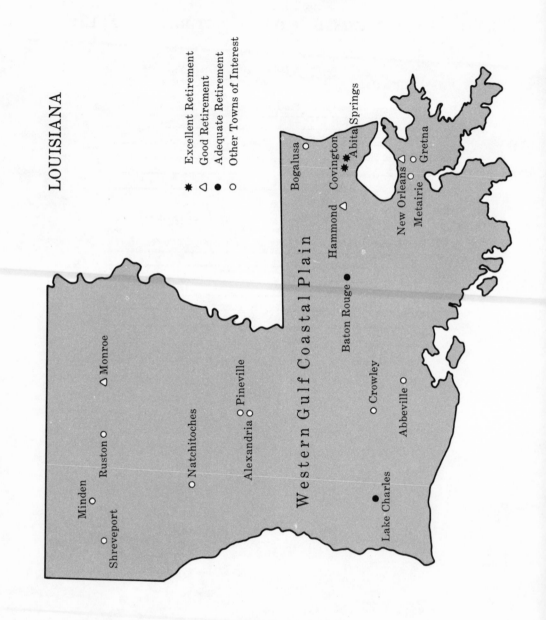

LOUISIANA

* Excellent Retirement
△ Good Retirement
● Adequate Retirement
○ Other Towns of Interest

Western Gulf Coastal Plain

Shreveport ○
Minden ○
Ruston ○
Monroe △

Natchitoches ○

Alexandria ○ ○ Pineville

Lake Charles ●

Crowley ○

Abbeville ○

Baton Rouge ●

Hammond △

Bogalusa ○
Covington ✳✳
Abita Springs

New Orleans △
Metairie ○
Gretna

X.

LOUISIANA—

LAND OF RICH IMAGES

Louisiana, the Pelican State, conjures up rich images: a boat floating on misty bayous, rural Cajuns trapping muskrat and fishing for shrimp, exotic Creoles concocting spicy recipes, flamboyant New Orleans where anything goes . . . Louisiana also has some of the finest retirement areas in the Sunbelt. The 2 major areas of retirement living are Baton Rouge and Shreveport.

Much of the state is a rich alluvial plain, with rolling hills in the north (535 feet is the highest point) to sea level and below in the coastal marshes of the south. Bluffs promenade along the banks of the Mississippi, while pine forests blanket the Ozone Belt north of Lake Pontchartrain. There is a strong French-Catholic influence in the southern part of the state while the central and northern parts are predominately Fundamental Protestant.

The 60-plus population in Louisiana numbers about 500,000 or about 13 percent of the state's total population.

Comfortable Summers and Mild Winters

Winter temperatures in Shreveport range from 10° F. to 60° F., and summer temperatures from 70° F. to 100° F. New Orleans' climate is even milder due to its proximity to the Gulf of Mexico: winter temperatures range from 28° F. to 70° F. while summer temperatures average 72° F. to 90° F. Annual precipitation totals about 59.9 inches. Humidity averages 73.3 percent annually in Shreveport; 78.8 percent annually in New Orleans.

You can wear drip-dry clothing from late April to early October; medium-weight clothing the remainder of the year. The mild climate and rich soil yield a vast array of flowers, shrubs, trees, and crops, which add floral and agricultural beauty. Forests cover about half of Louisiana; in other parts moss-draped cypress and oak trees, and lazy bayous (creeks) work their way to the sea.

Lowest Cost of Living

Louisiana's taxes and cost of living are the lowest of any Sunbelt (or other) state. Thanks in part to the legacy of the Longs, Louisiana makes a greater effort than other states to finance health, hospitals, welfare, and education. Forty percent of the tax burden falls on the rich oil and gas companies, relieving the individual taxpayer from personal taxes more than any other state. Louisiana is also less dependent on the state sales tax. This lessens the burden on lower income people, including retirees. But a note of caution: The oil and gas supplies in Louisiana are running out, and eventually the state will have to introduce new taxes or cut back services.

State income tax—2 percent on the first $10,000, rising to 6 percent over $40,000. State income tax exemptions include 10 percent gross income plus $2,500 personal exemption for a single person and $5,000 net for a couple.

Property taxes—Starting in 1978 all homes were assessed at 10 percent of fair market value and the homestead exemption is $5,000 for everyone. This means that a home assessed at $50,000 could be exempt from the average parish tax. Overall, property taxes range from 8.46 mills for cities to 45.8 mills for parishes (county). The average tax on a two-bedroom retirement home could be below $50.

Sales tax—The sales tax rate is 6 percent in most places. Current state rate is 3 percent and municipalities can and do levy a sales tax up to but not exceeding the state rate.

License plates—for cars cost $6 for 2 years; for house trailers and mobile homes, $10 per year; for boat trailers, $3 per year.

Baton Rouge has the lowest cost of living of any metropolitan area in the nation (about 88 percent of the national average). A retired couple can live in Baton Rouge on an intermediate budget for only about $8,014 a year. Alexandria, Lake Charles, Monroe, and Shreveport have costs of living comparable to Baton Rouge's; it costs even less to live in Louisiana's smaller cities and towns. Low housing costs—$30,000 for a two-bedroom retirement home—allow for much of the savings, although rates on mortgages have been going up.

Job opportunities exist for those with skills in shipping, shipbuilding, and the petrochemical industry. Retired military personnel have the added advantage of being near excellent commissaries and military hospitals.

Amazingly Low Housing Costs

Even in major cities like New Orleans, one-bedroom apartments rent for as little as $200 a month; two-bedroom apartments for $300 a month. Two- and three-bedroom houses sell from $30,000. In the Ozone Belt, some acreage and building lots sell for as low as $800 an acre, and Louisiana's building costs are among the lowest of any Sunbelt state.

Healthy and Unhealthy Areas

The Ozone Belt (see below)—the pine-covered section north of Lake Pontchartrain—is considered one of the world's healthiest regions. However, some areas of New Orleans, Baton Rouge, and other major cities are plagued by pollution from petrochemical plants and paper mills, despite industrial efforts to clean up.

Louisiana has 158 hospitals with a total of 24,948 beds. It also has 220 nursing homes with 16,172 beds. There are 5,457 physicians in the state. Good hospitals are located throughout the retirement areas, especially military hospitals in and around New Orleans. A semiprivate hospital room averages $92.55 daily, higher than in Mississippi, but still one-third below the national average of over $133 daily.

Folk Culture Galore

The Cajuns live in an area roughly defined by a line drawn from New Orleans northwest to midway between Alexandria and Baton Rouge, and then southwest across Lake Charles. They live in parishes (counties) with romantic names like Evangeline and Acadia, still speak French, and live as they have lived for generations. The Latin-blooded Creoles represent a special kind of aristocracy in New Orleans and other cities. New Orleans is America's original folk festival, combining the colorful Mardi Gras with exotic foods (a heady concoction of French recipes, Spanish seasoning, and American Indian herbs). In New Orleans I had a fabulous breakfast at Brennan's, one of the city's famous restaurants, that consisted of a Ramos Fizz (gin, cream, egg white, sugar, and orange-flower water), a spicy baked apple in cream, eggs Benedict with an outstanding hollandaise sauce, a strawberry mousse with brandy, and bitterstrong coffee. Louisiana has some of the best food anywhere in the country.

Widespread Services for Seniors

The active Bureau of Aging Services works through area agencies on aging serving all communities. Besides hot meal programs, transportation services (minibuses), and health programs, the bureau holds many public hearings and sponsors Senior Day rallies at the Governor's Conference on Aging. Outstanding information and referral services provide information for over 13,500 seniors a month, and an outreach program brings people in need together with available services.

The Parish Councils on Aging are the grass-roots focal point for services to the elderly. They carry out the many programs offered to Louisiana's older citizens in the 64 parishes throughout the state.

For further information:

> Office of Elderly Affairs
> Office of the Governor
> 4528 Bennington Dr.
> Baton Rouge, LA 70898

1. THE RED RIVER DELTA—COTTON AND CATTLE

This area is located along the Red River and extends from the northwestern tip of Louisiana to the central part of the state. It is a delta cotton and livestock production area. It is also the home of *Shreveport* (pop. 208,000), the second largest city in Louisiana. Shreveport's sister city, *Bossier City* (pop. 54,000) is one of the largest retirement areas for the military and the location of Barksdale Air Force Base, one of the world's largest air bases. *Natchitoches* (pop. 17,000) is the oldest settlement in the Louisiana Purchase and is an agricultural and college town—old yet new—a natural for retirement living. *Alexandria* (pop. 50,000) and *Pineville* (pop. 15,000), sister cities separated only by the Red River, provide a commercial center for the predominantly agricultural region.

Medical Facilities. The Red River Delta area has 20 hospitals, 40 nursing homes, 5 home health agencies, 550 doctors, 200 dentists. Shreveport and Alexandria house state-owned hospitals for low-income patients, and Alexandria also has a geriatrics hospital. The Home Health Agencies, operating under Medicare, provide medical services in the home.

Housing. Low-rent apartments, ranging from $50 to $100 a month depending upon income, are available in Alexandria, Bossier City, Pineville, Shreveport, and *Vivian.* Shreveport and Bossier have some 50 subdivisions with homes starting at $25,000 and one- to three-bedroom apartments renting from $200 to $500 a month. In the rural Alexandria-Pineville area, some two-bedroom homes rent for about $70 a month. In the cities costs begin at $300 a month for a three-bedroom home. One- to two-bedroom apartments rent from $250 a month, and subdivision homes sell for $25,000 to $200,000, with homesites selling for $5,000 to $50,000. Building costs are about $30 a square foot.

Recreation and Culture. Shreveport offers operas, drama, concerts, symphonies, and so on. The Shreveport Parks and Recreation Department provides art classes free to the public. Northwestern State University in Natchitoches features plays, musicals, concerts, art shows, and festivals. Alexandria offers community concerts, little theater, an art league, music clubs. Rodeo is popular in all parishes as well as thoroughbred racing.

You can enjoy golf, tennis, swimming, public parks and playgrounds, special-interest clubs (gardening, bridge, etc.) in every community throughout the area. Lakes offer year-round boating, fishing, duck hunting, sailing, water skiing, and scuba diving in every parish.

Special Services for Seniors. Shreveport's Randle T. Moore Senior Center has a planned program on weekdays and a dance each Friday night. Councils on Aging offering various services to older adults (senior centers and educational and crafts classes) include the Caddo-Bossier Council, the Natchitoches Council, and the Rapides Council. The recreation and parks department of Shreveport, Bossier, Alexandria, and Pineville also sponsor clubs and activities for older citizens. In addition, most of the churches have very active older groups composed of church members and nonmembers.

For further information:

Chamber of Commerce   Chamber of Commerce
Shreveport, LA 71101   Bossier, LA 71010

Chamber of Commerce   Chamber of Commerce
Alexandria, LA 71301   Natchitoches, LA 71457

Chamber of Commerce
Pineville, LA 71360

2. NORTH LOUISIANA UPLANDS—HOME OF YEOMEN

The term "yeoman farmer" applies to the inhabitants of this area because they are hardworking and independent. The farms are family sized and owner operated for the most part; the standard of living and the educational level of the farmers are relatively high.

Minden (pop. 15,000), located in Webster Parish, might be described as the South's most typical small city. It has a friendly, progressive community atmosphere without the confusion of a metropolitan area.

Springhill (pop. 7,000), also located in Webster Paris, is situated near Lake Erling and serves as the industrial and recreational hub of northern Louisiana and southern Arkansas.

Ruston (pop. 20,000) is an important trade distribution center.

Farmerville (pop. 5,000), nearly encircled by Lake D'Arbonne, is surrounded by forest on the land side, giving it a resort atmosphere.

Monroe (pop. 65,000) serves as the metropolis of north central and eastern Louisiana. Monroe is separated from its sister city, West Monroe, by the Ouachita River.

One man originally from Albany, New York, gave me the following reasons why he chose to retire in the Monroe area: The climate is mild but does have seasons, which avoids monotony; taxes are low (his are below $200 for a 2,800-square-foot house on a 2-plus-acre lot on the waterfront); it is within a day's drive of the ocean, mountains, and major cities like New Orleans, Houston, Dallas-Fort Worth, and an airport is nearby; Monroe is a major shopping, medical, and business center as well as a farming community, which makes the income fairly stable and relatively high.

Medical Facilities. The area has 14 hospitals, 21 nursing homes, 2 home health agencies, 170 doctors, 80 dentists. Monroe has a state-owned hospital for persons with low income.

Housing. The housing authorities of Farmerville, Grambling (Lincoln Parish), Homer (Claiborne Parish), Arcadia (Bienville Parish), Monroe, and Ruston have built apartments for elderly persons with low annual incomes. The privately owned Colonial Manor Apartments in Monroe are specially designed for the moderate- and upper-income elderly. One-bedroom apartments rent from $200 unfurnished and $250 furnished. Some rental housing is available from $200 a month. The cost of building a two- to three-bedroom home is about $30 per square foot. Two-bedroom homes sell for $30,000 and up.

Recreation and Culture. Monroe's Civic Center includes a theater, one of the South's most ultramodern centers for the performing arts; an arena (with a towering 70-foot roof) that hosts sporting events and major entertainment; and a convention hall, which offers space for conferences, displays, and banquets. Other cultural attractions include the Ouachita Valley Museum, Masur Museum of Arts, which sponsors an art show and Invitational Exhibit, Strauss Play House, operetta clubs, and the Northeast LA University Concerts Association.

Springhill has rodeos, bowling alleys, bridge clubs, hunting, fishing, and camping. The country club has a championship golf course.

The Minden area abounds with lakes and streams ideal for fishing, swimming, picnicking, and camping. Lake Bistineau to the south has rental cabins and facilities.

The Ruston Park and Recreation Board conducts a well-rounded recreation program for all ages throughout the year. D'Arbonne Lake, one of the largest in the state, is located in Lincoln and Union parishes. Farmerville is on this 15,000-acre lake, which is fed by springs from the surrounding hills, and offers camping, picnicking, boating, fishing, and hunting.

Monroe's parks, the Ouachita River, and bayous and lakes in the area offer the usual outdoor sports. In addition, Monroe has 4 indoor recreational centers which sponsor special programs for the elderly, 2 country clubs, and 3 municipal golf courses, a tennis club and 24 lighted courts.

Special Services for Seniors. The Ouachita Council on Aging has a comprehensive program of activities including instruction in various subjects. The Union Council on Aging in Farmerville and the Webster Council on Aging in Cullen sponsor projects to serve their elderly residents.

For further information:

Chamber of Commerce   Chamber of Commerce
Minden, LA 71055   Ruston, LA 71270

Chamber of Commerce   Chamber of Commerce
Springhill, LA 71075   Farmerville, LA 71241

Chamber of Commerce
Monroe, LA 71201

3. SOUTHWEST LOUISIANA—THE "RICE BOWL"

This is Louisiana's "rice bowl." Farms in this area require more than the usual cash outlay; people are industrious and more prosperous than the average. The inhabitants are mainly French, although there are settlements of Midwesterners.

Kinder (pop. 3,000) is the parish seat of Allen Parish and draws its revenue from agriculture, the forest industry, and natural resources of oil, gas, and gravel.

Lake Charles (pop. 80,000) is situated on the shores of 2 lakes and enjoys one of the few inland beaches between the Atlantic and Pacific coasts. The downtown area is alive and vital with 6 major shopping centers.

Sulphur (pop. 19,000), located in Calcasieu Parish west of Lake Charles, is primarily an industrial area and was named for the sulphur mining begun in 1888.

Jennings (pop. 13,000), the site of the first oil well in Louisiana, is located among meandering miles of scenic bayous in Jefferson Davis Parish.

Crowley (pop. 20,000), the Rice Capital of America, has the world's greatest concentration of rice fields and rice mills.

Cameron (pop. 2,000), the parish seat of Cameron Parish, is an area of sparsely populated marshlands.

Abbeville (pop. 14,000), the parish seat of Vermilion Parish, retains much of the charm of French villages and the 17th-century French dialect.

Medical Facilities. The area has 19 hospitals, 17 nursing homes, 5 home health agencies, 200 doctors, 100 dentists.

Housing. In the Lake Charles area people build on wooded lots. Prices for new homes range from $25,000 upward; there's something for everyone. There are plenty of apartments, ranging from one-bedroom unfurnished to three-bedroom furnished; rents are from $200 to $400 a month.

Apartments for low-income elderly have been built by the housing authorities of Abbeville; Church Point and Rayne; Crowley, Elton, Lake Arthur, and Welsh; Erath, Greydan, and Kaplan; Kinder, Lake Charles,

Oakdale, and Oberlin; Southwest Acadia Consolidated; Sulphur, Vinton, and Westlake. The apartment complex in Lake Charles provides space for group social activities and recreational programs.

Recreation and Culture. In Lake Charles, the Little Theatre, the Artists Civic Theatre Studio, and the Bayou Players annually stage a full season of dramatic, comic, and musical offerings. The 240-voice Messiah Chorus, the Lake Charles Civic Association, which sponsors guest attractions of national and international prominence, the Art Association, and the Lake Charles ballet societies reflect the enthusiasm Lake Charles residents have for cultural enrichment. Near Crowley is the Blue Rose Museum, housed in a typical old Acadia building, which portrays the story of the rice industry.

Southwest Louisiana offers endless recreational activities. The Gulf of Mexico provides "big-game" sportfishing, and Calcasieu Lake between Lake Charles and White Lake south of Jennings offers freshwater fishing, crabbing, and shrimping. You can also water ski and enjoy powerboat competition, sailing, and swimming.

Two large game preserves provide many opportunities for duck hunting; Sam Houston Jones State Park, located north of Lake Charles, has boat launching ramps, vacation cabins, and campsites. Sportsmen's clubs abound and all communities have golf courses, tennis courts, city parks.

Special Services for Seniors. The Calcasieu Council on Aging in Lake Charles sponsors a senior center and the parish has an active senior volunteer program. The Jefferson Davis Parish Council supports Jennings Senior Citizen Center.

The Recreation and Parks Department in Crowley, Lake Charles, Westlake, Hackberry (Cameron), and Abbeville sponsor clubs and activities for older adults.

For further information:

Chamber of Commerce
Kinder, LA 70648

Chamber of Commerce
Jennings, LA 70546

Chamber of Commerce
Lake Charles, LA 70601

Chamber of Commerce
Crowley, LA 70526

Chamber of Commerce
Sulphur, LA 70663

Chamber of Commerce
Cameron, LA 70631

Chamber of Commerce
Abbeville, LA 70510

4. THE FLORIDA PARISHES—THE DAIRY CENTER

This area was once part of Florida. It's now big dairy country and has major strawberry and vegetable crops. Many residents work as part-time farmers or in the forest products industries.

Baton Rouge (pop. 250,000) is a modern cosmopolitan city and center of the petrochemical industry. I enjoyed the landscaped parks and lake around the State Capitol, but as I approached along the Mississippi River, I found myself smothered in smog. Pollution controls may eventually cut down the smoke, but until they do, the pall will hang over the city.

Denham Springs (pop. 7,500) is near Baton Rouge but out of its industrial orbit.

Hammond (pop. 20,000) lies in the piney woods of Tangipahoa Parish, one of the growing areas of the state. It's the Strawberry Capital of the World.

Bogalusa (pop. 22,000) is the leading industrial city and trade center in the Pearl River Valley. Pine forests and streams enhance its beauty, but a paper mill adds pollution.

Medical Facilities. The area has 15 hospitals, 22 nursing homes, 4 home health agencies, 400 doctors, 180 dentists. The state operates 3 hospitals in this area for persons unable to pay high medical costs. In Baton Rouge, a Medicenter provides professional nursing care for recuperating patients, eliminating prolonged hospital confinement that would cost about twice as much.

Housing. The Hammond area has plenty of housing, with three-bedroom, 1,500-square foot, 1½-bath houses selling for $25,000 and up. Monthly rental for a three-bedroom house is from $300, and two-bedroom apartments rent from $200. The housing authorities of Bogalusa, Independence, and Pontchatoula, and East Baton Rouge Parish offer apartments to elderly families with low annual incomes. The Catholic-Presbyterian Apartments in Baton Rouge rent apartments starting at $200 for an efficiency and $250 for one-bedroom. Two-bedroom homes in Baton Rouge sell for $30,000 and up.

Recreation and Culture. Baton Rouge has a variety of cultural activities including a symphony orchestra, chamber music society, community concerts, and the Festival Arts Trio. The Baton Rouge little theater, Louisiana State University and Southern University drama departments, and touring Broadway plays provide a wide range of theater productions. Art exhibitions are located in the LSU and Southern art galleries, the Baton Rouge Gallery, the Old State Capitol, and several commercial galleries. LSU's Arts and Humanities Series brings visiting lecturers to Baton Rouge each year.

The Old Governor's Mansion has been converted into the Louisiana Arts and Science Center, which features exhibits and workshops along with the largest planetarium in the world.

Bogalusa's little theater group, the Mill Town Players, presents first-class performances. Music clubs and literary functions are also popular. In Hammond, Southeastern Louisiana College provides dramatic, musical, and lecture programs. Hammond also boasts a little theater group and an art league, which sponsors exhibits and workshops.

Most larger towns provide public recreation centers, swimming pools, gyms, golf courses, rodeo arenas, parks, playgrounds, and tennis courts. The countryside invites year-round hunting, fishing, and boating.

Special Services for Seniors. East Baton Rouge Parish has an active Council on Aging and an XYZ Senior Center sponsored by the First United Methodist Church. The XYZ Center offers crafts and other activities every weekday.

For further information:

Chamber of Commerce
Baton Rouge, LA 70801

Chamber of Commerce
Hammond, LA 70401

Chamber of Commerce
Denham Springs, LA 70726

Chamber of Commerce
Bogalusa, LA 70427

5. GREATER NEW ORLEANS—SUBLIME TO SUPREME

The New Orleans area combines the sublime health-giving qualities of the Ozone Belt north of Lake Pontchartrain with the supreme atmosphere of New Orleans. The marshy land isn't suited to agriculture, but the area has the highest level of living, due to its proximity to New Orleans. Even the rural Ozone Belt is only a short drive from the city over a causeway.

New Orleans (pop. 700,000). Despite its carnival atmosphere and its touristy Vieux Carré, New Orleans has a stable population which includes many retirees (18 percent of the residents are over 60). As a leading industrial, petroleum, and financial center, a wholesale and retail market, and a convention and tourist attraction, New Orleans is the business hub of this area. New Orleans has everything—history, beauty, atmosphere, culture (the jazz is spectacular). It is a good place to visit and a good place to live.

Metairie (pop. 150,000) contains more than half of Jefferson Parish's total population. For years it has been known as one of the finest residential sections in the Greater New Orleans Area.

Gretna (pop. 27,000), also in Jefferson Parish, is a neat, quiet, yet modern and streamlined community of orderly subdivisions and thriving shopping centers.

But the best retirement living lies across Lake Pontchartrain in St. Tammany Parish. Here, just north of the lake, lies the famous *Ozone Belt*, named for its healthful air, which is spiced by the rich fragrance of pine trees. There are only two other recognized ozone belts in the world—one in the Hartz mountains of Germany and the other in Arizona, around Pine and Payson.

The land here is high and dry and is covered with beautiful pine, oak, magnolia, beech, holly, and gum trees. In spring the area is a canvas of color when the azaleas, camellias, purple and white wisteria, dogwood, and rosebud are in bloom. The area is blessed with delicious, fresh water (it is shipped to other parts of the state). The woods are so healthy and the air and water are so clean and pure that many doctors consider the Ozone Belt one of the world's healthiest regions. (The number of doctors who have retired there is living proof!)

The main town in this area is *Covington* (pop. 10,000), 8 miles from the north toll gate of the Lake Pontchartrain Causeway (the world's longest). The causeway gives Covington residents direct access to the heart of New Orleans. The land around Covington is divided between flat green meadows and rolling hills. It is rich and fertile with many acres of standing timber. Covington is a dream town for sophisticated people of all ages who want a quiet, elegant life. Riverfront and country-club housing (Beau Chene Country Club, Tchefuncta Estates Country Club) costs $60,000 and up for two- and three-bedroom homes. But less expensive housing (from $30,000) is available within the city. Some apartment complexes exist, and more are under construction; rents range from $200 to $450 a month. Most have swimming pools and other forms of recreation.

Covington's excellent recreational and cultural advantages make this an ideal retirement community. It has a book club, the St. Tammany Art Association (largest in the area), community concerts, bridge clubs, garden clubs, an outstanding theater group, and several restaurants with cuisine that compares favorably to New Orleans'.

Another place to consider is *Abita Springs* (pop. 2,000), which boasts "country living with city facilities." A scattering of quaint homes tucked away in the woods, Abita Springs is so quiet that you can hear birds twitter as you walk down the main street.

Medical Facilities. The area has some 25 hospitals, 47 nursing homes, 4 home health agencies, 2,000 doctors, and 600 dentists. New Orleans has one of the most famous hospitals in the world, "Big Charity," which was established for persons of low income. It also has a Medicenter similar to the one in Baton Rouge. There are several excellent military hospitals in New Orleans as well as the new Tulane Medical Center. A semiprivate hospital room averages $102 daily—about $9 above the state average. Covington has Highland Park, a new modern hospital.

Housing. Many rental and for-sale apartments and houses are available in the New Orleans area and in the Ozone Belt. Two-bedroom furnished apartments rent from $250 a month ($200 unfurnished); two-bedroom townhouses rent from $300 a month; two-bedroom houses sell starting at $30,000.

Marrero in Jefferson Parish has a new 11-story, 200-unit apartment house for elderly persons, owned by Monsignor Wynhoven Apartments.

The Greater New Orleans Federation of Churches operates Stanton Manor, an apartment hotel for elderly Protestants. The rent includes three meals; however, all apartments have kitchens or cooking facilities.

Recreation and Culture. Besides being the birthplace of jazz, New Orleans offers other musical activities including concerts by the New Orleans Philharmonic Symphony, operas by the New Orleans Opera House Association, and the Summer Pops Concert series. The little theater groups and the professional Repertory Theatre present live stage performances. New Orleans has innumerable museums, art galleries, garden, social, civic, and patriotic organizations.

Southern Louisiana, with the largest acreage of coastal marsh land in the United States, is a fisherman's, hunter's, and trapper's paradise. The New Orleans City Park is one of the largest municipal parks in the United States and Audubon Park is the South's largest zoo.

Special Service for Seniors. Jefferson Parish has a year-round senior program including bowling, miniature golf, round dancing, crab and shrimp boils, social dances, field trips, and other outings. The First Street Methodist Church in New Orleans sponsors a senior center, and the Jewish Community Center in New Orleans offers crafts, workshops, and special programs for older adults.

Parish councils on aging are active in Jefferson, New Orleans, and St.

Tammany. St. Tammany's Council operates the Covington Senior Center, which offers varied activities.

For further information:

Chamber of Commerce
New Orleans, LA 70112

Chamber of Commerce
Gretna, LA 70053

Chamber of Commerce
Metairie, LA 70001

Chamber of Commerce
Abita Springs, LA 70420

Chamber of Commerce
Covington, LA 70433

SUMMARY

I was intrigued with the folkways and mysterious flavor of the people and places in Louisiana, but unless you are of French or Latin origin, you might feel out of place retiring in some parts of the state. Bests bets are one of the larger cities or the Ozone Belt. However, there is no doubt that retiring in Louisiana could add spice to life, and the Ozone Belt is so appealing (especially the towns of *Abita Springs* and *Covington*) that it should definitely be considered as a possible retirement haven.

Here are my ratings for Louisiana's major retirement areas:
Excellent—Covington, Abita Springs;
Good—New Orleans (area), Hammond, Monroe;
Adequate—Baton Rouge, Lake Charles;
Poor—Shreveport.

RATINGS FOR *LOUISIANA* MAJOR RETIREMENT AREAS

RED RIVER DELTA

Rating	Climate & Envir.	Medical	Housing	Cost of Living	Rec. & Culture	Spec. Senior Svces.
1						
2						
3						
4						
5						

NORTH LOUISIANA UPLANDS

Rating	Climate & Envir.	Medical	Housing	Cost of Living	Rec. & Culture	Spec. Senior Svces.
1						
2						
3						
4						
5						

SOUTHWEST LOUISIANA "RICE BOWL"

Rating	Climate & Envir.	Medical	Housing	Cost of Living	Rec. & Culture	Spec. Senior Svces.
1						
2						
3						
4						
5						

GREATER NEW ORLEANS

Rating	Climate & Envir.	Medical	Housing	Cost of Living	Rec. & Culture	Spec. Senior Svces.
1						
2						
3						
4						
5						

OZONE BELT-COVINGTON

Rating	Climate & Envir.	Medical	Housing	Cost of Living	Rec. & Culture	Spec. Senior Svces.
1						
2						
3						
4						
5						

FLORIDA PARISHES-BATON ROUGE

Rating	Climate & Envir.	Medical	Housing	Cost of Living	Rec. & Culture	Spec. Senior Svces.
1						
2						
3						
4						
5						

1 = Excellent   2 = Good   3 = Fair   4 = Poor   5 = Unacceptable

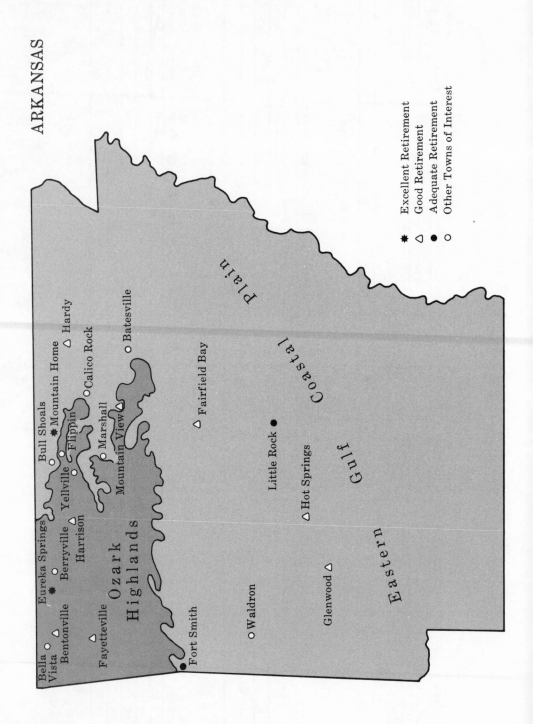

ARKANSAS

Ozark Highlands

Gulf Coastal Plain

Eastern

Bella Vista
Bentonville
Fayetteville
Eureka Springs
Berryville
Harrison
Bull Shoals
Yellville
Flippin
Mountain Home
Hardy
Calico Rock
Marshall
Mountain View
Batesville
Fairfield Bay
Fort Smith
Waldron
Glenwood
Hot Springs
Little Rock

Excellent Retirement
Good Retirement
Adequate Retirement
Other Towns of Interest

XI.

ARKANSAS—

RETIREMENT WITH

INDEPENDENCE

I felt more "at home" in Arkansas. Its topography, foliage, and people seemed more Midwestern than Southern, and I found it easier to strike up a conversation and easier to understand the people.

Most "Rackensackers" (the Indian name for Arkansas) are proud individualists, descendants of the Anglo-Saxon pioneers who founded the state. Arkansas is famous for its mountain hamlets. Their physical and cultural isolation has preserved such lovely traditions as the singing of Elizabethan songs and the plowing of fields with horses or mules.

Much of the "retirement land" lies northwest of a line drawn diagonally through the state from northeast to southwest. Here, retirees live in picturesque hamlets, surrounded by wooded hills and mountains, and can be reached only by two-lane roads that twist through smoky, misty valleys. The only major cities are Little Rock, Hot Springs, Fort Smith, and Fayetteville. Southeast of the diagonal, the land flattens to delta and coastal plains and there are no major retirement settlements of consequence.

Among the states Arkansas is second only to Florida in the percentage of retirees: Some 17.4 percent of the state's 2,144,000 population is 60 years of age or older, and some 12.6 percent are over age 65. Arkansas provides *more* state money in proportion to federal money for problems of the elderly than any other state.

Moderate Four-Season Climate

Climatic differences between Arkansas's northwestern mountains and southeastern plains aren't as great as the local differences between mountain and valley stations in the highlands. Generally, the climate of western and northern Arkansas is a little cooler with greater temperature extremes; humidity is lower, with less cloudiness.

Summer extremes rarely top 100° F. and winter extremes rarely fall below zero. The annual temperature averages 59° F.; the January average is 40° F. and the July average is 80° F.

Annual precipitation averages 45 inches, although the southeastern counties may get 5 to 6 inches more rainfall per year and some areas of the Ozark and Ouachita mountains might average 55 to 56 inches annually. Rain usually falls in showers, except during late fall, winter, and early spring when there are heavy local rains. Winter and spring are the wettest times of the year; December and January, and March through May are the wettest months. Snow falls mainly in the northwest and averages a foot annually.

Overall relative humidity averages 66 percent. Winter sunshine totals 55 percent of the possible amount; summer sunshine 74 percent of the possible amount. There are approximately 150 clear days and 100 cloudy days annually.

Low Taxes and Cost of Living

The only Sunbelt states with lower overall taxes than Arkansas are Florida, Louisiana, Mississippi, and Texas.

State income tax—1 percent on the first $2,999; 2.5 percent after that, rising to 7 percent on $25,000 and over. The state grants credits in lieu of personal exemptions: single persons, $17.50; married persons or head of family, $35 plus $6 for each dependent. Additional $17.50 credit for blind persons.

Property taxes—The state doesn't levy such taxes, but counties and municipalities do. The legal ratio of assessment is 20 percent, applied to the true market value of real property and the usual selling price of personal property. The rate in mills averages 70.5 per dollar of assessed valuation. Thus, a $10,000 house would be assessed at $2,000 and the tax would be $141 per $10,000 market value (70.5 × $2,000). Certain low-income residents aged 65 and older are allowed a cash rebate up to $500 from the state or a credit against their income tax for property taxes paid on the homestead.

Sales tax—The state levies a 3 percent sales tax, and some communities add 1 percent for a total of 4 percent.

Electricity rates may be higher in rural areas (Little Rock uses mainly natural gas). Food costs are comparable to those in other Sunbelt states. Many retirees have 5-acre farmettes where they raise their own vegetables and chickens and thus cut expenses. A retired couple should be able to live moderately on $8,500 to $10,000 annually in Arkansas.

Varied Retirement Housing

Arkansas offers various types of retirement housing, ranging from mobile homes to retirement villages. The state has some 12,392 housing units, scattered in 106 towns throughout the state. Residents age 65 or older occupy 4,332 of these units.

There are six retirement communities:

Horseshoe Development Corporation	Bella Vista Village
Horseshoe Bend, AR 72536	Bella Vista, AR 72712
Cherokee Village Development Corporation	Eden Isle
Cherokee Village, AR 72542	Eden Isle, AR 72543
Fairfield Bay	Woodland Hills
Post Office Box 105	Post Office Box 278
Shirley, AR 72153	Hardy, AR 72542

Housing authorities in Camden (71701), Fort Smith (72901), Magnolia (71753), North Little Rock (72119), Salem (72576), Searcy (72143), and Texarkana (75501) provide special housing facilities for seniors.

While total building costs may run $30 to $35 per square foot in Little Rock, they cost slightly less in Fort Smith, Fayetteville, and Rogers, and only $28 a square foot or less in rural areas.

Much rural acreage is available. Three years ago rural land sold for as little as $50 an acre; now it costs around $500 an acre. However, there is still much undeveloped scenic land that is quite beautiful in Arkansas. In most cases you should count on building your own housing. Building costs and restrictions have been rather loose; however, they are starting to tighten up. Ready-built two-bedroom retirement homes start at $30,000.

Extensive Medical Care

Arkansas's major medical centers are in Fayetteville, Bentonville, Rogers, Fort Smith, Hot Springs, and Little Rock—all in "retirement country." The state has 106 general hospitals and 1,740 doctors, all of whom will work with Medicare (not necessarily on "assignment"). The state has 204 nursing homes (72 are social service homes). Arkansas has some 650 dentists, 3,847 registered nurses, and numerous other medical personnel, although the ratio of doctors to population is below standard —1 doctor for every 930. Hospital rooms average $88.73 daily (semiprivate room), slightly less than in Louisiana, and more than one-third below the national average.

Culture and Recreation Abound

If you're self-motivated, you'll find many opportunities for culture and recreation in Arkansas. Besides the Ozark Folk Center at Mountain View (see below), small towns have their own musical and theatrical events. The state institutions of higher learning have waived tuition charges and fees for students who are 60 years of age or older. Arkansas boasts outstanding universities and colleges at such retirement centers at Fort Smith (Westark Community Junior College), Little Rock (University of Arkansas at Little Rock, Arkansas Baptist College, Philander Smith College), Batesville (Arkansas College), Fayetteville (University of Arkansas), Pine Bluff (Arkansas A, M&N), Russellville (Arkansas Polytechnic College), Hot Springs (Garland County Community College), and Harrison (North Arkansas Community College).

Hot Springs offers much organized entertainment as do Little Rock and other large cities. Golf and country clubs dot most of the retirement areas; greens fees are approximately $5.

Extensive Services for Seniors

About half the seniors in Arkansas are below the poverty level and need income help through Supplemental Security Income or other aid. The Office on Aging and Adult Services provides services for seniors of all income levels, including 70 nutrition sites, which serve a hot meal daily, and statewide social and recreational programs. It also provides transportation by minibus to the hot meal sites, but transportation is a problem in most areas, with the possible exception of Little Rock.

The state has an active Green Thumb program, which provides jobs for rural elderly to help beautify Arkansas. In addition, there is an active RSVP (Retired Senior Volunteer Program) effort and other volunteer programs which pay out-of-pocket expenses. The Arkansas branch of the American Association of Retired Persons, which lobbies for programs for seniors, is also very active. Low- and middle-income seniors participate in the Association of Community Organizations for Reform Now, popularly known as ACORN, which is made up of 120 neighborhood organizations. Headquartered in Little Rock, this organization performs such functions as pressuring local governments for better services and getting utilities to lower their rates.

According to a projection made by the Arkansas Employment Security Division, seniors can expect to find job openings through 1980 in the following categories: drafters, electronic technicians, engineering science technicians not otherwise classified, R.N.'s, clinical laboratory technologists and technicians, personnel and labor-relations workers, sales managers, office managers, retail sales clerks, secretaries, bookkeepers, counter clerks (except food), brick and stone masons, electricians, plumbers, pipefitters, job and die setters, jewelers and watchmakers, welders and assemblers, cooks, nurses' aides, orderlies, attendants, practical nurses, and air-conditioning, heating, and refrigeration mechanics.

For further information:

> Office on Aging and Adult Services
> 1428 Donaghey Blvd.
> 7th & Main St.
> Little Rock, AR 72201

1. NORTH CENTRAL ARKANSAS—FOLK MUSIC AND FOLKLORE

The Ozark Folk Center in *Mountain View* (pop. 3,000) is famous throughout Arkansas. Until a few years ago, this isolated hamlet in the Ozark foothills held only a handful of people, who liked to gather around the pot-bellied stove at the Stone County Courthouse on Friday nights to sing and play their five-stringed banjos, dulcimers, and guitars. Their songs and instruments have been handed down through generations by the original settlers from Tennessee and Kentucky. Some of the words are Elizabethan; the instruments handmade from centuries past.

Word of these "folk nights" spread and people from miles around came to hear the words and music. In 1963 the town held its first folk festival, to which 20,000 people came. By 1970 40,000 were attending, and from this festival grew the idea of a folk cultural center.

In 1973 the U.S. Economic Development Administration gave $3.4 million for the first national folk cultural center to be located in Mountain View. An ultramodern 1,000-seat auditorium was built (beamed and timbered to preserve the rustic look), as well as a series of cedar buildings where members of the Ozark Foothills Handicraft Guild and other craftsmen display their skills at woodcarving, basketry, chair making, pottery, blacksmithing, candle dipping, quilting, spinning, weaving, and so on.

The Ozark Folk Center operates as an Arkansas state park. It features motellike rooms in hexagon-shaped cabins in the woods. Large rooms, with picture windows facing the woods, rent for around $25 a night double occupancy. The resortlike dining center serves local specialties such as White River catfish, country ham, fried chicken, blackeyed peas, and cornbread.

As I drove to Mountain View from Little Rock, I couldn't help noticing the benches with advertisements on the back for the right-wing John Birch Society; signs that said FIGHT NEW TAXES, GET US OUT OF THE UN, SUPPORT THE RIGHT TO WORK LAWS. The conservatism is also reflected in the culture —the radio played soothing country folk music rather than the raucous country rock of much of the Sunbelt.

As you head north, the road twists and winds up oak-covered hills. Leaves, turning color as the seasons change, contrast with majestic pines. Mists and wood smoke float over the hills and through the hollows—there isn't a sign of plastic-and-neon civilization.

Many of Mountain View's residents work at the Ozark Folk Center. While lots sell for $2,500 to $5,000 an acre in the village, outside Mountain View lots sell for only $300 to $600. A large two-bedroom house can cost as little as $32,000 to build. A mild climate with an average temperature of 62° F. and a low tax base (69 mills in town and 59 mills in the county) make it a favorable location for retirees. The average 45 tc 50 inches of rainfall makes the land suitable for home gardening and beef and poultry production. Even if you don't consider Mountain View as a place to retire, you owe it to yourself to spend at least one night at the Ozark Folk Center. Stay at the lodge, eat the simple but delicious meals in the rustic dining room, and attend the concert that night. Next day, allow time to tour the arts and crafts shops and watch the people at work. Attractive shops with helpful, friendly clerks add to your pleasure.

For further information:

The Ozark Folk Center
Mountain View, AR 72560

South of Mountain View, on Greers Ferry Lake, lies one of Arkansas' largest retirement communities: *Fairfield Bay* (pop. 5,000), a 12,000-acre total living resort, recreation, and retirement community. Fairfield Bay is located on the north shore of the lake—one of the cleanest in the United States—which is 50 miles long with 343 miles of unspoiled shoreline. The annual temperature averages 73.1° F. and annual rainfall averages 56.2 inches.

Housing consists largely of single-family homes, condominium town-houses, and mobile homes. Housing is available in all price ranges, averaging $35,000 for two- to three-bedroom retirement homes.

Fairfield Communities Land Company has invested over $33 million in permanent improvements at Fairfield Bay, including "social improvements," that is, hiking trails, marina, golf course, riding stables, tennis complex, 2 swimming pools, and a civic center. Fairfield Bay is a self-contained community. Services include a post office, gift shop, bank, restaurant, beauty parlor, barber shop, general store, and miniature golf course. There is an outpatient clinic with doctors, nurses, and pharmacists; a community club, which sponsors group and service organizations and arts and crafts classes; a Special Events and Activities Committee, which sponsors Spring Festival and Water Festival; and complete shopping centers.

For further information:

> Fairfield Bay
> Post Office Box 3008
> Fairfield Bay, AR 72153

Northeast of Fairfield Bay lies *Batesville* (pop. 9,000), home of Arkansas College. It offers good outdoor recreation including golf, tennis, hunting, and fishing. Medical facilities include 2 hospitals (161 beds) and 2 nursing homes (260 beds). There are some 18 doctors in the area. Two- and three-bedroom homes sell from $30,000.

For further information:

> Chamber of Commerce
> 409 Vine Street
> Batesville, AR 72501

Mountain Home—The Northern Hub of Retirement Country

Mountain Home (pop. 6,950) is the hub of retirement in northern Arkansas. The retirement communities of *Hardy* (Cherokee Village), *Bull Shoals, Flippin, Yellville, Marshall,* and *Harrison* are located nearby.

To get here I drove on two-lane roads that snake up and down misty valleys and passed several antique stores offering local products—evidence of the area's thriving folk culture. I passed through the pretty town of *Calico Rock,* which is perched on a riverbank. Railroad tracks cross the entrance to the town.

Mountain Home is the center of retirement country and is, itself, a major retirement community. About one-half of the town is retired; many people come from the Midwest (mainly Illinois and Iowa) as well as from California and Florida to retire here.

Climate and Environment. The temperature averages 60° F. annually, with a high average of 80° F. in July and a low average of 38.7° F. in January. Rainfall averages 40 to 45 inches annually and snowfall 6 to 12 inches a year. Humidity averages around 50 percent annually.

The air is crisp and fresh, the mountains green and unspoiled. Nestled in the rolling hills are wide blue lakes—Norfolk and Bull Shoals—impounded by concrete dams. Game fish are plentiful here; the lakes are nationally famous for bass weighing up to 13 pounds. The cold rivers below the dams are stocked with rainbow and brown trout, some weighing over 30 pounds. *You can fish all year long.*

Medical Facilities. As I was driving through the area, the radio was broadcasting admissions and discharges at local hospitals. Area hospitals include a new 38-bed facility at Bull Shoals (complete surgery, X-ray, laboratory, and therapeutic equipment), Baxter General Hospital (complete services including surgery, laboratory, radiological department, emergency, hemodialysis, intensive and coronary care) with 97 beds, and a new nursing home with 72 beds, and Marion County Hospital, near Flippin (48 beds, an extended care unit of 32 beds, X-ray, radiology, and surgical facilities). There are approximately 40 doctors in the area, assuring good medical care.

Housing. Two- and three-bedroom retirement homes sell for as low as $30,000. However, newer, more modern homes average $35,000 to $50,000. Land sells for as low as $250 an acre. Some condominium townhouses sell for under $35,000, and there are many low-rent (around $75 a month) mobile home parks. Housing and land is available for all tastes and pocketbooks. In Hardy is Cherokee Village, a 15,000-acre planned community, where some 2,500 of the 2,800 residents are retired. Lots (100 feet by 150 to 180 feet) sell for around $10,000. Condominium townhouses, single-family homes, and mobile homesites are also available.

Cost of Living. Taxes seem unusually low: as little as $250 a year on a $30,000 house. Mountain Home real estate is assessed at 20 percent of its replacement value. The tax levy varies from 35 to 91 mills on the dollar assessment, depending upon location and school district. Personal property (autos, trucks, mobile homes, boats, airplanes, livestock, farm machinery and household furnishings and equipment at $25 per room) is assessed and the levy is the same millage as on real estate.

Recreation and Culture. Not surprisingly, most recreation centers outdoors: fishing, hunting, swimming, water sports. There is less organized recreation indoors, although the area has over 125 clubs, including arts and crafts, garden, political, and World War I Auxiliary clubs.

Special Services for Seniors. Since about 50 percent of the population is retired, services cater to seniors. Senior clubs include a branch of the American Association of Retired Persons, the Association of Retired Citizens of Baxter County, the National Association of Retired Federal Employees, and one unique organization—the Over-the-Hill Gang. This group of retirees helps out on civic projects. Recently, they restored a tornado-stricken boat dock in record-setting fashion.

For further information:

Chamber of Commerce
Hardy, AR 72542

Chamber of Commerce
Flippin, AR 72634

Chamber of Commerce
Harrison, AR 72601

Chamber of Commerce
Marshall, AR 72650

Chamber of Commerce
Mountain Home, AR 72653

Chamber of Commerce
Yellville, AR 72687

2. THE NORTHWEST CORNER—"LITTLE CHICAGO" AND "LITTLE SWITZERLAND"

West on U.S. 62 are *Harrison* (pop. 10,000) and *Berryville* (pop. 3,500). This part of Arkansas could be called Little Chicago because so many Windy City residents retire here. While most Midwesterners settle in comfortably, some city slickers think the natives are country bumpkins and cause hard feelings.

Harrison seems to be a tidy, sober city, but my impression of Berryville was of one vast liquor store. Arkansas has wet and dry counties and towns; Little Rock, Hot Springs, and Eureka Springs seem to be the only places where you can get a drink over the bar.

Toward *Eureka Springs* (pop. 2,000), the mountains get so steep they almost resemble the Alps (the Boston Mountain section of the Ozark Mountains is the largest and most massive in the state). Aptly, Eureka Springs is called "Little Switzerland."

Chalet-style motels and restaurants line the outskirts of Eureka Springs. The town is built on several elevations (1,400 to 1,700 feet) with homes facing one street and backing onto another 60 feet below. Two families living in the same house in upstairs and downstairs flats may be on different levels and streets, and may get their mail delivered at different times.

Victorian hotels with lacy iron railings, high ceilings, and broad porches grace the historic downtown area. The *entire* downtown Eureka Springs is listed in the National Historic Register. Each twist of the street reveals an atmospheric shop or building; Eureka Springs could be a stage setting for a Victorian melodrama. Most buildings were constructed in the 1880s when Eureka Springs was a fashionable international health spa, and reflect the grandeur of those days.

The following pertains to Eureka Springs as well as the nearby retirement communities of *Bentonville* (pop. 7,000) and *Fayetteville* (pop. 33,000).

Climate and Environment. This is the cooler part of the state; the annual temperature averages only 58° F. Average temperature in winter is in the 40s; in summer the average is in the 80s. About 39 days average over 90° F. and 77 days drop below 32° F. The noontime humidity averages 53 percent and the midnight humidity averages 77 percent. Average annual rainfall is 45 inches.

Medical Facilities. Eureka Springs has 1 hospital with 22 beds and a medical clinic; 4 doctors are in the area. Bentonville has 10 doctors and Bates Memorial Hospital with approximately 70 beds, including a cardiac care unit. Fayetteville also has a Veterans Administration hospital of 254 beds, and 2 nursing homes. Fayetteville has 60 doctors and excellent medical facilities connected with the University of Arkansas. The Carroll County hospital is located in Berryville, 64 miles away.

Housing. Building lots in Eureka Springs average $5,000. Some older housing is expensive, especially in the historic area where homes must be maintained in the original style, but two-bedroom houses in other sections sell for $30,000 and up. Carroll County has rigid building restrictions you should know about if you plan to build in the area (write to the Eureka Springs Chamber of Commerce). There are few rental apartments or houses available. However, only 7 miles from Eureka Springs is *Holiday Island,* a complete resort community with attractive wooded homesites and two-bedroom rustic lakeside condominiums that sell for around $35,000. It also includes facilities for boating, fishing, golf, tennis, indoor and outdoor swimming, horseback riding, cycling, and more. Bentonville has many individual housing units as well as the *Concordia of Bella Vista* retirement facility, which offers "life care" in a total living environment. Apartments sell from $25,000 to $36,000 and townhouses for $40,000 to $60,000. In Fayetteville two-bedroom homes sell for as low as $25,000 and up. Total building costs range from $25 per square foot; building lots range from $8,500 and up. Single-family homes rent from $200 a month; one-bedroom apartments rent from $125; two-bedroom apartments from $250. Fayetteville also has an adult center that provides housing for low-income elderly.

Cost of Living. Taxes in Eureka Springs total 74.5 mills per $100 value based on 20 percent of value. In Bentonville taxes total 78.5 mills. In Fayetteville, the total tax rate is 77 mills inside the city and 70 mills outside. Taxes on a $25,000 house would be $150 to $200 a year.

Recreation and Culture. Eureka Springs's Great Passion Play is held every night (except Mondays and Thursdays) from May 21 to October 30. The town also offers a wealth of activities geared toward retirees, including book clubs, hiking, gardening, square dancing, musical societies, and fraternal organizations. It has a public library, public golf course, tennis courts, swimming pools, and a country club. Bentonville has excellent golf courses and country clubs at Bella Vista. Nearby Beaver Dam is a 30,000-acre reservoir for water sports. Fayetteville, the home of the University of Arkansas, offers outstanding recreational facilities in connection with the university.

Special Services for Seniors. The Fayetteville Adult Center provides a full program for adults age 50 and older including china painting, square dancing, bowling, bridge, art classes, sing-alongs, potluck suppers, ceramics, canasta and other card parties, bingo, and lecture and slide programs. Fayetteville also has active chapters of the AARP and of the Retired Senior Volunteer Program. Bentonville sponsors a senior center and a variety of programs, and Eukera Springs has an active chapter of the AARP.

For further information:

Chamber of Commerce
Eureka Springs, AR 72632

Chamber of Commerce
Bentonville, AR 72712

Chamber of Commerce
Fayetteville, AR 72701

For further information about *Holiday Island:*
Holiday Island
Eureka Springs, AR 72632

For further information about *Concordia of Bella Vista:*
Concordia of Bella Vista
Bella Vista, AR 72712

3. SOUTHWEST ARKANSAS—THE HOT SPRINGS COUNTRY

I spent the night at *Fort Smith* (pop. 70,000), which I found to be a clean, compact city with good restaurants and shopping centers.

The next day offered scenic contrast; instead of climbing higher into hills and mountains, I descended toward the plains. As I curved down from the mountains vast expanses opened up and I was treated to picturesque scenes of pastoral beauty.

Glenwood (pop. 1,500) is an attractive retirement center featuring ranch-style homes on large plots of land. Georgia Pacific and International Paper have facilities here; the attractive commercial center includes a new bank and city hall building. Glenwood is popular for retirement because of the good fishing, hunting, riding, and gardening; the mild climate; the scenic hills and lakes. Land sells for $500 an acre and up; cabins rent for $50 a week; three-bedroom homes sell for as low as $25,000. Glenwood is only 32 miles from Hot Springs and 53 miles from Little Rock.

I confess at first I wasn't impressed with *Hot Springs* (pop. 38,000). It is an "older" town, started around 1836, the year John C. Hale and his wife arrived from Tennessee. At that time the settlement consisted of 6 or 8 rude cabins and a small hotel. The Hales purchased some land, built a two-story hotel, and, in 1854, constructed the first bathhouse in Hot Springs. Before that time, many people had come to bathe in the natural water holes in the mountains (the Indians considered this hallowed ground; warriors laid aside their arms and, regardless of tribe or tongue, bathed in peace).

Hot Springs is famous for its baths, which are considered beneficial for gout and rheumatism, arthritis, neuritis, diabetes, Bright's disease, heart disorders (especially those associated with high blood pressure), chronic kidney diseases, stomach disorders, catarrhal diseases of nose and throat, malaria, anemia, skin diseases, and defective elimination.

While most people bathe in the water, it is also quite drinkable. Unlike most mineral water, it doesn't taste like rotten eggs. I drank some (there are free drinking fountains all over town) and was quite pleased by the natural taste. My taste test was confirmed when a bird came down to drink directly out of one of the two springs that are kept open so visitors may see waters emerging naturally.

The other 45 springs are sealed and water is collected, carefully cooled, and piped to central reservoirs for bathhouse and therapy use. Complicated collecting and cooling systems provide visitors with pure water in properly heated baths.

The federal government supervises the base and approves the rates. In 1979, 1 bath cost $3.80; 18 baths cost $64.70 ($3.59 a bath). One massage cost $5.00; 18 massages cost $83.25 ($4.62 a massage). Many visitors stay for weeks and spend all their time at the baths.

Most of the central part of the city along Bathhouse Row looks as though it was developed in the early part of this century. There were some seedy-looking brick buildings and some seedy-looking people. I walked up Central Avenue to the Arlington Hotel, passing palm readers and diamond appraisal shops. The Arlington Hotel looked like a hospital from the outside. Old men sat on the porch tilting back their chairs to get the warmth of the sun. Inside, the lobby was filled with people reading the papers with magnifying glasses.

I then took the Promenade walk in back of the baths where I saw many very elderly people (80s, 90s) hobbling along carrying large jugs to fill up at the conveniently located fountains. In some instances they clustered on benches surrounding a fountain, watching the endless parade of cars that would pull up and fill countless 5-gallon cans with the free water. I talked to some, who said they not only bathed in and drank the water, but used it to cook with. One man in his 90s assured me: "You'll live to be 100 if you drink this water."

Climate and Environment. Hot Springs is the eastern gateway to the Ouachita Mountains. The terrain to the north and west of the city is rugged and mountainous, while to the south and east it is hilly and rolling. Elevation of city streets runs 600 to 800 feet, while surrounding mountain heights run to 1,450 feet.

The climate is mild, with a mean annual temperature of 63° F. The growing season is relatively long, averaging 221 days from late March to early November. Winter is short; the coldest month is January with a mean temperature of 43.4° F. Summer is long and hot, July averaging 82.3° F. Rainfall averages 53.19 inches and is well distributed throughout the year. Snowfall averages 4.5 inches, but there is no snow in the mountains from

April to October. Humidity averages an ideal 55 percent; Hot Springs receives 60 to 65 percent of possible sunshine.

Medical Facilities. Hot Springs has the nationally famous Physical Medical Center for arthritics. It also has 4 hospitals, as well as clinics, rest and nursing homes, and a state-owned rehabilitation center. The town has 70 licensed physicians registered by the federal government to prescribe treatments in the baths. There are 573 hospital beds and 89 physicians in the area. Semiprivate hospital rooms average about $70 daily.

Housing. Although there hasn't been much home building in Hot Springs recently, there are several two-bedroom homes available for $25,000 and up; several new retirement homes available for $30,000 to $50,000. On the outskirts of Hot Springs, in Hot Springs Village, many homes are priced from $25,000 to $40,000. While rentals are scarce, Benedictine Manor, a retirement home owned and operated by the Olivetan Benedictine Sisters, and other retirement apartments for seniors are available, including new ones being built on Whittington Avenue, one of the main arteries off Bathhouse Row.

Cost of Living. The Hot Springs tax rate in mills is 79.5, based on property assessed at 20 percent of actual value. Taxes on a $20,000 home are around $300 a year in the city and $260 outside the city limits. Utilities run from $100 to $150 a month for a two-bedroom all-electric house, but are somewhat less for a gas-heated home. Food costs, especially in restaurants, seemed a bargain.

Recreation and Culture. Hot Springs offers the whole spectrum of entertainment from topless dancers to church bazaars. It's a place where people come to have fun, and the entertainment and nightclubs draw guests from Little Rock. Whiskey flows about as freely as the water, and Hot Springs is one of the few Arkansas towns (outside of Eukera Springs and Little Rock) where you can buy drinks over the bar.

Hot Springs has a Fine Arts Center which is the home of the Southern Artists Association (notable for their spring and fall outdoor art shows) and a lively little theater group called the Community Players. A very active historical society meets monthly and publishes an annual yearbook. The Hot Springs Community Concert Association sponsors an entertainment series that features widely known artists. Hot Springs also boasts much local talent, including 25 to 30 musicians between the ages of 55 and 100 who make up the Hot Springs National Park Adult and Senior Citizens Concert Band. Since it began in 1974, the band has played for bank and park openings and has participated in many local and state events.

The town also features art, music, book, literary, federated, garden, and study clubs; duplicate bridge, square dance, geology, and other hobby groups; the major civic, patriotic, and fraternal organizations. Three scenic fishing and recreation lakes offer outdoor sports.

This is the Bridge and Bible Belt and there are more than 100 churches of every denomination. There is also an excellent 174,000-volume public library and various schools for adult education.

Special Services for Seniors. Hot Springs houses several retiree clubs: AARP/NRTA, National Association of Retired Federal Employees, Retired Officers Association, 50-plus clubs, and the Retired Senior Volunteer Program. The Community Adult Center and the Neighborhood Senior Citizens' Center provide retirees with a place to spend leisure hours, with recreation, study, handicrafts, games, and other pursuits. Hot Springs has federally funded offices of the Senior Community Service Employment Program, supervised by the Garland County Council on Aging.

For further information:

Chambers of Commerce at:
Fort Smith, AR 72901
Glenwood, AR 71943
Hot Springs, AR 71901

Little Rock—The Beginning and the End

I started and ended my visit to Arkansas in *Little Rock* (pop. 150,000). Located in the center of the state, at a point where the Ozark-Ouachita highlands meet the central coastal plains, this clean, modern capital city is a pleasant blend of Southern charm and Midwestern friendliness.

Climate and Environment. Little Rock has a temperate climate that averages 41.3° F. in winter and 82.1° F. in summer, with a comfortable average annual humidity of 69.3 percent. The moderate climate is ideal for cultivating roses, and the city has been appropriately nicknamed City of Roses. But it is also an industrial center, with 378 manufacturing plants including Allis-Chalmers, Armstrong Rubber, Timex, Remington Arms, Jacuzzi, Westinghouse, General Electric.

Medical Facilities. Little Rock has 10 hospitals, including the University of Arkansas Medical Center, 2 VA hospitals, and Arkansas State Hospital for Nervous Diseases. Hospital rooms average $96.79 (semiprivate) —about $8 more per day than the state average. There are some 600 doctors in the area (about 1 per 250 residents), assuring about the best medical care in the state.

Housing. Good housing is relatively scarce and expensive. However, there are some two-bedroom homes for sale at $25,000 up and for rent at around $300 a month and some two-bedroom apartments and duplexes for rent for as low as $250 a month. Two-bedroom mobile homes sell from $3,000 and rent from $150 a month.

Cost of Living. Cost of living is higher in Little Rock than in other parts of the state; it costs about $10,000 annually for a retired couple to live here comfortably.

Recreation and Culture. Cultural facilities include the University of Arkansas at Little Rock campus, including the School of Graduate Technology; Arkansas State Symphony, Arkansas Arts Center, 3 major public libraries, and a convention center. MacArthur Park has live theater, ballet, opera, and symphony concerts as well as classes in theater arts, pottery, and glassblowing. War Memorial Park contains 202 acres of golf, picnicking, and a zoo; Burns Park has 1,575 acres of golf, tennis, boating, fishing, wildlife trails, and camping.

Services for Seniors. Little Rock has a number of senior organizations and facilities, including a chapter of the American Association of Retired Persons, Heritage House Activity Center, Campus Towers Activity Center, and Senior Citizens Activities Today, a private organization that caters to senior needs. Little Rock is also home to the Association of Community Organizations for Reform Now (ACORN), a collection of 120 neighborhood organizations in low-to-middle-income communities in 6 states. ACORN fights state and local governments for better services and facilities in low-income neighborhoods and it fights the utilities on everything from high rates to pollution.

For more information:

> Chamber of Commerce
> Continental Building
> Markham and Main Streets
> Little Rock, AR 72201

SUMMARY

I liked the people, the places, and the scenery in Arkansas. I felt at home here and was reluctant to leave. If you're a self-motivating individualist, you could retire here comfortably on little money—especially in the quaint towns of Mountain View, Mountain Home, Eureka Springs, and even Hot Springs.

About the only unfavorable aspects for retiring in Arkansas are the roads (which aren't good) and the distances between towns (often over twisting, two-lane mountain roads). Also, there is a feeling of isolation in some of the mountain hamlets; unless you can stake out your own "territory" and social life, you might feel lonely. And I wouldn't advise any city slicker to try to put anything over on the natives—they're a lot smarter than you think.

Here are my personal ratings for Arkansas's major retirement areas:
Excellent—Mountain Home (area), Eureka Springs;
Good—Mountain View, Fairfield Bay, Hardy (Cherokee Village), Harrison, Bentonville, Fayetteville, Glenwood, Hot Springs;
Adequate—Fort Smith, Little Rock.

RATINGS FOR *ARKANSAS* MAJOR RETIREMENT AREAS

MOUNTAIN HOME

Rating	Climate & Envir.	Medical	Housing	Cost of Living	Rec. & Culture	Spec. Senior Svces.
1						
2						
3						
4						
5						

FAYETTEVILLE

Rating	Climate & Envir.	Medical	Housing	Cost of Living	Rec. & Culture	Spec. Senior Svces.
1						
2						
3						
4						
5						

LITTLE ROCK

Rating	Climate & Envir.	Medical	Housing	Cost of Living	Rec. & Culture	Spec. Senior Svces.
1						
2						
3						
4						
5						

RATINGS FOR *ARKANSAS* MAJOR RETIREMENT AREAS

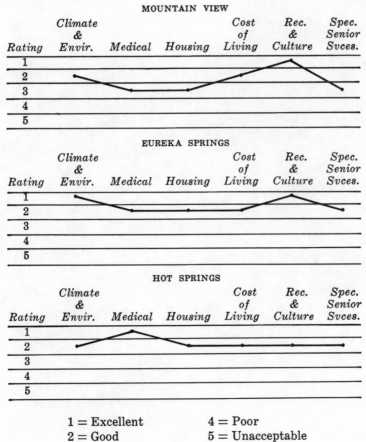

1 = Excellent   4 = Poor
2 = Good   5 = Unacceptable
3 = Fair

TEXAS

Wichita Falls △

Great Plains   Western

○ Midland   △ Tyler

Gulf

△ San Angelo   Coastal

Plain

Texas Hills Johnson
City

△ Alpine   Fredericksburg △ ○   △ Austin

✹
Kerrville

✹ San Antonio

Aransas Pass ○
Corpus Christi ●
○ Port Aransas

Padre
Island

△ El Paso

Harlingen
△
Great   McAllen ○
Plains   Weslaco △
△   Brownsville
Alpine

Inset

✹ Excellent Retirement
△ Good Retirement
● Adequate Retirement
○ Other Towns of Interest

See Inset

XII.

TEXAS—

WHERE THE SOUTH

MEETS THE WEST

A Big State with Climate to Match

Texas makes up 7½ percent of the total land area of the United States, with almost 300,000 square miles of land and 624 miles of coastline. Yet only about 13,000,000 people live here (43 per square mile); about 13 percent are age 60 or older. Within the state, many younger people are moving to the cities while the older population remains in the rural areas. Many counties in the state have had a 50 percent increase in the older age group in the last 10 years.

Much of the state is dry and flat, with the exception of the hill country near Austin and the mountains around El Paso and Alpine.

The Texas climate is generally hot in summer, cool in fall, mild in winter, and balmy in spring. Rainfall and humidity shrink from east to west while winter temperatures increase from north to south. Austin may occasionally have a light blanket of snow; Brownsville hasn't had snow in almost 100 years. San Antonio may have a drought; Corpus Christi swelters in high humidity. In Corpus Christi the mean annual temperature is 71° F. (January 57° F., July 83° F.) and rainfall averages 26 inches. But farther up the coast in Galveston, there is as much as 41 inches of rain a year.

City	Jan. aver. temp.	July aver. temp.	Sunny days	Aver. humidity	Aver. precipitation
Austin	57.9°	79.0°	221	67.5%	26.07 ins.
Dallas	54.1°	79.4°	233	63.5%	24.45 ins.
Houston	59.0°	77.4°	199	78.3%	50.80 ins.

Very Low Cost of Living

Food, housing, and gasoline are cheaper in Texas than in many other Sunbelt states. And, in spite of their size, Dallas, Houston, and Austin have living costs that are 5 to 10 percent below the national average. A retired couple can live on an intermediate budget in Texas for less than $8,500 annually.

Property tax—Counties, cities, and school districts set the property taxes, and the state assessed a tax of 12 cents per $100 of county valuation (based on only a percentage of actual market value). However, the state tax reduced to 10 cents after January 1978. The state allows a $3,000 homestead exemption from the value of the property as assessed by the county. Local taxing authorities have the option of granting an *additional homestead exemption* of $3,000 to persons 65 years of age or older. Generally, property taxes in Texas are the second highest in the Sunbelt, and averaging $206 per $10,000 valuation.

Personal property tax—Some local taxing authorities levy a tax on personal property, such as automobiles and household furnishings.

Intangible property tax—Although a tax on intangible property such as stocks, bonds, and bank accounts is authorized by law, it is rarely assessed.

Income tax—Texas has *no* tax on personal or corporate income.

Sales tax—The state imposes a 4 percent tax on most items except for groceries, prescription medicines, and products used in agricultural production. Most Texas cities impose an additional 1 percent sales tax.

For additional information write:

> Tax Information Division
> Comptroller of Public Accounts
> 111 East 17th Street
> Austin, TX 78774

In Texas call toll free: 1-800-252-5555.

Various Housing Available at All Price Ranges

Throughout Texas's retirement areas low-to-moderate ($25,000 to $40,000) two-bedroom retirement homes are available, including single-family homes within a regular community and townhouses or condominiums in adult communities. There are also many low-rent (averaging $75 a month) mobile home parks and subdivisions. Large developments at Lake Travis have condominiums that sell from $40,000 and mobile home lots that sell for $10,000. Horizon City near El Paso has vacation and second homes that sell for $40,000. At Lake Mathis, single-family two-bedroom homes sell for as low as $35,000.

Medical Help at All Levels

Texas has good medical facilities, especially in the larger cities. Adult day care centers, where the physically disabled may spend the day in a sheltered environment, receiving social, nutritional, and medical help, are located throughout the state. In Hidalgo County, a Senior Companion Service provides paid volunteers to work with the aged, mentally ill, or disabled. These volunteers not only provide companionship in homes but also in nursing homes and day care centers. Many communities also offer homemaker services, which help the elderly remain in their homes.

Texas has 571 hospitals with a total of 57,056 beds; 873 nursing homes with 74,430 beds; 94 personal care homes with 615 beds. There are 18,421 doctors in Texas, which means 1 doctor for every 696 residents, not as good a ratio as in Florida. A semiprivate hospital room averages $99.54 daily—about $11 more per day than Arkansas, but still almost one-third below the U.S. average of over $133 a day.

Plenty of Low-Cost Recreation Available

The larger retirement cities provide plenty of community activities—clubs, dances, indoor and outdoor sports—at low cost.

Although Texas lists some 376 museums, some with renowned art and historical collections, many smaller communities don't offer much in the way of culture. However, they feature active social and recreational programs, and offer many opportunities for service work and volunteer activities. Texas estimates that nearly 1 out of every 4 residents is involved in some type of voluntary activity. The average volunteer contributes 9 hours a week to hospitals, schools, civic, political, and community groups, and so on.

Hunting and fishing are also very popular in Texas; *residents over age 65 don't need a license.*

Many Services for Seniors

The Governor's Committee on Aging (through 28 Area Agencies on Aging) conducts or coordinates many programs for seniors including a hot meal program for some 30,000 seniors each day; a Retired Senior Volunteer Program (RSVP) in such cities as Fort Worth, Dallas, Waco, Lufkin, Austin, Houston, Galveston, Kerrville, San Antonio, Corpus Christi, Edinburgh, Harlingen; a Senior Texans Employment Program (STEP), which employs elderly for conservation, restoration, beautification, recreation, and other community service projects; Green Thumb, which provides beautification jobs for older workers in rural areas; a rural transportation program that furnishes 500 vans and drivers to seniors in rural Texas counties; a Center for Studies in Aging at North Texas State University (located in Denton) ; Senior Community Service and Senior Community Aides programs, which provide jobs for seniors in cities such as Dallas, El Paso, Houston, Laredo, Mission, Waco, San Antonio, and Brownsville; Foster Grandparents Programs; Service Corps of Retired Executives (SCORE) ; and the Senior Companion Service previously mentioned.

Job opportunities in cities such as Houston are among the best in the nation. Among those needed: accountants; chemical, electrical and mechanical engineers; medical and engineering technicians; registered and licensed practical nurses; bookkeepers, cashiers, checkers, office clerks, secretarial, and other office personnel; salespeople in most fields; tailors, auto mechanics, bricklayers, electricians, farm equipment mechanics, instrument and laboratory technicians; maintenance repair persons, millwrights, plumbers, tire service people, stationary engineers, tractor-trailer truck drivers, arc welders.

For further information:

> Governor's Committee on Aging
> Post Office Box 12786
> Capitol Station
> Austin, TX 78711

1. THE LOWER RIO GRANDE VALLEY—RETIREMENT WITH A MEXICAN FLAVOR

I had served in the Army in Texas (near Tyler) and had returned many times since, mainly to the larger cities: Houston, Dallas, Fort Worth. This time I headed directly to the southern tip—the lower Rio Grande Valley—which contains some of the best retirement country in the Lone Star State.

I flew from Little Rock to Houston, then to McAllen. I knew I was near the border when I stepped off the plane—the radio was playing Strauss' "Die Fledermaus" with a Latin beat!

There is a Hispanic flavor to the lower Rio Grande Valley (which is actually a delta). Most retirement towns are on the border or within 10 miles of it, and some 79 percent of the people in the area have Spanish surnames. Most of the help in stores and restaurants is of Mexican descent; while they do speak English, they sometimes speak Spanish among themselves, which seems to annoy some non-Spanish-speaking Anglos.

I drove down *McAllen*'s (pop. 58,000) palm-lined avenues (this is the City of Palms) to my first-class motel, which charged only $16 a night. I was pleasantly surprised to see gasoline selling for as low as 54 cents a gallon. Local residents get bargains by shopping in Reynosa, the Mexican town just 8 miles south of McAllen. However, *avoid* eating in Mexican restaurants. While a restaurant may look clean in the dining area, it may be dirty in the kitchen. Some restaurants mix leftover food with fresh food, which could cause food poisoning, and also buy spoiled chicken or other fowl, dip them in vinegar to kill the taste, and cook them up as fresh.

Climate and Environment. McAllen enjoys cool night breezes in summer and warm Gulf breezes in winter. These usually blow at 5 to 15 miles an hour; during the summer you can open doors or windows to take advantage of the wind. The temperature averages 65° F. in January and 84° F. in July, with a mean annual temperature of 72° F. Annual rainfall averages 20 inches and mean relative humidity stays around a steady 70 percent. Tornadoes, dust storms, and hurricanes are unusual.

Medical Facilities. McAllen has a fully accredited general hospital of 272 beds and complete facilities. It is staffed by 85 doctors, many of whom are specialists, representing every field of medicine. The hospital offers excellent laboratory and X-ray facilities, including a Radiation Treatment Center.

Housing. Tidy frame and stucco two-bedroom bungalows sell for as low as $25,000 and up; one-bedroom apartments rent for $150 and up. For

$350 a month you can rent a luxurious furnished two-bedroom apartment with utilities. Rents are somewhat higher in winter. The chamber of commerce maintains a courtesy rental listing. Cockroaches and mosquitos may be a problem so be sure your house or apartment has adequate protection.

Cost of Living. Housing, fuel, and recreation are cheaper in McAllen than in some other parts of Texas, as well as locally-grown fruits and vegetables. Excellent shopping centers offer everything from groceries to furniture.

Natural gas is abundant and cheap in McAllen; electricity rates are a bit higher. During July and August it may cost $125 to $200 a month to completely air-condition a house.

McAllen property taxes are a bit lower than average for Texas: about $200 per $10,000 true market value of a home. A $25,000 two-bedroom retirement home would be taxed at around $500 annually.

Recreation and Culture. The city maintains municipal swimming pools and a municipal golf course, in addition to facilities operated by the country club; residents can play year-round. There are 50 churches and 1 synagogue in town. All the large civic clubs, as well as numerous women's clubs are represented. McAllen has excellent museum, garden, library, and community concert programs. The Tourist and Social Club features arts and crafts, buffet suppers, cards and games, dances, pool and billiards, shuffleboard, and special events.

Special Services for Seniors. Most of the senior clubs have chapters here; there is also a chapter of SCORE (Service Corps of Retired Executives), and the Telephone Pioneers of America.

For further information:

> Chamber of Commerce
> Post Office Box 790
> McAllen, TX 78501

Other Retirement Centers in the Lower Rio Grande Valley

From McAllen, I dipped toward the border and turned east on State Route 281. I passed vast fields of sugar cane and saw palm trees on the horizon. Most of the music on the car radio was Mexican. If you plan to settle here it is a good idea to understand at least some Spanish.

I turned up to old Route 83 at Weslaco (the center of the valley), then continued east again to:

Harlingen (pop. 40,500), which offers many tourist and retirement attractions including Six-Shooter Junction, a theme-and-crafts park featuring demonstrations by crafts people, food, and rides from the 1880s era, and the Confederate Air Force, the only complete collection of World War II aircraft in the world. Harlingen is the home of the Life Begins at 40 golf tournament, and it has a splendid municipal course. At Anson House, retirees can participate in various activities including shuffleboard, cards, and bus tours. Two-bedroom retirement homes sell for around $30,000, and attractive mobile home villages rent space from $75 a month. Harlingen is in the medical center of southern Texas and has the Valley Baptist Medical Center and Radiation Treatment Clinic, Rio Grande Center for Mental Health, and the Harlingen State Chest Hospital. There are 566 hospital beds, with 137 medical doctors, dentists, and chiropractors.

For further information:

> Chamber of Commerce
> P.O. Box 189
> Harlingen, TX 78550

Brownsville (pop. 80,000) is the largest city in the lower Rio Grande Valley and it has the advantage of being only a few miles from the Gulf of Mexico. Gulf breezes fan the city in the summer, making it a degree or so cooler in summer than most other valley towns. Housing is available in all price ranges; high-rise apartments for seniors rent for as low as $70 a month, based on 20 percent of the tenant's income. Mobile home parks rent space from $70 a month; two-bedroom retirement houses average $35,000. At the Brownsville Country Club you can purchase lots for around $9,000. Although the city is a seaport and industrial community, the streets are lined with palm trees and bougainvillea. Many homes and gardens border on winding waterways (some mansions belong to international celebrities). There are some 80 doctors in the area and hospital facilities at the 117-bed Valley Community Hospital, 162-bed Brownsville Medical Center, and 3 nursing homes are outstanding, as are the recreational facilities (including golf). Just across the border is the vibrant town of Matamoros, where you can shop for bargains, attend bull fights, and swim on white sandy beaches.

For further information:

> Chamber of Commerce
> Post Office Drawer
> Brownsville, TX 78520

You may also write:

Rio Grande Valley Chamber of Commerce
Post Office Box 975
Weslaco, TX 78596

2. THE TEXAS "RIVIERA"—FROM SOUTH PADRE TO CORPUS CHRISTI

Highway 77 from Brownsville to Corpus Christi is a flat, dull route passing hundreds of miles of flat, dry, dull land. But a few miles to the east lies one of the most fascinating strips of Texas—*Padre Island* (pop. 500).

This 110-mile sandy scimitar has some of the best beaches and best fishing in Texas. It's been hailed as the Miami Beach of the 1980s; if construction of high-rises make it so, it could well win this dubious title. Many high- and low-rise dwellings, from condominiums to beach houses, are available, ranging in price from $30,000 to over $100,000 for two-bedroom units.

In spite of the "civilization" there are miles of gently sloping beaches that are perfect for swimming or surf fishing. The beaches are intriguing to beachcombers—yielding bright shells, driftwood, and occasional flint points of the Karankawa Indians, who once roamed the area. Padre Island still remains remote, and the best facilities—shopping, recreation, medical —are available in Brownsville and Corpus Christi, reached via a free causeway.

For further information:

Chamber of Commerce
South Padre Island, TX 78578

Corpus Christi (pop. 250,000) is a fine seaport and the home of major Navy and Army facilities. Although the area is a livestock and industrial center, the fine landlocked harbor makes the city a resort area with fishing, swimming, and water sports.

Corpus Christi offers many cultural and educational facilities, including the Corpus Christi Museum, Symphony, Del Mar College, Corpus Christi State U. and a 2,600 seat exhibition hall, which features Golden Age dances. The city also has several community centers where you can play shuffleboard, cards, attend movies, lectures, and 2 municipal golf courses and 4 country clubs.

Corpus Christi is a delightful place to visit. The town has many tasty Bar-B-Que pits where you can get an order of ribs, cole slaw, beans, and beer for less than $3.50. The only disquieting note is the "adult entertainment strip" near the waterfront. I was told not to walk the streets at night and, looking out my hotel window, I could see what looked like prostitutes and policemen. The city has an annual crime-rate ratio of 1 crime per 21.1 people, every 2 years. It ranks 301st in safety out of U.S. cities with populations over 50,000.

Climate and Environment. The mean annual temperature is 71° F.; January averages 57° F., April, 71°, July 83°, October, 71°. The average annual humidity is a not-uncomfortable 69 percent, although some summer days are hot and humid. Rainfall averages 26 inches.

Medical Facilities. Medical facilities include 10 hospitals with a total of 1,497 beds. There are some 300 doctors in the area, assuring adequate medical care.

Housing. Many two-bedroom retirement homes sell for $25,000 to $40,000; one-bedroom apartments rent from $200 a month and up, and two-bedroom apartments rent from $250 a month and up. Effective tax rate: $2.8047 per $100.

Recreation and Culture. Corpus Christi has public beaches and fishing piers on the bay and along the Gulf of Mexico. The Art Museum of South Texas is located here—a striking building right on Corpus Christi Bay. Along the bay, 2 T-heads and an L-head thrust into the bay at the heart of downtown offering mooring for pleasure craft and free fishing for residents. A causeway from Corpus Christi leads to Padre Island National Seashore, where you can swim, beachcomb, and fish.

For further information:

> Chamber of Commerce
> P.O. Box 640
> Corpus Christi, TX 78403

Before turning inland, I visited *Aransas Pass* (pop. 8,500) and *Port Aransas* (pop. 1,500), where many folks retire because "the fish bite every day." Aransas Pass lies between Mustang and St. Joseph Island; it is on the mainland but connected to Mustang Island by causeway and ferry. Port Aransas and Aransas Pass are modest towns with modest homes. You can retire here comfortably on $500 to $600 a month. Lots sell from $3,500; modest two-bedroom retirement homes cost $25,000 to $40,000. The causeways and surrounding areas aren't pretty, but these towns are only about 28 miles from Corpus Christi, where recreation, shopping, and medical facilities are available. There are 7 doctors in the towns.

For further information:

Chamber of Commerce
Aransas Pass, TX 78336

Chamber of Commerce
Port Aransas, TX 78373

3. SAN ANTONIO AND THE TEXAS HILL COUNTRY

As I drove north-northwest toward San Antonio, the landscape was big, open, and flat. It was relieved mainly by clumps of trees and historical markers that told of some pioneering activity—usually a tragedy. Much of this country was originally settled by Germans and other Europeans and still has evidence of their cultures.

San Antonio (pop. 760,000). I can see why so many people (especially the military) want to retire here. It's a large city (with skyscrapers) with a small-town atmosphere and environment—clear, clean air and neat, tidy houses.

Climate and Environment. San Antonio is located on the edge of the Gulf coastal plains. It has a modified subtropical climate, predominantly continental during the winter months and marine during the summer. Normal mean temperatures range from 52° F. in January to 84° F. in July. Although the summer is hot, with daily maximum temperatures over 90° F. over 80 percent of the time, extremely high temperatures are rare. Mild weather prevails during much of the winter months; below-freezing temperatures occur on about 20 days each year.

Normal annual rainfall averages 27.84 inches, with the heaviest amounts in May and September. Relative humidity averages 80 percent during the early morning hours most of the year, dropping to nearly 50 percent in the afternoon. San Antonio is known as the place where the sunshine spends the winter. About 50 percent of the possible amount of sun shines during the winter months and more than 70 percent during the summer.

Medical Facilities. Hospital and medical facilities in San Antonio's private and governmental hospitals provide more than 9,000 beds. The total number of physicians in Bexar County is over 1,200. The Bexar County Medical Society, 202 West French Place, San Antonio, TX 78212 will assist newcomers in locating a family physician.

Housing. Prices of new homes in subdivisions range from $30,000 to $90,000 depending on location, size, and features offered. For information on new homes contact the Greater San Antonio Builders Association, 8925 IH 10 NW, San Antonio, TX 78230. There are usually 1,000 homes for sale in the local market at any given time. Average monthly rentals for a three-bedroom residence range from $200 to $400. One-bedroom apartments rent from $150 a month and two-bedroom apartments rent from $200 a month.

For additional information contact the San Antonio Apartment Association, 901 N.E. Loop 410, San Antonio, TX 78209.

Cost of Living. Costs are generally low, and San Antonio has unusually good shopping centers. The central shopping district comprises about 30 blocks in the downtown section of the city, and the city features dozens of neighborhood and suburban shopping centers. Natural gas used to be unusually cheap in San Antonio, and retirees paid only $10 a month for utility bills in a two-bedroom home. Since the energy crisis, rates have jumped to about $40 a month and up.

The county tax rate is 91 cents per $100 valuation, based on 20 percent of market value. The city rate is $1.65 per $100, based on 45 percent of market value, bringing the actual assessment ratio to 33.4. Like most other Texas cities, San Antonio levies a sales tax of 1 percent on all items purchased at retail except groceries, prescription drugs, rent, mortgage payments, and gasoline. There's also ½ percent transit tax.

Recreation and Culture. The San Antonio Symphony Society and other local musical groups sponsor many annual events. Permanent art galleries include the noted McNay Art Institute. San Antonio boasts 2 major museums: the Institute of Texan Cultures and the Witte Museum. Theaters and various dramatic groups offer several theatrical productions.

Park facilities include a zoo, an aquarium, sunken gardens, one outdoor theater, swimming pools, golf course, lakes, recreation buildings, and more. San Antonio also has an extensive library system including a number of research libraries, a medical library, and libraries at the colleges and universities. Most of the usual private, fraternal, and professional organizations are represented in San Antonio. There are many local civic, church, school, and special interest groups as well.

Special Services for Seniors. Besides many senior centers, San Antonio has many special senior organizations, including the following:

> Senior Citizens Council of Bexar County
> Post Office Box 64
> San Antonio, TX 78291

Texas Senior Citizens Association
822 Fair Avenue
San Antonio, TX 78223

AARP
234 Eastley
San Antonio, TX 78217

For further information:

Chamber of Commerce
602 Commerce Street
San Antonio, TX 78296

As I left San Antonio, the land became rolling, wild, and woolly. I was approaching the Hill Country, or LBJ Country, of Texas, home of many favorite retirement towns including:

Kerrville (pop. 15,000). At an elevation of some 1,650 feet and surrounded by cedar and live-oak hills, this area has some of the most ideal scenery and climate in the nation. Summers average 79.8° F. and winters average 47° F. At the south edge of the town is Kerrville State Park, 500 acres for camping, swimming, fishing, nature study, and hiking. One-third of the town's residents are retired, and they are active in art, music, and literary pursuits. Brick and stone homes (prices average $40,000 for two-bedroom houses) are tucked in the hills along winding, spacious streets and lots. One of the several attractive subdivisions is Loma Vista, a medium-cost adult community with club-type activities. There's also an all-adult mobile home park where two-bedroom units sell for around $25,000. Taxes on average retirement homes are around $500. Kerrville has an ultramodern hospital and some 25 doctors in the area, assuring better-than-average medical care. Kerrville has a branch of the Retired Senior Volunteer Program (RSVP).

For further information:

Chamber of Commerce
Kerrville, TX 78028

Leaving Kerrville, I wound up even steeper hills until I came upon a delightful surprise: *Fredericksburg* (pop. 7,000). The main street of this town looks like a stage setting for a German beer garden! In fact, some of the most prominent signs are beer steins with Gothic printing and German words. Fredericksburg was founded by German pioneers in 1847.

The town grew slowly and stolidly, and its German heritage has kept Fredericksburg clean, orderly, conservative, and law-abiding.

You don't have to be German to retire here, but you should like hearty German breads, sauerbraten, beer, and other German foods. German is spoken as often as English and old customs, such as Saengerfests (song fests) and Schuetzenfests (marksmanship tournaments) are regularly observed. Annual events include Easter Fires Pageant (hillside fires) ; horse races around July 4; a night in Old Fredericksburg with Old World music, food, and costumes.

Hunting (turkey and deer) is especially good here, and you can enjoy golf, swimming, tennis, cycling (good trails in the area), gardening, and hiking year-round. Lady Bird Johnson Park, a 190-acre outdoor recreation center, is only 3½ miles to the south.

Fredericksburg shares the healthy Hill Country climate of Kerrville, and this has made it a mecca for health seekers—especially those with respiratory and cardiac problems. Summer temperatures average 78° F. and winters 48° F. Annual rainfall is 28 inches. A modern hospital with 15 doctors provides good medical care.

Two-bedroom homes sell for $30,000 and up, and there are some rentals (homes and apartments) for $250 a month and up. Although Fredericksburg doesn't have retirement communities as such, it does have 2 senior citizen groups—the Happy Agers and the AARP. Seniors are welcome in all community activities. The area is especially interesting to "rock hounds" as there are many 1-billion-year-old rocks lying exposed to the surface.

For further information:

> Chamber of Commerce
> Post Office Box 506
> Fredericksburg, TX 78224

Heading toward Austin via Johnson City, I saw a number of signs pointing to the *Highland Lakes,* where retirement and other homes sell for $40,000 to $125,000. Lake Travis World of Resorts is one of the many developments here—a 5,500-acre community with 3 adjoining villages. At Highland Lakes, in a contemporary design village, condominiums sell from $40,000. Other developments include Lago Vista and Horseshoe Bay, with a large marina, yacht club, golfing, and tennis; Bar K Ranch, with an airstrip, golf, and riding; Point Venture, with marina, pool, tennis, and golf; Lakeway, where condominiums start at $75,000; Kingsland on Lake LBJ (a year-round vacation and retirement community), which has the largest

shopping center on the lakes. There is a 150-mile "stairway" of lakes leading into Austin.

For further information:

Highland Lakes Tourist Association
Post Office Box 1967
Austin, TX 78767

Austin (pop. 331,577, city; 396,436 metropolitan). Although this is the
state capital, it looks like a small town, with its low buildings. The pink
granite Capitol Building, second in size among the capitol buildings only
to the Capitol Building in Washington, D.C., looks like a giant hen brooding
on the horizon. Yet Austin is the commercial center for 10 counties, and a
major industrial center with 450 manufacturing firms.

Climate and Environment. The climate is moderate: Temperatures
average 57.9° F. in winter and 79° F. in summer. The humidity averages a
comfortable 55 percent. Rainfall is 32.49 inches annually.

Medical Facilities. Austin is a major medical center with 9 hospitals
(1,346 beds), 461 physicians, and 231 dentists. This assures above-average
medical care.

Housing. Retirees are also attracted to Austin because of its low-cost
housing: Many two- and three-bedroom houses sell for $30,000, and two-
bedroom apartments rent for about $300 a month. Many one-bedroom
apartments rent for around $150 a month. Unfurnished homes and
duplexes (two- and three-bedroom) are available for $250 a month and
up. Mobile homes sell from $8,000 and rent from $100 a month. Mobile
home lots rent for as low as $60 a month.

Recreation and Culture. Austin is also a major cultural center with
the University of Texas system and the University of Texas at Austin. It
has the Lyndon Baines Johnson Library and several other major research
centers; Texas Memorial and Texas Art museums; 4 small colleges; 4
local theater companies; the Austin Symphony, and 2 ballet companies.
Recreation facilities include 2 lakes, 7,000 acres of parks, pools, 9 golf
courses, 47 tennis courts, and 2 annual festivals.

Special Services for Seniors. While Austin isn't geared to retirement,
it does have 3 senior centers and the Adult Friendship Center where you
can meet and mingle with other retirees.

For further information:

Chamber of Commerce
901 West Riverside
Austin, TX 78767

4. OTHER TEXAS RETIREMENT TOWNS OF INTEREST

Tyler (pop. 69,000). This is the Rose Capital of the World—half of the field-grown roses in the U.S. come from here. The moderate climate (annual average temperature is 67° F.) allows azaleas, redbuds, dogwood, and wisteria to flourish. Azalea Trails and spring flower shows from late March to early April herald the arrival of spring; the Texas Rose Festival draws 150,000 spectators in October.

Many lovely retirement homes nestle among the blossoms. Two-bedroom townhouses sell from $30,000 and two-bedroom homes from $40,000. Ten miles south on 18-mile-long Lake Palestine is a 600-acre planning community called Lake Village. Building lots on or near the lake start at about $7,500. There are 2 mobile home communities near Tyler, where lots rent from $60 to $75 a month.

Tyler is a cultural center; it is the home of Texas College, Texas Eastern University, and Tyler Junior College. Local community groups stage plays and there are also art and music groups.

There are 1,150 hospital beds in the area and 201 physicians, assuring good medical care.

For further information:

Chamber of Commerce
Tyler, TX 75701

Wichita Falls (pop. 106,800). This gateway to Texas (from Oklahoma) is a major trade and industrial (oil) center. It is also home to Sheppard Air Base, a technical and jet pilot training center for the U.S. Air Force.

Wichita Falls offers unusually good cultural and recreational facilities, with the Wichita Falls Museum and Art Center, Midwestern State University, a municipal golf course, and fishing, boating, swimming, and water skiing at both Lake Wichita and Lake Arrowhead. The moderate temperature (average 42.8° F. in winter; 68° F. in summer) permits outdoor activities all year long.

Two-bedroom homes average $30,000 and apartments are available from $250 a month. There are 2 rental mobile home parks in the area; rents average $70 a month. Wichita Falls has sufficient hospital facilities (1,032 beds) but it has only 169 physicians, which is just barely adequate for the population.

For further information:

Chamber of Commerce
Wichita Falls, TX 76307

San Angelo (pop. 70,000). This is primarily a ranching (sheep and cattle) community and is the largest primary wool market in the United States. It is also a center for excellent fishing (black and smallmouth bass, crappie, catfish, bream perch) and hunting (deer, turkey, mourning dove, ducks, blue and bobwhite quail, squirrel, rabbit, javelina hog). San Angelo has a symphony orchestra and is home to Angelo State University. It has a municipal golf course and swimming pool; fishing and boating in nearby Lake Nasworthy and North Concho Lake. Fort Concho, among the best preserved Texas frontier military forts, is nearby.

San Angelo boasts good retirement housing in Rio Concho Manor, a 253-unit apartment complex designed especially for semiretired or retired persons. Rents range from $100 to $200 a month including utilities. Other two-bedroom apartments rent from $250 a month, and two-bedroom homes are available from $30,000. San Angelo has some 600 hospital beds and 125 doctors.

For further information:

Chamber of Commerce
San Angelo, TX 76901

Midland (pop. 78,000) lies on the former Chihuahua Trail, the immigrant road to California. It got its name because it is halfway between El Paso and Fort Worth. Midland is headquarters of the vast Permian Basin oil activity, and it houses more than 800 petroleum and related businesses. It is also the home of several unusual museums, including the Midland Man Museum (remains of a prehistoric man 22,000 years old), Museum of the Southwest (art, history, science), Midland County Museum (Indian and pioneer relics), Permian Basin Petroleum Museum (history of petroleum in the area), and the Pliska Aviation Museum (first airplane flown in Texas). The city also has good recreation areas including parks, pools, tennis courts, and golf course. Midland also has a symphony orchestra, theater, and Midland College.

Two-bedroom homes start at $30,000 and two-bedroom apartments rent from $200 a month. Taxes are approximately $200 per $10,000 market value. There are only 250 hospital beds in the area and 150 doctors.

For further information:

Chamber of Commerce
Midland, TX 79701

Alpine (pop. 7,000) at 4,485 feet is one of the highest locations in the state. It lies between the Davis Mountains to the northwest and Chisos

Mountains to the southeast and is the county seat of Brewster County, the largest county in Texas (Brewster County is bigger than the state of Connecticut). Its location and elevation make for a temperate climate; January, the coldest month, averages 46° F. and July, the hottest month averages 77.2° F. The annual average is 62.9° F. Annual rainfall totals 15.21 inches.

For a town its size, Alpine has unusual cultural and recreational facilities. It is the home of Sul Ross State University with 2,000 students and a 70,000-volume library. There is a 35,000-volume public library, and adult and continuing education courses are offered in all fields. Other facilities include 10 tennis courts, a golf course, a summer outdoor theater, a community center, and a senior center. There are some 50 clubs in town, including a chapter of the American Association of Retired Persons, and a senior citizens' club.

Alpine is the gateway to Big Bend National Park and the starting point of scenic tours of the Davis Mountains including Fort Davis, a state park, McDonal Observatory, and various ghost towns. Lakes Amistad and Balmorhea and the Rio Grande River provide good fishing; there's good hunting for deer, antelope, javelina, dove, and quail.

Housing is scarce. The few two-bedroom houses that are available sell for around $35,000. But Alpine and Brewster County (as do most Texas counties) give a $3,000 tax exemption for persons over age 65.

Alpine has 50 hospital beds, 8 doctors, and 1 dentist in the area, making medical facilities less than adequate.

For further information:

Chamber of Commerce
Alpine, TX 79830

El Paso (pop. 400,000) is well-known as a retirement center because of its sunny climate, low humidity, low cost of living (95 percent of national average), and varied recreational, cultural, and social activities.

Climate and Environment. The 3,700-foot elevation causes large differences in temperature between day and night. Temperatures on summer days are frequently in the high 90s, but at night they drop to the 60s. Winter daytime temperatures may rise to an average of 60° F. but at night they often drop to below freezing. Humidity is low, averaging around 20 percent, and dust and sandstorms occur most frequently in March and April.

Medical Facilities. El Paso has 15 hospitals providing 2,531 beds, and 424 doctors and 127 dentists. St. Joseph Hospital has a Cardiac Rehabilitation Center and Cancer Treatment Center. William Beaumont Army Medical Center, one of the largest military medical centers, has 463 beds.

Housing. New homes in the best residential areas sell for about $35 a square foot, but some two-bedroom homes sell for as low as $25,000 and one-bedroom apartments (furnished, with utilities paid) rent for as low as $150 a month. There are 4 major housing projects for low-income elderly.

Recreation and Culture. Outdoor sports are available in El Paso year-round; there are few days when you can't play golf, tennis, swim, or hike. Cultural facilities include the El Paso Symphony, which provides a full concert season and summer pops concerts. The art museum houses the work of contemporary artists and traveling exhibits. El Paso's central library, one of the most complete in the Southwest, is located downtown with branch units in residential areas. Amateur and professional theatrical groups are active year-round and the University of Texas at El Paso sponsors ballet and other cultural activities.

Special Services for Seniors. El Paso makes an effort to help retirees through discounts on merchandise and an active Council on Aging, which is devoted exclusively to helping older people with their problems.

El Paso is the largest U.S. city on the Mexican border, and it's directly across from Juarez, which is the largest Mexican city on the U.S. border. As in McAllen, much of the help is Mexican and it pays to speak some Spanish. Texas border towns do have problems with illegal immigrants, petty thievery, and other crime. However, El Paso ranks 205th in safety nationally, with only 1 crime per 28.7 persons every 2 years. This makes it safer than many northern cities of comparable size.

For further information:

> El Paso Council on Aging
> 600 Chelsea
> El Paso, TX 79903
>
> Chamber of Commerce
> El Paso, TX 79944

SUMMARY

I liked the low cost of living, the food, and the low-humidity climate of Texas. Outdoor sportsmen (everything from golf to hunting) or those interested in volunteer or service work could retire comfortably here. However, it pays to learn some Spanish if you settle in places like El Paso, McAllen, Harlingen, or Brownsville.

I felt the general lack of culture in most of the small Texas towns and would be unhappy if I retired in an area virtually devoid of any intellectual stimulation. Also, the haphazard zoning in some areas makes the outskirts of some towns look like junkyards. Severe wind and dust could be a problem for people with allergies or other respiratory problems.

Here are my personal ratings for Texas's major retirement areas:
Excellent—McAllen, Kerrville, San Antonio, Midland;
Good—Brownsville, Austin, Fredericksburg, Wichita Falls, Tyler, Alpine, San Angelo, El Paso, Harlingen;
Adequate—Corpus Christi.

RATINGS FOR TEXAS MAJOR RETIREMENT AREAS

LOWER RIO GRANDE VALLEY (MCALLEN AREA)

Rating	Climate & Envir.	Medical	Housing	Cost of Living	Rec. & Culture	Spec. Senior Svces.
1						
2						
3						
4						
5						

CORPUS CHRISTI

Rating	Climate & Envir.	Medical	Housing	Cost of Living	Rec. & Culture	Spec. Senior Svces.
1						
2						
3						
4						
5						

KERRVILLE-FREDERICKSBURG

Rating	Climate & Envir.	Medical	Housing	Cost of Living	Rec. & Culture	Spec. Senior Svces.
1						
2						
3						
4						
5						

SAN ANGELO

Rating	Climate & Envir.	Medical	Housing	Cost of Living	Rec. & Culture	Spec. Senior Svces.
1						
2						
3						
4						
5						

SAN ANTONIO

Rating	Climate & Envir.	Medical	Housing	Cost of Living	Rec. & Culture	Spec. Senior Svces.
1						
2						
3						
4						
5						

AUSTIN

Rating	Climate & Envir.	Medical	Housing	Cost of Living	Rec. & Culture	Spec. Senior Svces.
1						
2						
3						
4						
5						

RATINGS FOR *TEXAS* MAJOR RETIREMENT AREAS

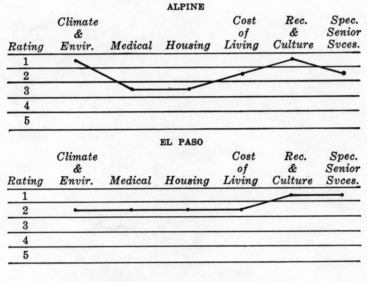

1 = Excellent   4 = Poor
2 = Good   5 = Unacceptable
3 = Fair

NEW MEXICO

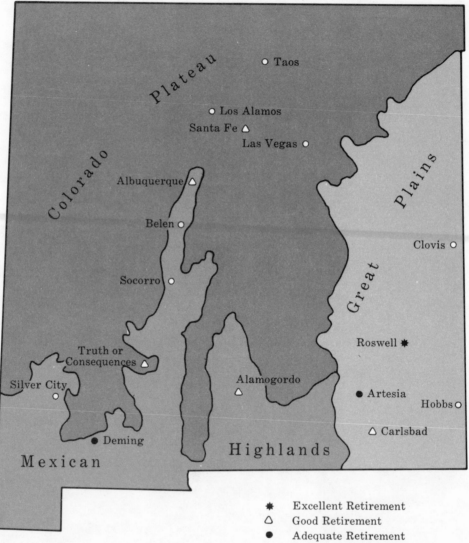

Taos ○

Los Alamos ○

Santa Fe △

Las Vegas ○

Plateau

Colorado

Albuquerque △

Belen ○

Socorro ○

Truth or
Consequences △

Silver City ○

Deming ●

Mexican

Alamogordo △

Highlands

Great Plains

Clovis ○

Roswell ✳

Artesia ●

Hobbs ○

Carlsbad △

✳   Excellent Retirement
△   Good Retirement
●   Adequate Retirement
○   Other Towns of Interest

XIII.

NEW MEXICO—LAND OF

ENCHANTING RETIREMENT

I've always been fascinated and frightened by New Mexico—fascinated by the stark beauty of its moonlike landscapes and frightened by its immensity.

I flew from Dallas to Albuquerque. Even though I had just left flat, open Texas, I was still awed at the expansiveness of New Mexico. It's the fifth largest state in the Union but one of the most sparsely populated. Only 1,200,000 people live here—about 8 per square mile. Even the outskirts of Albuquerque, the state's largest city, are surrounded by the desert, which looms ready to sand it over.

New Mexico's older population constitutes over 10 percent of the state's total; it increased 40 percent between 1960 and 1970 and about 15 percent in the last 5 years. Not all of New Mexico is good retirement territory. The best part is the 300-mile strip of the Rio Grande Valley which begins at Taos and runs south through the capital of Santa Fe to

Albuquerque and Truth or Consequences, then continues into El Paso, Tex. Another prime retirement strip in the east covers Clovis, Roswell, Artesia, Hobbs, Carlsbad.

A Land of Contrasts

As altitude governs climate, New Mexico offers contrasts both in geography and temperature. The habitable altitude ranges from 2,850 feet in the south to 9,500 feet in the north. In the northern part of the state, it is as high, cool, and green as in Switzerland. In the southern part of the state, it is warmer and drier. Overall, the climate is semiarid and continental (the Continental Divide runs through New Mexico). Winter days are sunny and dry with some powdery snow in the north. Summers are warm in the north and hot in the south, but the nights are cool and crisp. Temperatures average from 47° F. to 82° F. in the mountains and 60° F. to 94° F. in the south. In Albuquerque, January temperatures average 44° F. and July 69.4° F. with 42.3 percent humidity (annual average) and 16.52 inches of rain. In Roswell (southeastern New Mexico) the January temperature averages 48.1° F. and summer 71.8° F. with annual humidity of 48.8 percent and 26.4 inches of precipitation.

Roughly two-thirds of the state is mountainous; 85 percent lies above 4,000 feet in elevation. The low point is 2,850 feet on the lower Pecos River area near Carlsbad; the high point is 13,150 feet at Wheeler Peak near Taos. This variation in altitude can make a difference in where you settle.

The sun shines 70 percent of the days in New Mexico. The number of inches of rainfall also varies, from 8.10 at Belen to 25.19 at Cloudcroft.

Many retirees say the climate is good for rheumatism, arthritis, sinus, asthma, emphysema, and other respiratory ailments.

Live Like the Natives—And Save Money

New Mexico isn't a land of millionaires; if you live simply like most of the people, you'll be able to live on less. Living costs are 5 to 10 percent below the national average, as is the per capita income.

Taxes are fairly low, New Mexico ranks thirty-sixth in tax burden; only the Sunbelt states of Arkansas, Florida, Louisiana, Mississippi, and Texas have lower taxes.

State income tax—Married joint return and head of household rates range from $8.00 on the first $2,000 to $14,686 plus 9 percent of the excess of income over $200,000. Special rates are provided for married persons filing separately. Single rates are $ 8 .00   on the first $1,000 to $7,203 plus 9 percent over $100,000. Credits are provided for medical and dental expenses and for installation of solar energy units. A credit is allowed for state and local taxes paid during the tax year by taxpayers with modified gross income of $8,000 or less. The credit ranges from $6 to $268 based on income and number of exemptions. If the credit exceeds the tax liability, the excess will be refunded. The income tax exempts most types of retirement pensions.

Property taxes—A constitutional limitation of 33⅓ percent of assessment keeps this tax below national average. Average effective rate is about $156 per $10,000 valuation.

Sales tax—A 4 percent tax applies to almost everything, and most cities add 1 percent.

For tax information write:

> Bureau of Revenue
> Bataan Memorial Building
> Sante Fe, NM 87501

or:

> Taxpayers Association of New Mexico
> 219 Shelby Street
> Santa Fe, NM 87501

Housing—Both the Good and the Bad

New Mexico has few retirement communities as such, and those that exist have been in trouble. The problem is that developers buy up vast tracts of land and then subdivide them, selling what they paid $40 an acre for to retirees and others at $6,000 an acre.

It sounds like an outright fraud, and, in some instances it is. However, much of this land is available only in vast tracts, and large developers are the only ones who can afford to buy up the land. Still, by any standard, most of the land isn't worth more than $200 an acre; without services or utilities, it isn't fit to build on. New Mexico has clamped down on some of these subdividers and has brought some to trial for fraudulent selling tactics.

Before buying land from any developer, make sure you get a copy of the "property report" the U.S. Department of Housing and Urban Development (HUD) requires developers to furnish to prospective buyers. This report answers *some,* but not all, pertinent questions about the land to help you, but it can't judge or evaluate the land for you. Also check to see what land is selling for just outside the subdivision.

If you feel you are being cheated, contact the Federal Office of Interstate Land Sales Registration (451 Seventh Street, S.W., Washington, D.C. 20411). This office has obtained refunds in several instances.

If you build in New Mexico you might be tempted to use adobe, but you'll find it expensive. Frame, stucco, and brick still remain the best building tools at the most reasonable prices here. Also, *be sure to check your title carefully.* Some titles go back to Spanish land grants that are shaky at best.

Although there is a general shortage of housing throughout New Mexico, there are some retirement residences in Santa Fe and other larger towns. You can get extremely good buys on single-family houses in places like Roswell, Truth or Consequences, Carlsbad, Hobbs, Silver City, and Deming where two-bedroom retirement homes sell as low as $20,000.

Health Care Could Be a Problem

While health care is generally good in the larger cities, some rural towns are pleading for doctors. Also, from personal experience, I can sum up health problems of someone considering retirement in New Mexico in this phrase: *Watch out for the altitude!*

My mother, who is in her 80s, has a bad heart. The last time she went to Santa Fe (elevation about 7,000 feet) she suffered a heart attack—because of the high altitude. I've talked to other retirees who say you must either learn to *adjust* and *live* in the high altitude—or stay away from it.

However, once you've learned to adjust to high altitudes, you might improve your chances of survival. A team of doctors from Harvard, Case Western Reserve, and New Mexico universities found that the death rate from coronary heart disease was 28 percent lower among men who lived above 7,000 feet than among those who lived at 3,000 to 4,000 feet. The doctors theorized that men get more exercise when they work in a thin mountain atmosphere and once they become acclimatized, this helps deter development of high blood pressure. New Mexico has the *lowest* death rate from heart attacks of the 48 continental states.

Check with your doctor to see if he or she feels that a high altitude would be good or bad for you, especially if you have heart-related or respiratory problems.

New Mexico has 54 hospitals with a total of 6,484 beds; 43 nursing homes with 2,649 beds; 23 personal care homes with 696 beds. There are 1,714 doctors, or 1 for every 694 residents—less than the desired ratio and less than the national average (1 doctor for every 575 persons). However, daily hospital costs for a semiprivate room average only $115.45, well below the national average of $133.

New Mexico is trying to make up for any lack of physicians in rural areas by inaugurating home health care programs, but at present they operate mostly in Santa Fe and Albuquerque. The state has a nursing home ombudsman who helps keep the elderly from being institutionalized through use of such community services as home-delivered meals, home-maker visits, visiting nurses, and health aides.

Plenty to See and Do

New Mexico offers attractions ranging from sophisticated grand opera in Santa Fe to simple picnics in primitive forests. It features ancient Indian ruins and modern skyscrapers.

The state is a rockhounder's paradise with plenty of semiprecious and precious stones (opal, turquoise, agate, azurite, pyrope) and metals (silver, gold, zinc, lead) available. You can trace the development of the atom bomb in Los Alamos; ride a tram near Albuquerque to dine above the clouds; fish, hunt, swim, ski, and cycle; attend concerts, visit art museums, shop and dine in intriguing surroundings.

Religion and folk culture dominate New Mexico. The shrine of healing in the primitive town of Chimayo draws natives and visitors from all over; Santa Fe's Indian festivals, where you can buy outstanding (and expensive) pottery, jewelry, leatherwork, rugs, and so on are world-famous. The pueblos at Taos and Santa Clara attract thousands of residents and tourists.

In general, people coming into the state have an opportunity to build cultural wants because they aren't developed fully. Budding groups in many communities offer retirees opportunities to get involved in activities. Retirees in New Mexico are always aware that they are surrounded by nature and learn to accept it on its terms. It helps if you're outdoors- or nature-minded if you retire here. Another vital point: *Be prepared to furnish your own transportation.* Albuquerque is the only New Mexico city with a transit system.

Some Services for Seniors

There are senior clubs and organizations and a hot meal program in every county and in most communities. In some communities, such as Roswell, there is a special "retirement division" to help retirees get settled. Most communities have area or local councils on aging that provide information and services.

The expanding Commission on Aging helps some of the elderly needs areas—especially health care, income, transportation, and housing—by providing funds and assistance to communities and local organizations.

For further information:

> State Agency on Aging
> Chamian Hull Bldg.
> 440 St. Michaels Dr.
> Santa Fe, NM 87501

1. NORTH CENTRAL NEW MEXICO— MOUNTAINS AND MESAS

Northern New Mexico is a land of mountains and mesas, ranging in altitude from 5,314 feet at Albuquerque to 7,050 feet at Taos. The high altitude makes for cool days and nights; winter temperatures occasionally reach zero (with snowfalls), but summer days seldom go over 90° F. Nighttime temperatures may drop to half the daytime high. Average rainfall is only around 12 inches, yet the annual snowfall averages 30 inches and more. Relative humidity is around 50 percent, higher in summer and lower in winter. The sun shines about 75 percent of the possible hours most of the year. June and October are the sunniest months, February and July are the least sunny.

The main retirement areas include Albuquerque, Santa Fe, and Taos and surrounding towns.

Albuquerque (pop. 300,000, city; 400,000 metropolitan). About one-third of the entire population of the state lives in Albuquerque and surrounding Bernalillo County. Albuquerque is the fastest-growing city and the only metropolis in the state; it also provides the state's only transit system.

Medical Facilities. Albuquerque has 11 hospitals with some 2,362 beds and 821 doctors, assuring adequate medical care for at least the metropolitan area. A semiprivate hospital room averages $105.20—about $10 a day less than the state as a whole.

Housing. Finding good housing in Albuquerque can be a problem. Some 96 percent of the existing apartments are filled and the single-family housing situation isn't much better. Most of the houses that are being built are presold, and planners estimate that another 5,500 new housing units a year will be necessary to accommodate the expanding population. However, in 1979 there were several apartments for rent (around $200 a month for one bedroom) and some houses for sale for $40,000 and up for two-bedroom units. Albuquerque also has Encino House, an 11-story apartment complex for low-income elderly, and Camlu Apartments, a proprietary activity home designed to meet complete food and housing needs of older people. About 35 miles south of Albuquerque lies *Belen* (pop. 5,000) which features several retirement facilities including a country-club-type mobile home and recreational vehicle park. Rentals run $75 to $100 a month. New two-bedroom homes sell for $45,000 and up.

Recreation and Culture. Albuquerque has a symphony orchestra, 50 art galleries, 10 museums, and 8 libraries. It also has Sandia Peak ski area with the longest tramway in North America; 125 city parks, 29 swimming pools, 9 golf courses, 146 tennis courts, Cibola National Forest, and Rio Grande Zoo. It is also home to the University of New Mexico, situated on an unusually beautiful 700-acre campus. On the pueblo-style campus are several museums and places of interest, Albuquerque also has the University of Albuquerque, which offers adult education classes and the Indian Pueblo Cultural Center.

Special Services for Seniors. Albuquerque's transit system offers reduced fares for seniors. Seniors may also get reduced tickets to concerts, little theaters, and other special events. The city operates 20 senior centers and has active chapters of senior organizations.

For further information:

Chamber of Commerce
Albuquerque, NM 87102

Santa Fe (pop. 50,000) is the capital and the cultural center of the state.

Climate and Environment. Situated at the base of the towering, 13,000-foot Sangre de Cristo Mountains, Santa Fe is also a very picturesque city. Santa Fe has a large Plaza and the Palace of the Governors where Indians sit and display their wares; many abode homes and buildings; quaint Canyon Road with its artists and craftsmen and shops; unique restaurants serving savory Mexican and Indian dishes; and the renowned outdoor opera. The altitude of 7,000 feet, however, could be hard on someone with heart, lung, or related problems. The dry, arid air with a high pollen count can aggravate some health conditions; check with your physician before moving.

Medical Facilities. While Santa Fe has enough doctors (a total of 100, or about 1 per 500 residents) hospital care may be expensive. There is one major hospital with 250 beds and 3 smaller hospitals. But the average semiprivate room rate is $122.50 daily—$7 above the state average.

Housing. Housing for sale or rent is scarce, but Santa Fe has some expensive and inexpensive homes for rent or sale (an average two-bedroom house costs around $50,000). It has 2 major retirement residences: Plaza del Monte, formerly a home for Presbyterian ministers but now open to all, with independent cottages and living quarters; and El Castillo, an extremely attractive retirement residence on the Santa Fe River, within easy reach of shopping centers and medical facilities. However, there is a 2-year waiting list for units. A 400-square-foot studio apartment sells for $17,500, and a 1,260-square-foot two-bedroom apartment sells for around $45,000. Monthly fees range from $250 for 1 person to $350 for 2, including utilities, cleaning, 24-hour emergency nursing service, and lifetime nursing care. Santa Fe has some rental units for $250 a month and up (2-bedrooms) ; building costs are $37 per square foot.

Cost of Living. Santa Fe is probably the most expensive city in New Mexico, both in taxes (41 mills per $1,000 vs. a county tax of under 35 mills) and cost of living. However, you *can* live inexpensively here; one advantage of a larger city is that it offers more opportunities to hunt for bargains. Shopping is picturesque in Santa Fe, whether you buy from an Indian at the Palace of Governors, at a shop along the Plaza, at the La Fonda Hotel, or on Canyon Road. Eating in Santa Fe is also a pleasure; I ate at Steaksmith, featuring quality aged beef, crab, lobster tails, prime ribs and fine wines for 10 to 20 percent less than in New York.

Recreation and Culture. Culture abounds in Santa Fe's Museum of Navajo Ceremonial Art, Palace of the Governors, Santa Fe Opera, art and music festivals, Museum of Fine Arts, Museum of International Folk Art, and Institute of American Indian Arts.

Special Services for Seniors. The Santa Fe County Senior Center's program is one of the most sophisticated and well-organized in the United States. It has a total of 3,700 members, 17 staff members, and 21 different services provided countywide at 10 centers and 6 meal sites. Its pharmaceutical program is unique: Seniors can get needed medicines free of charge if they qualify under federal low-income guidelines. The city supports a senior center, which provides hot lunches.

For further information:

> Chamber of Commerce
> P.O. Box 1928
> Santa Fe, NM 87501

Taos (pop. 3,000) is actually three towns: Taos proper, the Spanish-American settlement into which Anglos have moved; Taos Pueblo, the Indian town 2½ miles north; and Rancho de Taos, 4 miles south. Each is distinct yet all are closely allied.

Medical Facilities. Taos has a general hospital and access to medical facilities in Santa Fe. There are over 10 doctors in Taos, assuring adequate medical care for the population.

Housing. Country homes on over an acre of land sell for as low as $30,000. Country estates, 5,000-square-foot homes on 10 acres of land, sell for $250,000. Building lots cost around $10,000 but other land sells for as low as $100 an acre in large tracts.

Recreation and Culture. Taos proper is more compact than Santa Fe, and its shops, plazas, and restaurants are even more colorful. Despite its small size, Taos is culturally very active. It has a famed art colony, many picture galleries, craft shops, antiques, and imports. Nearby is the famous Rancho de Taos church.

Set in a high mountain valley, surrounded by the Sangre de Cristo Mountains, Taos is an outdoor paradise with deer, elk, bear, wild turkey, quail, and mountain trout. Horseback riding, skiing, and hiking are popular year-round sports.

Services for Seniors. Taos has an active senior club for retired teachers and a Senior Citizens League of Taos County. The Taos-Rio Arriba Senior Citizens Program is one of the largest in the state, with 900 regular participants and 450 meals served at 14 sites. Dancing is popular with seniors in this area and special dances are held at the center.

There are also active senior centers in Los Alamos, Maxwell, Springer, Raton, and other areas. The Las Vegas-San Miguel County Senior Citizens Programs offers an average of 40 daily meals, transportation, and information and referral services. Las Vegas also has an RSVP (Retired Senior Volunteer Program) with 150 volunteers in 14 work stations. Mora County has the Wagon Mound Senior Citizens Program, which provides meals, transportation, and other services for seniors in the area.

For further information:

Chamber of Commerce
Taos, NM 87571

If you plan to settle in north-central New Mexico be sure to check on the water situation. While Albuquerque seems to have an adequate water supply for the next several years, Santa Fe suffers from a water shortage.

2. THE EASTERN RETIREMENT STRIP— CLOVIS TO CARLSBAD

From Santa Fe I drove southeast toward the retirement country of Clovis, Roswell, Artesia, and Carlsbad. The altitude drops several hundred feet—from 7,000 feet at Santa Fe to 3,111 feet at Carlsbad. As I descended in altitude I gained in longitude; the scenery and landscape expand for miles in all directions. The vast distances freed my spirit and the silences eased my mind.

I drove for hours without seeing anyone or anything. The nearest "town" of any size was *Vaughn* (pop. 867), where I stopped at a well-equipped cafe (it was the only bus stop for hundreds of miles). Then I was on my way again, with more vast miles and empty hours before I reached the retirement country.

The relatively moderate elevation prevents the extreme cold of the area to the north and the heat and humidity of the area to the south. While summer temperatures average 77.5° F., the relatively low humidity (only 30 percent in mid-afternoon) moderates the heat. Frequent showers (average annual rainfall is 12 inches) from June to September break the heat. In the fall, the rainfall tapers off and frosty nights alternate with warm days. The temperature averages 59.5° F. In winter, subfreezing nights are tempered by warming days. The sun shines 70 percent of the possible amount, allowing for a rapid rise in temperature. The average winter temperature is 41.2° F. Winter has the least precipitation; rain falls only 5 days and snow falls only 7 days. Spring is the driest season; moderate winds (25 mph) blow most days from February to May. Average spring temperature is 59.4° F.

Clovis (pop. 34,000), at 4,280 feet, is the highest of the eastern towns. It is a railroad, agricultural, dairy, and military center, located on the edge of the Great Plains.

Medical Facilities. Hospital costs in Clovis are low, however there is a shortage of physicians in the area. There are only 25 doctors in Clovis—1 doctor for over 1,000 residents, which is less than adequate. But there is a Retirement Living Facility and Nursing Home licensed by state and federal agencies for Medicare and Medicaid. A semiprivate room there averages only $105.34 daily, $10 less than the state average.

Housing. Existing two-bedroom homes average $30,000 and new homes average $40,000. Clovis has several mobile home parks where two-bedroom mobile homes rent for $200 a month. It also has Grand Avenue Home, a public housing facility for low-income seniors; rent depends upon income.

Cost of Living. Food prices aren't necessarily lower in this area, but other costs, including taxes, are. The property tax is based on 33⅓ percent of appraised value, at a rate of between $30 and $40 per $1,000. Taxes on a $35,000 house might be about $400 a year. Monthly utilities (water, sewer, garbage collection, gas and electricity) average about $75 a month. Recreation and cultural costs are usually lower.

Recreation and Culture. Clovis boasts the only zoo (over 100 acres) in eastern New Mexico and western Texas. The zoo is located in Hillcrest Park, which also features golf, swimming, and picnicking. The town sponsors 2 municipal senior centers: Hospitality House, which includes Baxter Hall, and Friendship Center at Grand Avenue Home, a public housing facility. There are 7 privately organized senior centers here.

For further information.

Chamber of Commerce
Clovis, NM 88101

Roswell (pop. 50,000) is the largest town in this area—an urban oasis in the midst of the desert. Farming, ranching, livestock, and oil and gas exploration surround the town, making it the area's commercial and industrial center.

Medical Facilities. Roswell has the most medical facilities in the area: 3 general hospitals with a total of 540 beds. A semiprivate room averages $108.50 daily, slightly more than Clovis but still below the state average. There are some 65 doctors in the area, not quite adequate for the population. But Roswell is the home of the New Mexico Rehabilitation Center, part of the New Mexico Department of Education, which offers physical, educational, and vocational rehabilitation. It has 52 beds and outpatient care. Roswell has 24-hour emergency service and a doctor on call at all times.

Housing. Although Roswell claims its average retiree has an income of around $10,000 a year, you could live here on less. Several two-bedroom homes are advertised for as little as $20,000 and $25,000, and three-bedroom homes from only $35,000. Roswell has several apartment houses where furnished efficiency apartments rent for as low as $150 a month and two-bedrooms for $200 a month. There is also public housing for seniors; efficiency apartments rent for as low as $100 a month, although there is a long waiting list now. Taxes run about the same as Clovis (preceding).

Recreation and Culture. Roswell offers Memorial Recreation Center with games, square dances, pot luck suppers, and various club activities. The Recreation Center also features classes and facilities for ceramics, decorating, creative writing, drawing and sketching, knitting and crocheting, leatherworking, macrame, oil and watercolor, photography, sewing, silversmithing, wood carving, and many other subjects. The town provides Hi Neighbor bus trips that go all over the United States and parts of Canada and Mexico. There are 3 golf courses, a little theater, symphony orchestra, community concerts, and RSVP programs.

Special Services for Seniors. Besides 2 senior centers and 11 privately organized senior citizen clubs, Roswell features Retirement Service, Incorporated, which helps retirees get settled.

For further information:

> Retirement Services
> Roswell Chamber of Commerce
> P.O. Box 70
> Roswell, NM 88201

Artesia (pop. 13,000), primarily an agricultural center, got its name from the vast underground water supplies which once rushed up through drilled wells, but are now pumped to irrigate the many acres of farmland in the area.

Artesia has a 50-bed general hospital and a 62-bed nursing home. There are 7 physicians and surgeons in the area—inadequate for proper medical care. However, residents can use medical facilities in Roswell (44 miles north) and Carlsbad (35 miles south).

Two-bedroom homes sell from $25,000 and apartments rent from $150 a month (advertised rents are as low as $50 a month).

The City of Artesia Recreation Program provides activities for young and old. Some of the programs offered include arts and crafts, softball, exercise classes, swimming, and tennis. Artesia has a country club with year-round golf. There are 3 privately organized senior clubs and a federally supported community services program.

For further information:

Chamber of Commerce
Artesia, NM 88210

Carlsbad (pop. 28,000) is a jumping-off place for Carlsbad Caverns, and many hotels, shops, and restaurants display "caveman" or "cavern" themes. The Pecos River flows through the city, assuring a good water supply.

Medical Facilities. Carlsbad has a 134-bed general hospital, offering specialized services including intensive and coronary care units, physical therapy, inhalation therapy, radiation and cobalt therapy, and isotope screening. The Lakeview Christian Home of the Southwest is a 159-bed nursing home. Rates are geared to Blue Cross-Blue Shield approved rates. There are about 31 doctors in the area—inadequate for the population.

Housing. Carlsbad houses cost slightly more than in neighboring areas, but you can still buy two-bedroom houses for around $30,000 and three-bedroom homes for only slightly more. Luxury apartments for seniors run from $300 to $600 a month, but some two-bedroom apartments are available for around $250 a month. A nearby rental trailer park offers a full recreation program. Fees average $75 a month.

Recreation and Culture. Carlsbad has the Bridge Center—a building designed for the comfort, convenience, and pleasure of bridge players. It also has the only lake within the residential area of any city in the Southwest. This 2-mile-long lake is spring-fed and provides swimming, boating, and water skiing. Hunting for big game, game birds, and small animals, and fishing for rainbow and brown trout, bass, catfish, perch, and bluegills are popular sports. The surrounding area—Carlsbad Caverns, Guadalupe Mountains National Park, Mescalero Indian Reservation—adds to Carlsbad's appeal.

Special Services for Seniors. Carlsbad has several retirement clubs and centers, and a special committee that caters especially to retirees.

For further information:

The Retirement Committee
P.O. Box 69
Carlsbad, NM 88220

Seventy miles east of Carlsbad is the town of *Hobbs* (pop. 36,000), an important livestock, ranching, agriculture, and petroleum center. While not a retirement center, you might want to investigate Hobbs if you like this eastern New Mexico "retirement strip."

For further information:

Chamber of Commerce
Hobbs, NM 88240

3. THE SOUTHWEST—A LONG WAY FROM ANYWHERE

From Carlsbad, I cut into a corner of Texas before popping back up into New Mexico and encountered the spookiest country I'd ever seen. It was desolate—nothing out there except miles upon miles of nothingness. At times the road climbed a high butte, and I'd be poised over half the world. At other times the road would *sink below* the bottom of what was once a seabed (the land is encrusted with salt). It was fascinating and frightening—I was glad to see El Paso with its sprawling suburbs. Heading north again into New Mexico, the first large town I saw was Alamogordo.

Climate and Environment. Alamogordo (pop. 29,000) lies at 4,350 feet and enjoys a dry, warm climate. Average summer temperature is 91° F. with a high of 110°; winters average 37° F. with a low of −14°. But with an average humidity of only 19 percent, neither the summer heat nor the winter cold feel too extreme. Rainfall averages only 10 inches annually and the sun shines approximately 80 percent of the time. Winds generally average about 10 miles per hour but are stronger in spring.

Medical Facilities. The town offers good health care with a 100-bed hospital including a large geriatric ward, and a modern nursing home.

Housing. Alamogordo features numerous new two- and three-bedroom homes for sale, ranging in price from $30,000 to $65,000. Some rentals are available; an average two-bedroom home rents for $250 and up a month, depending upon quality and location.

Recreation and Culture. The town sponsors many clubs including senior clubs, rockhounds, coin collectors, and many other activities including a GLO and GRO program, which meets daily and offers supervised arts, crafts, and recreational activities. For the culturally inclined, there are art galleries, Arts 'n' Authors Club, and Desert Art League. There are several musical groups providing entertainment and instruction. The local library houses 50,000 books and receives 190 periodicals, and the Alamogordo Branch of New Mexico State University has a 560-acre campus in town.

For further information:

Chamber of Commerce
Alamogordo, NM 88310

Truth or Consequences (pop. 8,000). Named in 1950 for the famous television show, this town was originally known as Hot Springs. The baths still draw people; the chemically uniform thermal waters offer relief for arthritis and rheumatism.

Climate and Environment. The average humidity is only 15 percent and rainfall averages only 7.1 inches. The average winter temperature is 46° F.; average annual temperature, 77° F. The temperature in summer often stays in the 90s, but the low humidity of 15 percent makes it tolerable.

Medical Facilities. Truth or Consequences has 2 major hospitals; one is for crippled children and the other is said to be one of the most modern and best-equipped hospitals in the Southwest. Rates average a low $90.71 daily for a semiprivate room.

Housing. The town has numerous apartments, motels, hotels, and mobile home parks; most offer weekly or monthly rents. Retirement housing starts at $30,000; rents at $250 a month.

Cost of Living. Taxes are somewhat lower here than elsewhere in New Mexico; they are one-third the assessed valuation and range from $29.37 per $1,000 inside the city to $23.03 outside.

Recreation and Culture. Nearby are Elephant Butte State Park and Caballo Lake, featuring resort inns, boating, fishing, and all water sports.

Special Services for Seniors. Truth or Consequences boasts the largest senior center facilities in the state; activities range from golf to community theater.

For further information:

Chamber of Commerce
Truth or Consequences, NM 87901

Deming (pop. 12,000). My most vivid impression of Deming was a sign I saw which read: DEMING NEEDS DOCTORS! (a frightening omen for retirees!). There are many retirees here and the town has 3 privately organized senior clubs. Deming boasts that its water is 99.99 percent pure, coming naturally from deep wells. The climate is somewhat the same as those of Truth or Consequences and Alamogordo, but the humidity drops to as low as 5 percent. Deming claims that doctors from all over the country send their patients here to take advantage of the mild climate and low humidity (if the sign is true, the patients should send the doctors to

Deming). There is a modern 52-bed hospital and a 34-bed nursing home, but only 8 doctors at last count—1 doctor for 1,500 residents—*way below standard.*

Two-bedroom homes sell for $25,000 to $40,000 and mobile homes sell for $2,000 to $5,000. Deming Ranchettes (building lots) sell for $4,500, but other land sells for as low as $150 an acre. At the Kingdom of the Sun Retirement Center, low-income elderly can rent efficiency apartments, one-bedroom apartments, and two-bedroom units. The center offers recreational facilities and is within 6 blocks of a shopping center. Apartments are air-conditioned, insulated, and soundproofed. However, there's a waiting list for units. Deming has 11 parks, a country club, auditorium, museum, and rockhound and hiking clubs. The community library houses 26,200 volumes. Deming has an Area for Aging office where a hot lunch is served daily. There's also a Meal on Wheels program.

For further information:

Chamber of Commerce
Deming, NM 88030

Socorro (area). Socorro county's (pop. 12,000) population over age 60 is slightly over the national average of 10 percent. Neighboring Sierra County boasts 34 percent over age 60, due largely to hot springs and an abundance of low-cost apartments, many submarginal. Many retirees move here for remedial help for arthritis and other health problems (there's a 45-bed hospital in the area, and a clinic, and 5 doctors). The Socorro Senior Citizens Club built 40 garden-type apartments for the elderly under FHA loans, with supplemental rental features (rates depend upon income). Other housing is available without subsidies for $30,000 and up.

Being 4,600 feet above sea level, Socorro's air is dry and clean. The average mean temperature is 58° F. It is not unusual to have a spread of 30 to 50 degrees F. between day and night. Average rainfall is 8.5 inches with 8.71 inches of snow. The January monthly average temperature is 37° F. and July, 79° F. Socorro is the home of the New Mexico Institute of Mining and Technology. The college golf course is open to the public and the city-owned Olympic-size pool is available to the public at low rates. The area supports an art league, a community chorus, and 3 senior centers, providing noontime meals and supporting services under federal, state, and local funding. Taxes average about 1.3 percent of true market value ($130 per $10,000 valuation).

For further information:

> Southern Rio Grande Council of Governments
> 575 South Alamdea Street
> Las Cruces, NM 88001

Don't overlook *Las Cruses* (pop. 46,000) which has a campus of New Mexico State University, museums, White Sands Missile Range, ghost mining towns, extinct volcanoes, ancient forts, and mountains in the area.

SUMMARY

I liked New Mexico's vast vistas and low-humidity climate. Housing is a fantastic bargain in places like Roswell, Carlsbad, and Clovis; however, the housing situation isn't good in Albuquerque or even Santa Fe. I liked the Indian lore and Mexican folk culture, and I could see that an anthropologist, archeologist, rockhound, or outdoorsman could retire here comfortably. If you want culture, you would have to confine yourself to Albuquerque or Santa Fe (which could be expensive).

I don't like the higher altitudes for health reasons: *Check with your doctor if you plan to retire in the higher elevations.* And I confess to being somewhat frightened by the isolation of some of the towns. On the 4-hour drive from Santa Fe to Roswell, I didn't pass 10 people or see 25 homes. I was constantly surrounded by an overwhelming nature and would have been scared out of my wits if I had had a breakdown and was stranded on a lonely road at any time of day or night.

Here are my personal ratings of New Mexico's retirement areas:
Excellent—Roswell;
Good—Albuquerque, Carlsbad, Santa Fe, Alamogordo, Truth or Consequences, Las Cruses;
Adequate—Deming, Artesia, Socorro.

RATINGS FOR *NEW MEXICO* MAJOR RETIREMENT AREAS

ALBUQUERQUE

Rating	Climate & Envir.	Medical	Housing	Cost of Living	Rec. & Culture	Spec. Senior Svces.
1						
2						
3						
4						
5						

SANTA FE–TAOS

Rating	Climate & Envir.	Medical	Housing	Cost of Living	Rec. & Culture	Spec. Senior Svces.
1						
2						
3						
4						
5						

ROSWELL

Rating	Climate & Envir.	Medical	Housing	Cost of Living	Rec. & Culture	Spec. Senior Svces.
1						
2						
3						
4						
5						

CARLSBAD

Rating	Climate & Envir.	Medical	Housing	Cost of Living	Rec. & Culture	Spec. Senior Svces.
1						
2						
3						
4						
5						

ALAMOGORDO

Rating	Climate & Envir.	Medical	Housing	Cost of Living	Rec. & Culture	Spec. Senior Svces.
1						
2						
3						
4						
5						

DEMING

Rating	Climate & Envir.	Medical	Housing	Cost of Living	Rec. & Culture	Spec. Senior Svces.
1						
2						
3						
4						
5						

RATINGS FOR *NEW MEXICO* MAJOR RETIREMENT AREAS

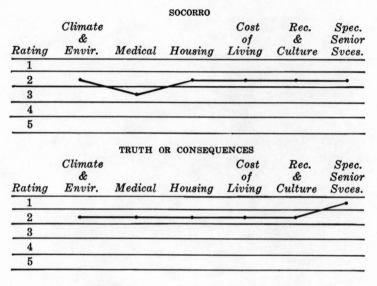

SOCORRO

Rating	Climate & Envir.	Medical	Housing	Cost of Living	Rec. & Culture	Spec. Senior Svces.
1						
2						
3						
4						
5						

TRUTH OR CONSEQUENCES

Rating	Climate & Envir.	Medical	Housing	Cost of Living	Rec. & Culture	Spec. Senior Svces.
1						
2						
3						
4						
5						

1 = Excellent   4 = Poor
2 = Good   5 = Unacceptable
3 = Fair

ARIZONA

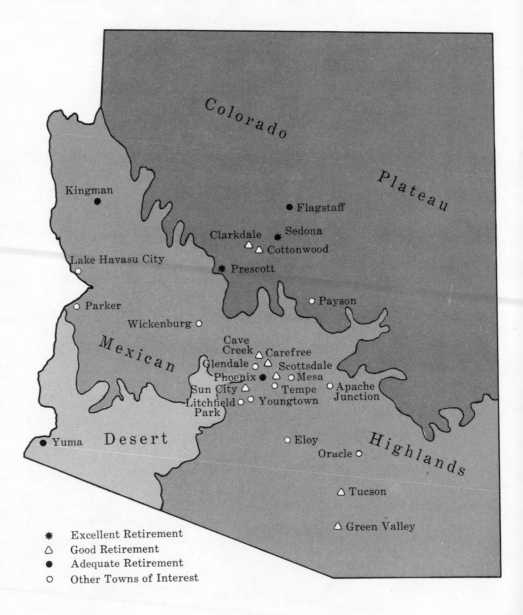

Colorado

Plateau

Kingman

● Flagstaff

Clarkdale ✳ Sedona
△ △ Cottonwood

✳ Prescott

Lake Havasu City ○

○ Parker

Payson ○ Payson

Wickenburg ○

Mexican

Cave
Creek △ Carefree
Glendale ○ △ Scottsdale
Phoenix ● △ ○ Mesa
Sun City △ ○ Tempe ○ Apache
Youngtown Junction
Litchfield ○ ○
Park

● Yuma   Desert

Eloy ○ Eloy

Oracle ○

Highlands

△ Tucson

△ Green Valley

✳   Excellent Retirement
△   Good Retirement
●   Adequate Retirement
○   Other Towns of Interest

XIV.

ARIZONA–

CONTRASTS IN RETIREMENT

Arizona is my southwestern "home." I lived here a year when I was editor of the weekly newspaper in Prescott; I owned 6 acres of retirement land in Carefree; my mother "pioneered" here in the 1930s and still lives in Scottsdale; my stepmother lives in Green Valley (south of Tucson).

Arizona's scenery is much the same as its neighboring states', but without the monotonous flatness of Texas or the limitless expanses of New Mexico. Arizona is more diversified and picturesque. Desert cacti or shrubs usually line the side of the road; canyons and arroyos split the landscape; mountains post sentinel on the distant horizons.

Arizona *is* a state of amazing contrasts. In the north (starting a few miles below Prescott) are majestic pine forests, steep rocky mountains, high plateaus, and rich, colorful canyons, including the granddaddy of them all, the Grand Canyon. In the south (from Wickenburg to the border) the land resembles a saucer with Phoenix and the Valley of the Sun at the bottom and Tucson near the elevated rim. Here is where 80 percent of the population lives and most people retire. But Phoenix and Tucson are as urban as Cleveland; if you want the Old West you must explore the northern part of the state, from Prescott upward.

Arizona's climate varies, but the norm is high sun and low humidity. This magnet draws Midwesterners (especially from Illinois, Iowa, Michi-

243

gan, Wisconsin, and Minnesota) who want to thaw out for a winter or for
the rest of their lives. The sun shines 86 percent of the time in Arizona,
rising to 99 percent in summer and fall—more sun than Florida and the
rest of the Sunbelt. Arizona is the original "health" state; people traditionally come here to seek relief from tuberculosis, asthma, arthritis, rheumatism, and related diseases. However, the southern part of the state—
especially around Phoenix and Tucson—isn't as healthy as it once was and
is plagued by dust, air pollution, hard water, and congestion. Despite this,
there are many places in Arizona where you can retire in a healthy, low-
cost environment and find suitable housing and activities.

The Highs and Lows in Climate

As in New Mexico, the altitude governs the temperature. In the north,
where altitudes vary from 5,000 feet to 12,000 feet, there is a moderate
4-season climate. Winters may vary from 15° F. to 45° F. with 18 to 70
inches of snow. Summers vary from around 50° F. to 90° F. However, the
low humidity (average 45 percent) in the summer makes it feel cooler, and
the brilliant sunshine in the winter usually melts much of the snow. Spring
and fall are distinctive; blue, red, and yellow mountain flowers carpet grass-
lands from April through June, and fall foliage adds its golden harvest
from September through November.

In southern Arizona (from 3,000 feet and below) "perpetual summer"
lasts from April through November. Temperatures start to climb in April,
hitting the 90s in May and October and soaring to 100° F. and above during
June, July, August, and September. However, the low humidity—often only
15 percent—makes temperatures of 100° F. comparable to those in the 80s
in more humid areas.

A point to remember: *The temperature often drops 30 degrees and
more from day to night.* I've swum in a pool in Phoenix during a December
afternoon with the temperature in the 70s only to have that same pool
freeze over at night when the temperature dropped into the 20s.

A wonderful bonus about Arizona—you can go from winter to summer
just by going down a mountain. When I lived in Prescott (6,000 feet) I
would visit my mother in Phoenix (1,083 feet). In winter, I'd leave snow
behind in Prescott and swim in a pool in Phoenix that same afternoon!

Arizona Isn't Necessarily Cheap

A recent study by Arizona State University in Tempe indicated that a
retired couple in good health, with Medicare, living in a separate house-

hold would need around $9,000 annually to retire adequately in the Greater Phoenix area.

On a comparative cost-of-living scale for urban retired couples, the Greater Phoenix area ranks behind Boston, New York, Honolulu, Buffalo, San Francisco-Oakland, Cleveland, Seattle, Washington, D.C., Philadelphia, Milwaukee, Los Angeles, Chicago, Minneapolis, St. Louis, Detroit, Kansas City, Baltimore, and San Diego. However, rising costs are bringing Phoenix more in line with such cities as Denver and Pittsburgh. Cities with living costs lower than Phoenix include Cincinnati, Dallas, Houston, and Atlanta. The cost of living in smaller communities in Arizona is generally less than it is in Phoenix and Tucson.

Gas for heating and hot water costs about $50 a month for the average two- to three-bedroom home. To air-condition such a house in summer costs from $60 to $90 a month. Water costs vary from about $10 a month in winter to about $25 a month in summer, depending upon how much water you use (especially in cooling).

Sales and excise tax—The state assesses a 4 percent sales tax on everything, including food. Phoenix and 19 other cities assess an additional 1 to 2 percent tax. The state and some cities also tax luxury items (liquor, cigarettes, tobacco). Total tax on gasoline is 11 cents a gallon.

State income tax—Taxes begin on net annual incomes of $2,000 or gross incomes of $5,000 per couple after exemptions. The rate varies from 2 percent to 8 percent of the net taxable income. If the individual or couple must pay federal income tax, the amount paid can be deducted from gross income before the state income tax is figured.

Arizona has a $1,000 widow's tax exemption that is seldom used because most people don't know about it. It's worth inquiring about if you qualify.

Persons aged 65 or over are granted an additional $1,000 personal exemption in filing their state income tax returns. They are also allowed medical and dental expenses without reference to the statutory limitation of $5,000 for a married couple or $2,500 for a single person. If either husband or wife is aged 65 or over, medical expense of both spouses are exempted. In general, state income tax averages 10 percent of federal withholding.

Property taxes—Taxes vary according to the county, city or town, and district. As a rule, the base for residential property tax is an assessment of approximately 88 percent of the property's full cash value, times 15 percent. The resulting figure is then applied against the tax rate effective in that particular district. Generally, property taxes run about 1.55 percent of true market value ($155 per $10,000). Arizona also has a 4 percent rent tax—persons who rent are required to pay the rent plus 4 percent for the first 3 months, and 1 percent extra after that. Mobile homes 8 feet by 40 feet and larger are taxed as unsecured personal property. Taxes are based on 82 percent of the suggested retail price of the manufacturer when the home was new, and gradually decrease to 15 percent of this value over a period of 15 years. Mobile homes smaller than 8 feet by 40 feet are taxed as automobiles and require license plates.

One point to remember: Arizona, like California, Idaho, Louisiana, Nevada, New Mexico, Texas, and Washington, is a *community property state*. This means that real or personal property acquired by either spouse during marriage is the common property of both. If property was owned separately by one spouse before moving to Arizona, however, the title to and any income accruing from the property remains separate.

Varied Housing at Moderate Prices

Nationwide surveys show that, dollar for dollar, Arizona—particularly in the southern and central sections—offers some of the best home values in the United States (from 5 to 15 percent below national average). However, costs are going up; one retiree bought a townhouse in 1972 for $30,000 that now sells for $60,000. Building costs in the higher elevations may run as high as in other areas with similar climates.

Arizona has all types of housing, from mobile homes to high-rise condominiums. Only Florida and California rival Arizona in the number of retirement communities. But beware of two factors concerning housing: (1) only 17 percent of Arizona's land is available for building—the rest is owned by the state or federal governments, or Indian tribes; (2) some parts of Arizona—particularly around Tucson—are running short of water.

Most of Arizona's water comes from deep wells. Since the water is consumed 5 times faster than it is replaced, the ground levels are dropping and wells must be dug deeper. A development that may save Arizona is the Central Arizona Project, which will pump water from the Colorado River to the Phoenix and Tucson areas. But California wants its share of this water, and even the Colorado is being overused. Make sure that your land has an adequate water supply *first*.

Arizona, like New Mexico, has suffered from land frauds, and the state has prosecuted some developers. But the rules for buying land, as outlined in Chapter III and in the chapter on New Mexico, apply here. *Don't buy land site unseen,* and don't buy unless you understand all the problems you might have building on that land. I once owned 6 acres of land in Carefree (northeast of Phoenix), for which I paid $3,500 in 1958. I sold it in 1973 for over $20,000. I was lucky; for every 1 as lucky as I, there are 3 who have been left holding a worthless piece of land or a fraudulent mortgage.

If you have any questions regarding subdivisions or land parcels offered for sale, write to:

> The Arizona Real Estate Department
> State Office Building
> 1624 West Adams
> Room 401
> Phoenix, AZ 85007

Selective Health Care

As in most Sunbelt states, Arizona's medical facilities are good in urban areas and varied in rural areas. Phoenix and Tucson provide the medical centers, and anyone within the surrounding areas has access to good health care. Prescott, Flagstaff, Kingman, and some larger mountain towns also have adequate medical facilities. But, again, check these out. Arizona has 82 hospitals with a total of 9,929 beds. It also has 61 nursing homes with a total of 4,697 beds and 25 personal care homes with 1,537 beds. It has 1 doctor per 557 residents, making it second-best (to California) in the numbers of doctors per resident. A semiprivate room averages $117.94 a day, slightly more than New Mexico, but still $18 a day below the national average. Arizona has a Medical Aid for the Aged (MAA) program that will help make payments for Medicare and Medicaid if the person is eligible or qualifies by low income and residency (you must be a resident for a year before you can receive nonemergency medical care at county expense).

While Arizona's climate is generally healthy for most respiratory problems, some problems become aggravated when the humidity drops below 10 percent. This happens often in the central, southern, and western regions. Persons with certain skin ailments or sun allergies may also have problems in Arizona. The dust and smog in and around Phoenix and Tucson can trouble otherwise healthy people. While the air is clean and the water pure in Prescott, the 5,389-foot elevation may bother those with heart or related problems. Check with your doctor before making any move for health reasons.

For information on medical care in certain areas write:

Arizona State Department of Health Services
1740 West Adams
Phoenix, AZ 85007

Outdoor Living and Indoor Pleasures

Arizona's superabundance of sunshine and mild temperatures encourages many outdoor activities: golf, swimming, boating, horseback riding, cycling, camping, sightseeing, barbecuing, hunting, fishing, and camping. Arizona has many nature and wildlife parks, Indian ruins, and state and national park preserves (including the Grand Canyon). It pays to be sports- or nature-minded if you settle in Arizona.

However, the larger metropolitan areas (Phoenix, Tucson, Prescott, Flagstaff, Kingman) offer surprisingly sophisticated activities. The Phoenix Parks and Recreation Department publishes an annual "Activities and Facilities Guide," which lists all the recreational and cultural events scheduled for that year. Write: Parks and Recreation Department, 251 West Washington Street, Room 401, Municipal Building, Phoenix, AZ 85003. Included are the Phoenix Arts and Crafts Center, which has summer and winter programs of interest to retirees, including photography, casting and soldering jewelry, metal crafting, oil and acrylic painting, lapidary, ceramics, macrame, batik, and tie dyeing. The Tucson area publishes a "Program Guide," which lists similar facilities and activities during the year. Write: Tucson Parks and Recreation Department, 900 South Randolph Way, Tucson, AZ 85716. Tucson's primary recreation center is centrally located in Randolph Park and features a 36-hole golf course; a recreation center that includes a huge swimming pool and tennis complex; the park proper, which includes lakes, picnic areas, gardens, concert areas, and a stadium. Tucson's Salvation Army sponsors a summer campout for senior citizens at Camp O'Wood near Oracle in the Catalina Mountains.

Special Services for Seniors

Arizona has many senior organizations, including chapters of the American Association of Retired Persons, National Council of Senior Citizens, National Association of Retired Federal Employees, and the Arizona Council for Senior Citizens. This last group has been the leader in the battle to obtain equal rights and opportunities for retired residents in Arizona. It also promotes the organization of senior citizen councils on a county level and helps to coordinate their activities.

For further information:

> Arizona Council for Senior Citizens
> Cottage 4A
> 2101 East Maryland Avenue
> Phoenix, AZ 85016

Arizona also has an active Bureau on Aging that helps finance and coordinate the activities and programs for seniors at local levels.

For further information:

> Aging and Adult Services
> 1400 W. Washington Ave.
> P.O. Box 6123
> Phoenix, AZ 85007

1. SOUTHERN ARIZONA—LAND, SAND, AND MOUNTAINS

Green Valley is an adult community of some 6,000 people about 25 miles south of Tucson. My stepmother moved here because she suffers from arthritis (she thought the sun and warmth would be good for her). When I last saw her in Detroit, she could hardly walk without a brace because she was so crippled. When I saw her in Tucson, she was walking almost normally. (Not all of this is due to the sun and warmth. She had an operation which helped her walk, but she does credit the warmth and sun for making her feel better and function more easily than in Michigan.)

She leases a townhouse in Green Valley for $300 a month. These townhouses sell for $35,000 and up. Utilities—gas and electricity—cost about $100 a month. Higher-priced units rent for $500 a month furnished, and some townhouses in the foothills sell for $50,000. Other housing ranges from $40,000 to $125,000 and includes single-family houses, apartments, and mobile home estates. June is "murderously hot" but cooling rains fall in July. Winters are warm.

Green Valley is a self-contained community, with an extensive shopping mall, good library (a branch of the Tucson Library System), country club, recreation center (each area has its own center, which includes a tennis court, whirlpool baths, and game rooms) and several churches. Green

Valley has oven 20 doctors, a 197-bed medical center, a privately owned clinic, and a 60-bed nursing home. Extended-care facilities are available in Tucson. Most residents are WASPs (white Anglo-Saxon Protestant) from the Midwest.

For further information:

Fairfield Green Valley
Green Valley, AZ 85614

Tucson (pop. 300,000 city; 500,000 metropolitan) is still the dominant retirement city in Arizona. I knew Tucson in the 1950s when the highway ran through the town and it didn't take 10 minutes to get from one side to the other. Recently it took me over an hour to get from only one eastern "gateway" to the town to the bypass freeway that exits from Tucson. The town has *exploded*—in population, buildings, freeways, businesses. The population has more than tripled since the 1950s. *And* some 2,000 people arrive each month!

Climate and Environment. Many newcomers are retirees who come here for the abundant sunshine, the moderately priced housing, the special retirement communities and facilities. Tucson is located in a desert valley, surrounded by mountain ranges on all sides. The city limits cover some 90 square miles, and the elevations range from 2,400 feet in the city to over 9,000 feet at the top of Mt. Lemmon. The climate is warm and sunny throughout most of the year, with relatively low humidity (average 39 percent annually). The annual maximum temperature averages 82° F.; the annual minimum temperature, 54° F. Rainfall averages 10.63 inches a year. From November to mid-February the pollen count is practically nil.

This warm, dry air has proven beneficial to those suffering from most respiratory infections, including sinus, asthma, and bronchitis, and those afflicted by arthritis and other diseases. The city's Senior Health Improvement Program (SHIP) provides disabled older persons with excellent day care at greatly reduced costs.

But Tucson has its climatic and health drawbacks. At times, smoke from copper smelters and auto exhausts envelops the city. Tucson could also be facing a water shortage as the ground levels subside (no one really knows how long the water will last—guesses range from 10 to 500 years). Experts say municipal water tables are dropping as much as a foot a month, and the city is ripping out green turf on street curbs to put in less thirsty palms and crushed brick. Tucsonians have been told they are taking water from their underground supply almost 5 times faster than it is being replaced by nature. The deeper the city must go for water, the less efficient the pumping is and the more expensive. Water rates have already gone up, some rising from $50 to $200 a month (in July), although others went up only a few dollars. Tucson is now very "slow growth"-conscious.

Medical Facilities. Tucson has good health facilities with over 300 doctors, 6 large community hospitals, and many private homes and sanitariums. A semiprivate hospital room averages $113.29 daily, about $20 below the state average.

Housing. Two-bedroom homes sell from $30,000 and three-bedroom homes from $40,000; residential lots in desirable areas start at $9,000, and desert and mountain lots sell from $750. Some 200 mobile home parks in the area provide low-cost housing; rentals run $75 to $100 a month.

Cost of Living. Residential property is assessed at 15 percent of market value for land and improvements. The rates per $100 valuation are $1.50 state; $3.1590 city; $0.5982 Pima College, for a total of $6.6072. This equals about $99 per $10,000 valuation. Retail sales tax (state and city) totals 6 percent. Food and prescription drugs are tax-exempt.

Recreation and Culture. Tucson's community center features all sports and cultural activities (art, music, crafts). The outstanding Pima Council on Aging provides services and activities to seniors including information and referral, a monthly newspaper for seniors, a council of senior citizens organizations (there are more than 145 in the area), and a Sun Fair, which provides seniors an opportunity to display their handicrafts and hobbies. The University of Arizona in the heart of Tucson offers many facilities, exhibits, and ongoing programs of interest to seniors, including the Arizona State Museum, athletic facilities, geological museum, museum of art, and library.

Special Services for Seniors. Of special interest to seniors is the Volunteer Bureau, where seniors can match their skills with needs. The bureau is located at 3833 East 2nd Street, Tucson, AZ 85716.

For further information on Tucson itself write:

Chamber of Commerce
Tucson, AZ 85702

Other Retirement Areas Around Tucson

Arizona City (pop. 2,000). About 12 miles from Casa Grande (northwest of Tucson) lies the "Golden Corridor" and the master plan for Arizona

City, a residential/retirement community of 3,500 acres. Residential areas include homesites, single-family homes, and apartments. Recreational facilities include golf course, swimming, tennis, shuffleboard, 48-acre lake, and a community center with all facilities.

For further information:

> Arizona City Development
> Box 188
> Phoenix, AZ 85223

Oracle (pop. 3,000) is a hill town (4,500 feet altitude) about 30 miles northeast of Tucson with an expanding population that is mostly retirees. Oracle has a small library and an attractive park. Three-bedroom homes range from $40,000 to $60,000.

For further information:

> Chamber of Commerce
> Oracle, AZ 85623

Toltec-Eloy (pop. 7,000) is also located in the "Golden Corridor." Toltec is a planned community begun on 13,000 acres and annexed by the city of Eloy. Residential areas are interspersed with parks and playgrounds; a recreation center features most activities.

For further information:

> Chamber of Commerce
> Eloy, AZ 85231

Yuma (pop. 50,000). Tucked in the far southwestern corner, right on the border, Yuma has long attracted retirees. The Yuma Recreation and Parks Department sponsors the Golden Roadrunners, which plans recreational activities for residents and winter visitors 50 years of age and over. Year-round activities include card games, community singing, crafts, dancing, dinners, movies, picnics, tours, and special programs. Two-bedrooms sell from $35,000; apartments rent from $250 a month.

Yuma has been called the "sunniest city in the United States" with some 93 percent of possible sunshine throughout the year. It is also Arizona's warmest city with an average daily high of 69.7° F. in January. There are 221 hospital beds and some 60 physicians in the area, assuring adequate medical care.

For further information:

> Chamber of Commerce
> Yuma, AZ 85364

Tubac (pop. 600). This tiny, picturesque community has become a haven for artists and the retired. It was the site of the first Spanish Presidio in Arizona and still retains its historical atmosphere. The old Spanish Presidio and the area immediately surrounding it are now a state historical park.

For further information:

> Tubac Village Council
> Tubac, AZ 85640

Arizona Sunsites. Horizon Corporation, a nationally known planner and developer, is building on 41,000 acres of land in the Sulphur Springs Valley, about 90 miles southeast of Tucson. Some 500 homes and apartments have been completed and are now occupied by more than 1,150 residents. There is a community center building, a small mobile home and RV park and a 30-shop commercial center with Western facades and covered porticos. Sunsites has its own fire station and first-aid station, medical clinic, motel, and service station. Recreational facilities include golf, tennis, swimming, and more. Homes including lots range from $37,000 to $70,000. Golf course lots sell from $7,500 to $10,000. Apartments rent for $250 to $300 monthly (efficiency or one bedroom). Daily and weekly rates also available.

For further information:

> Horizon Corporation
> 4400 East Broadway Boulevard
> Tucson, AZ 85726

Southern Arizona also boasts such colorful towns as Patagonia, Nogales, Bisbee, Douglas, and Benson, which you shouldn't overlook if you investigate retirement housing in this area.

2. CENTRAL ARIZONA—THE METROPOLITAN SPRAWL

Apache Junction used to be a remote outpost consisting of a service station and a store. Now it is all but engulfed by developments, including *Apache Villa Retirement Community,* which offers single-family homes with views of the brooding Superstition Mountains. This is just one of the several communities that ring *Mesa* (pop. 140,000), once a quiet Mormon town several miles from Phoenix but now part of the urban sprawl, and center for mobile home and other retirement communities. Mobile home spaces rent from $70 a month; two-bedroom homes average around $35,000.

Around Mesa are *Velda Rose Estates,* which features single-family residences along with a community center, clubhouse, swimming pool; *Fountain Hills,* 12,000 acres with mountain-view homes, a picturesque golf course, 60 commercial buildings, and some 100 businesses and services; *Golden Hills Leisure World,* with a mineral spring health spa, an 18-hole golf course, recreation center, and gatehouse and security; *Golden Hills Country Club Estates,* with the longest 18-hole golf course in the Valley of the Sun and regular adult activities; *Apache Wells Mobile City and Country Club,* one of the largest (400 lots) adult mobile home centers in the country; *Desert Sands Golf and Country Club,* a mobile home community designed for mobile-home owners on a fixed income; and the *Fountain of the Sun.* The area has three general hospitals and several nursing facilities.

Fountain of the Sun (pop. 1,000) combines luxurious conventional housing and a mobile home community. It is built around an 11-acre central park with an 18-hole golf course, lake and casting pond, swimming pool, clubhouse, banquet and dining rooms, tennis courts, driving range, putting greens and more. There is 24-hour gate security. Residents pay only $15 a month for use of the facilities.

Single-family homes and condominiums start at around $40,000. A $65 and up monthly maintenance fee on the condominiums includes water, sewer, insurance on dwelling, maintenance of common area, and more.

Fountain of the Sun is primarily a blue-collar community. The average age is 55 and most residents come from the Midwest—Illinois, Michigan, Wisconsin, Iowa. Persons with moderate incomes can live comfortably here. Residents use the medical facilities in the Phoenix-Tempe-Mesa-Scottsdale metropolitan area, which includes some 25 hospitals with 6,500 beds and over 1,600 doctors (150 in Mesa), which assures good medical care.

For further information:

> Fountain of the Sun
> 8001 East Broadway
> Mesa, AZ 85208

For information on other communities in and around Mesa write:

> Chamber of Commerce
> Mesa, AZ 85201

From Mesa it's just a short drive (20 miles) to *Scottsdale* (pop. 80,000). My mother settled here in the 1940s. When I first saw her house in 1949, I could walk 2 miles in a straight line (no buildings) from the center of town, which was just a 4-block-long crossroads with a drugstore, saloon, gas station, and grocery store to her house. At one time I could have bought the weekly paper (now a daily) for only $2,000. For many years Scottsdale was known as the West's Most Western Town because horses *did* have the right of way, and there were hitching posts in front of the stores. Authentic cowboys wore authentic Western clothes. It *was* the Wild West.

No more. Scottsdale is now one of the largest cities in the state, complete with fake-brick sidewalks, shopping malls, and adult bookstores. What used to be 2-lane roads are now superhighways; where my mother's house stood in splendid isolation is now a subdivision. Where she now lives (in a "casita" [small house] in a subdivision), high-rise condominiums are being built in what 2 years ago was a cotton field. Eighteen percent of Scottsdale residents are retired.

Climate and Environment. Scottsdale is a healthier place to live in than Phoenix. Its elevation (about 2000 feet) and distance from the center of Phoenix improves the quality of the air.

Medical Facilities. The city has a 340-bed hospital, 5 extended-care nursing homes, 220 doctors, and 79 dentists, assuring its residents excellent health care.

Housing. Housing is expensive here. The median price of homes is around $50,000, and many cost more. At Scottsdale Shadows, a total apartment community with high-rise condominiums, a large recreation building, golf course, swimming pool, tennis courts, and so on, you might pay $75,000 to $100,000 for a two-bedroom unit. At McCormick Ranch, a 4,200-acre ranch that is being developed into homesites and various types of housing, two-bedroom units cost $75,000. Similar expensive housing is available at Scottsdale House, an elegant community for affluent adults who like condominium community living with a clubhouse and a wide range of hotel-like services, and at Villa Octillo, a plush apartment complex with catered services. Less expensive housing is available at 3 mobile home communities in the area.

Cost of Living. Property taxes are reasonable: $12.11 per $100 valuation, which is about $180 per $10,000 market value of home.

Recreation and Culture. The Scottsdale Center for the Arts sponsors concerts, plays, ballets, and art exhibits featuring national and internationally renowned artists.

Special Services for Seniors. The new senior citizens center (7375 East Second Street) provides a full recreation program, including card parties, pot luck suppers, travelogues, and arts and crafts.

For further information:

Chamber of Commerce
Scottsdale, AZ 85251

Sun City (pop. 48,000) was begun by Del Webb in 1960. When I first saw Sun City in 1963 it was a community of some 2,000 homes and some apartments, with fewer than 4,000 people.

I've been back several times since, each time amazed at the progress. Sun City is now the seventh-largest city in Arizona, covering some 9,000 acres. It has 6 recreational centers, including the Sundial Center, which features Arizona's largest indoor swimming pool, first indoor air-conditioned shuffleboard courts, and the state's only synthetically surfaced bowling green. Another newly opened recreation center houses a 40,000-volume library and the community's first handball and volleyball courts. Other recreation areas feature exercise rooms, pool and billiards, therapy baths, miniature golf, boating and fishing, tennis, ping pong, bocci, weaving, bowling, picnic areas with scenic waterfalls, cabanas, barbecues, and small lakes. Residents get all this for only $40 per person per year (with a small fee for bowling). Sun City also has the 7,500-seat Sun Bowl, where top entertainers and the 70-member Sun City Symphony play (season tickets are only $12 for 6 shows), a college campus where 1,000 students attend, ten 18-hole golf courses, a 261-bed medical center with 200 doctors.

Sun City offers 21 floor plans featuring 4 modes of living: single-family homes, duplexes, garden court apartments, and patio apartments. Base prices range from $45,990 to $87,490. Some homes are on acre or larger lots, with ranch-fenced corrals and optional stalls and tack rooms. Bridle paths wander through the area with access to desert areas nearby. Rentals are $150 a week during the winter season (October 16 through May 31).

The average retiree living in Sun City needs to have an income of around $850 a month. Taxes are very reasonable, averaging $10.50 per $1,000 market value ($525 on a $50,000 home). The majority of those living in Sun City are retired teachers, government employees, accountants, shopkeepers, engineers, and other middle-class Americans. They hail mainly from California, Illinois, Michigan, New York, Minnesota, Wisconsin, Ohio, Colorado, Iowa, Missouri, and Washington. No one under age 18 is permitted residency. A new community, *Sun City West*, is opening up.

Sun City is an amazing place and worth a look. For further information write:

> Del E. Webb Development Company
> Post Office Box 1750
> Sun City, AZ 85351

Sun City has a counterpart is *Youngtown* (pop. 2,000), which borders it on the west. Like Sun City, it restricts children under 18. Youngtown started before Sun City and most of the residents have grown older with the town (the average age is 70). Most housing is single-family units, which sell for around $30,000; however, there are some duplexes and single-story apartments. Youngtown covers 632 acres; 15.5 of these acres are devoted to parks and recreational areas, including a stocked lake. Youngtown is self-sufficient; there is no property tax. It has a shopping center and other community services. Medical services are provided in a 60-bed hospital. There are 15 doctors in the area, assuring good medical care.

For further information:

> Town of Youngtown
> 12030 Clubhouse Square
> Youngtown, AZ 85363

Carefree (pop. 2,500) used to be just an area surrounding *Cave Creek*, a quaint artsy-craftsy town about 25 miles northeast of Scottsdale. The land is about 1,500 feet higher than the Phoenix area, which makes 2 important differences: It's cooler in the summer, and the higher elevation supports unique desert plants like the beautiful giant saguaro cactus.

Now Cave Creek is a country village and Carefree is a country subdivision. While all age groups are represented, retired executives and military leaders predominate.

Taxes are low (only $9.81 per $100 assessed valuation) and there's no city tax. Cave Creek-Carefree has a 24-hour medical clinic and it does have 7 doctors and 3 dentists. Besides single-family homes, the area has 5 apartment complexes, 5 condominiums, 1 hotel of 197 units, 1 motel with 16 units, and 3 mobile home parks (rentals average $75 a month). "Tennis villas" sell from $35,000 (two-bedroom) to from $45,000 (three-bedroom). Many similar developments are available ranging to $75,000 and up for two-bedroom units.

For further information:

> Cave Creek-Carefree Chamber of Commerce
> Carefree, AZ 85377

Other Central Arizona Retirement Communities of Interest

Chandler (pop. 25,000), home of the nationally known San Marcos Resort Hotel and a popular resort and winter vacation area, has many mobile home parks. Chandler has 18 doctors.

For further information:

Chamber of Commerce
Chandler, AZ 85224

Glendale (pop. 85,000), a residential community adjoining Phoenix, is home of Glencroft Retirement Community, a 40-acre complex sponsored by the Congregational Church in the Phoenix area. The community consists of 240 housekeeping units in 8 courts, 100 residential living units in a 4-story building with central dining, and a medical center with 160 nursing beds. There are 25 doctors in the area. Glendale also has numerous mobile home parks where rents average $75 a month. Good hospital facilities in area.

For further information:

Chamber of Commerce
Glendale, AZ 85301

Litchfield Park (pop. 4,000) is another resort area which is turning into a retirement center. Site of the plush Wigwam Resort Hotel, Litchfield Park includes a series of villages that will have an eventual population of 75,000. When the villages are completed, they will center around a core of department stores, shops, restaurants, hotels, office buildings, and so forth. Each village will have a central theme and a neighborhood and community center as well as the central core area. Lots sell for $35,000 and up and unfurnished garden apartments near the country club range from $250 to $300 a month.

For further information:

Litchfield Park Properties
P.O. Box 747
Litchfield Park, AZ 85340

Then, of course, there's *Phoenix* (pop. 700,000 city; over 1,350,000 metropolitan). Unfortunately, Phoenix suffers from the ills of other major metropolitan areas. It has more than its share of congestion, pollution, noise, and crime, although the farther you are from the city core, the less pollution and congestion.

Phoenix is no longer the quaint little city I first saw 30 years ago. It is now the center of an urban sprawl that includes Scottsdale, Tempe, Chandler, Mesa, Apache Junction, Glendale, Peoria, Sun City, Litchfield Park, Avondale, Buckeye, and smaller communities. In the immediate Phoenix area, the Valley of the Sun is about 20 miles wide, and you can see mountains in all directions.

Climate and Environment. Phoenix's relatively low elevation (1,086 feet) prevents it from having a moderate climate, such as in Tucson. January, the coldest month, averages 49.7° F. and July, the hottest month, averages 89.8° F. The average annual temperature is 70.5° F. Rainfall averages 7.20 inches a year and relative humidity averages 33 percent. July is the wettest month with .77 inches of rainfall; April the driest with .32 inches. There are 294 days of sunshine.

Medical Facilities. Phoenix has 27 hospitals with a total of 6,795 beds and 52 nursing homes. There are 2,130 doctors in the area, assuring good medical care for the population.

Housing. Recently, Phoenix has had a housing shortage. Good two- and three-bedroom houses, when available, cost $50,000 and up. Rentals are scarce, but when available (off-season in summer) are from $250 a month for two-bedroom units. The quality and cost of housing in the central Phoenix area ranges from very low in the districts south of McDowell Avenue to high in the north and northeast (toward Carefree and Scottsdale). However, there are many mobile home parks in the area where two-bedroom units sell from $15,000 and rent for about $150 a month. Union, fraternal, and church-sponsored retirement housing is available for sale ($30,000 and up) and for rent ($200 a month and up).

Cost of Living. Phoenix ranks ninth out of 25 metropolitan areas in the U.S. for which living costs are compiled. A retired couple would need around $9,000 annually to retire here. The sales tax totals 5 percent and the average property tax is about $12 per $100 assessed value (about $180 per $10,000 market value of a house).

Recreation and Culture. There are some 1,258 clubs and organizations in Phoenix, including many senior citizen clubs. The main cultural attractions include little theater, legitimate theater, the Civic Plaza, Arizona State University, the art museum, symphony, Arizona state fairgrounds, Celebrity Theater, Grady Gammage Memorial Auditorium, and Sun City Bowl. Fifty golf courses, an inland surfing beach, ice skating rinks, an amusement park, and pro hockey, basketball, baseball, and football (home of the annual Fiesta Bowl) are available. Phoenix also has desert botanical gardens, Japanese flower gardens, and a zoo.

For further information:

Chamber of Commerce
805 North Second Street
P.O. Box 10
Phoenix, AZ 85001

3. NORTHERN ARIZONA—
MOUNTAINS, CANYONS, AND MESAS

I fell in love with *Prescott* (pop. 17,000 city, 23,000 area) in 1949. I drove from the north through Flagstaff, colorful Oak Creek Canyon, Sedona, and Jerome, over Mingus Mountain and through a broad valley before I arrived at the picturesque Granite Dells (featured in many movies) which mark the northern approach to the town. Prescott lies at 5,389 feet (it's called the Mile-High City). The southern entrance to town is as picturesque as the northern but different: You drive through the Prescott National Forest, which has some of the largest Ponderosa pine tracts in the world. Prescott was—and is—a summer resort. In the days before superhighways and big cars, people from Phoenix would wind their way here in summer; wealthy Phoenicians started resorts and it was fashionable to have a "cabin" in Prescott. While wealthy Phoenicians now spend summers in air-conditioned comfort in the Valley of the Sun or in San Diego, many tourists and retirees still come to Prescott.

Climate and Environment. Prescott has an "old-fashioned" look. There's something nostalgic about the town built around the tree and grass-covered courthouse square that has the stately old homes and the quaint "Whiskey Row," with the swinging doors of the Palace Bar. Besides the picturesqueness of the town and surrounding areas, Prescott is *healthy.* The pines to the south filter the air, making it crisp and pure. Many prominent citizens originally came here for relief from asthma and stayed on to settle (93 percent of asthmatics say they find total relief in Prescott). However, be careful of the altitude. Even as a 23-year-old, I found my heart pounding when I went up to Prescott from Phoenix. And 2 beers on Whiskey Row were enough to turn me into a Saturday-night drunk.

Altitude aside, the climate is about perfect. Summers average 70° with a maximum of 87° F. in the afternoon. The temperature at night usually breaks to a low of 53° F. Humidity is nearly ideal, with a year-round average of 45 percent. In winter the average maximum temperature is 58.6° F. and the average minimum 31.8° F. Rain or snow falls nearly every month of the year; rain averages 20 inches a year and snow about 20 inches.

Medical Facilities. Because of its reputation as a health center, Prescott has unusually good medical facilities. The Yavapai Community Hospital has 147 beds and a medical staff of 34 (semiprivate rooms average around $100 daily—$17 below the state average), and Whipple Veterans Administration Center has 236 beds and a 232-bed domiciliary. Whipple was originally founded for tuberculosis patients but now has general medical and surgical patients. Prescott has more doctors per capita than most towns its size: 26 doctors and surgeons, 20 dentists, and 10 other medical specialists.

Housing. Most people have single-family cabin-type resort and vacation homes. Costs are equivalent to similar housing in other resort areas but higher than in southern Arizona. Some "cabins" in wooded areas are available from $25,000 for two- to three-bedroom units. Conventional two-bedroom homes sell from $50,000 in the newer subdivisions, but some older houses sell for as low as $35,000. Some rentals are available for one or two persons, ranging from a low of $200 a month. About 14 miles southwest of Prescott, the Prescott Country Club Properties offers lots for conventional homes as well as mobile homes. Community facilities include an 18-hole golf course and a clubhouse. Lots sell for around $12,000. Prescott Gardens Mobile Home Park on the outskirts of town has a recreation hall and shuffleboard courts. Monthly rentals range from around $75 and up.

Cost of Living. Living costs aren't cheap, because food and other supplies must be brought in from Phoenix and other distant points. City taxes are $11.27 per $100 assessed valuation at 15 percent of full value (about 1 percent of market value of house).

Recreation and Culture. Prescott has always been keen on arts and crafts. It has a Mountain Artists' League, Fine Arts Association, arts and crafts center, a well-stocked library, and a junior college and high school that offer extension courses. About 25 percent of the residents are retired and they engage in wide-ranging cultural and recreational activities including golf, theater, museum, art center, and the Prescott Adult Activities Center, which sponsors a daily program for seniors ranging from movies to hula dancing. Prescott seems to have more clubs than it has people to become members.

Prescott isn't perfect, but it certainly merits close attention if you're considering retiring in Arizona.

For further information:

> Chamber of Commerce
> Prescott, AZ 86301

Driving from Prescott to Flagstaff and the Grand Canyon you cross Prescott Valley and wind up to Mingus Mountain (7,743 feet). Then you plunge down through the town of *Jerome* (pop. 250) until you come to the floor of the Verde Valley (but it's not very green). Here, the towns of *Clarkdale* (pop. 1,000), which used to be a company town, and *Cottonwood* (pop. 3,000), a ranching center, offer retirement possibilities. The land is a delicate yellow until, almost suddenly, it changes to almost a rusty red. This is Oak Creek Canyon, regarded as the second most beautiful canyon in the Southwest (after the Grand Canyon). Red- and taffy-colored rock spirals like soft ice cream into towering peaks, some shaped like Chinese pagodas and others like cathedrals, bells, courthouses, and coffee pots. Alongside the road grow lush evergreens; oak, maple, and apple trees; and wild blackberry bushes. Oak Creek splashes over sculptured rock. Hundreds of Western films were made here; if you recall any beautiful red-rock scenery, the film was probably made in Oak Creek Canyon.

In the heart of Oak Creek lies *Sedona* (area pop. 36,790). Not surprisingly, Sedona has attracted many artists and writers. The town lies at 4,240 feet, so its climate is a bit different from Prescott's. Summers may be hotter, but winters are milder. Sedona is only 27 miles from Flagstaff, which presents a completely different weather picture (see below).

Sedona isn't equipped for recreation per se, although there are 2 golf courses, 10 art galleries, and a library. There is also a health clinic with 2 doctors in attendance (15 doctors in the area). Most people live in individually built homes, some quite expensive, but there's a planned community and mobile home park nearby. The average two-bedroom retirement house starts at around $60,000; taxes on such a house average around $550.

For further information:

Chamber of Commerce
Sedona, AZ 86336

Flagstaff (pop. 35,000) sits at 7,000 feet in the midst of pines and quaking aspen. It gets much snow in the winter; the Arizona Snow Bowl (skiing) is located near here as is Lowell Observatory. Flagstaff is also home to Northern Arizona University and gateway to scenic attractions including the Grand Canyon and many Indian ruins. The Museum of Northern Arizona is a splendid introduction to the area.

I've never been wild about Flagstaff itself—it's a combination tourist stop, student hangout, and cowboy's Saturday night, but it does feature a symphony orchestra and numerous festivals. It also has more than 50 churches and fraternal clubs (including senior clubs), and it's noted for its year-round hunting and fishing.

Again, beware of the high altitude and cold (Flagstaff averages only 27.3° F. in January, often accompanied by snow). Annual snowfall averages 73.3 inches per year. It's not as warm as Prescott in summer; although August days may get into the 80s, the temperature drops into the 40s at night.

New three-bedroom homes sell for $45,000 and up; some older homes sell for slightly less. Rentals aren't plentiful, but when available cost from $150 to $350 a month. Combined taxes run $9.2478 per $100 of assessed value, based on 15 percent of full valuation (slightly lower than Prescott). A 110-bed community hospital and some 60 physicians assure good medical care.

For further information:

Chamber of Commerce
Flagstaff, AZ 86001

Kingman (pop. 15,000) is a town 25 percent of whose residents are 55 or older. More and more retirees are settling here. According to a Kingman chamber of commerce official: "Many people look toward the West and toward retirement for the same thing: a new beginning. Kingman, as a remote, rural community needs qualified talented people. Our clubs and organizations, museums, libraries, and so on depend heavily upon volunteer resources, and a person can find many opportunities to participate in the community from the start. There is, therefore, the opportunity for recognition and status within the community." Beyond that, Kingman has many cultural activities, including 4 professional concerts a year. It's near enough to Las Vegas (100 miles) for a resident to drive in for an evening's entertainment. The Colorado River, offering boating and fishing, is only 25 miles away.

Another major attraction is the relatively low cost of living in Kingman. Residential property taxes for a standard house is around 1 percent of the value of the house each year. The taxes on a typical home are between $350 to $500 a year. Construction costs are around $30 a square foot, including the price of the lot (around $35,000 for new 3-bedroom house). Lots which have utilities range from $4,000 for a one-sixth-acre lot to $10,000 for a 1-acre lot in the best section of town.

Being at a relatively low elevation, Kingman's average winter high is 57° F.; some January days get up to 75° F. Average July days are 95° F.

with low humidity. Kingman gets some 4 inches of snow a year, with rainfall of about 6½ inches a year.

Activities also include a municipal golf course, the Senior Citizens
Center, and numerous activities and organizations geared toward the retiree (especially courses in silversmithing, rockhounding, and lapidary).
Kingman has an 83-bed general hospital with a staff of 19 doctors as well as
a 120-bed extended-care facility.

One note of caution: Much of the land toward the northwest (Las
Vegas) is unusually barren and was once the site of early land fraud. Be
careful when buying property here.

For further information:

> Chamber of Commerce
> Kingman, AZ 86401

Other Northern Arizona Retirement Communities of Interest

Lake Havasu City (pop. 15,000) is the site of the famous London
Bridge reconstruction. This beautiful monument has now been reassembled
at a point where Pittsburgh Point juts out into the lake. The city of London
has built an English village, featuring a pub, restaurant, and other facilities, on land next to the bridge. Besides this obvious tourist attraction, the
city, built on 16,630 acres, offers many recreational facilities, including
golf courses, tennis courts, and beaches and marinas along the 45-mile-long
lake. There are 22 doctors and 2 hospitals in the area; about one-third of
the residents are retired.

For further information:

> Chamber of Commerce
> Lake Havasu City, AZ 86403

Parker (pop. 2,500). Constructed 11 miles below Parker Dam, this
town consists mainly of mobile home and trailer parks. Residents can fish,
boat, and swim in the Colorado River. Parker has about the same summer
climate as Phoenix, but gets cooler in winter.

For further information:

> Chamber of Commerce
> Parker, AZ 85344

Payson (pop. 3,600). Located just below Arizona's famous Mogollon
Rim, Payson is noted for its scenic beauty and surrounding recreation

areas. Nearby is *Switzerland in Arizona,* a community of Alpine-type homes. At an altitude of almost 5,000 feet, Payson's climate is similar to that of Prescott. This is an area for the outdoor-minded.

For further information:

Chamber of Commerce
Payson, AZ 85541

Wickenburg (pop. 4,000). Although officially not in northern Arizona, Wickenburg lies in a cooler-than-Phoenix altitude of over 2,000 feet. It was one of the original retirement areas of Arizona and became known as the Dude Ranch Capital of the World. It still offers many luxurious facilities for retirees, who comprise about 60 percent of the inhabitants. Housing consists of single-family homes, motels, guest ranches, apartments, mobile home parks, and other facilities. Two-bedroom homes are available from $40,000.

For further information:

Chamber of Commerce
Wickenburg, AZ 85358

SUMMARY

I like the contrast in Arizona, the mountain versus valley climate. I also like the desert cacti (especially the saguaro), the pine forests, trees, shrubs and other plants that make Arizona more varied than the other Southwestern states. Arizona offers a variety of housing and the choice between completely urban and completely rural living.

I *don't* like the congestion around Phoenix or Tucson, and I was appalled when I had to wear a necktie to dine in a fancy restaurant. New York, yes; Arizona, no. Also, Arizona has the highest per-capita crime rate in the U.S. and is the main conduit for drug traffic in the United States.

Nevertheless, I still like Arizona and will return to places like Prescott when I seek my retirement haven.

Here are my personal ratings for Arizona's major retirement areas:
Excellent—Prescott, Sedona;
Good—Green Valley, Tucson (area), Cave Creek-Carefree, Verde Valley area (Clarkdale, Cottonwood), Scottsdale;
Adequate—Phoenix (area), Yuma, Flagstaff, Kingman.

RATINGS FOR ARIZONA MAJOR RETIREMENT AREAS

GREEN VALLEY

Rating	Climate & Envir.	Medical	Housing	Cost of Living	Rec. & Culture	Spec. Senior Svces.
1						
2						
3						
4						
5						

TUCSON (AREA)

Rating	Climate & Envir.	Medical	Housing	Cost of Living	Rec. & Culture	Spec. Senior Svces.
1						
2						
3						
4						
5						

MESA (AREA)

Rating	Climate & Envir.	Medical	Housing	Cost of Living	Rec. & Culture	Spec. Senior Svces.
1						
2						
3						
4						
5						

PHOENIX (AREA)

Rating	Climate & Envir.	Medical	Housing	Cost of Living	Rec. & Culture	Spec. Senior Svces.
1						
2						
3						
4						
5						

SCOTTSDALE

Rating	Climate & Envir.	Medical	Housing	Cost of Living	Rec. & Culture	Spec. Senior Svces.
1						
2						
3						
4						
5						

SUN CITY

Rating	Climate & Envir.	Medical	Housing	Cost of Living	Rec. & Culture	Spec. Senior Svces.
1						
2						
3						
4						
5						

PRESCOTT

FLAGSTAFF-SEDONA

Rating	Climate & Envir.	Medical	Housing	Cost of Living	Rec. & Culture	Spec. Senior Svces.
1						
2						
3						
4						
5						

LAKE HAVASU CITY

Rating	Climate & Envir.	Medical	Housing	Cost of Living	Rec. & Culture	Spec. Senior Svces.
1						
2						
3						
4						
5						

KINGMAN (AREA)

Rating	Climate & Envir.	Medical	Housing	Cost of Living	Rec. & Culture	Spec. Senior Svces.
1						
2						
3						
4						
5						

CAREFREE-CAVE CREEK

Rating	Climate & Envir.	Medical	Housing	Cost of Living	Rec. & Culture	Spec. Senior Svces.
1						
2						
3						
4						
5						

1 = Excellent
2 = Good
3 = Fair
4 = Poor
5 = Unacceptable

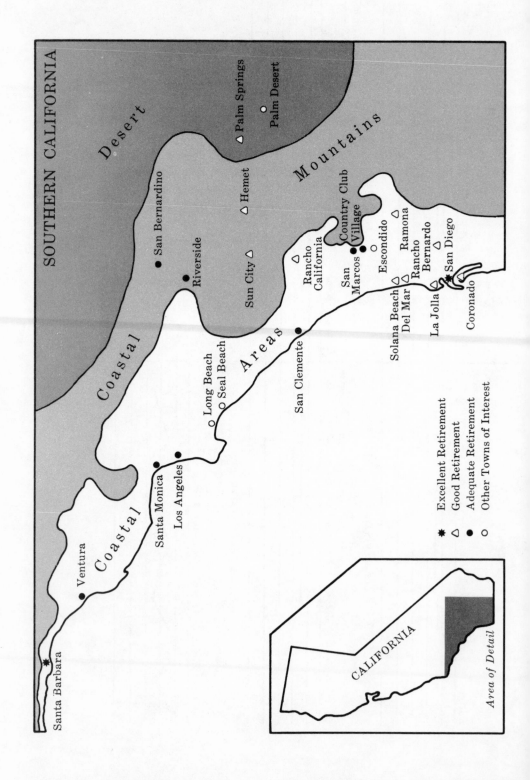

SOUTHERN CALIFORNIA

Desert

Mountains

Coastal

Coastal

Areas

Santa Barbara

Ventura

Santa Monica
Los Angeles

Long Beach
Seal Beach

San Clemente

San Bernardino

Riverside

Sun City

Hemet

Palm Springs

Palm Desert

Rancho
California

Country Club
Village

San
Marcos

Escondido

Ramona

Rancho
Bernardo

Solana Beach
Del Mar

La Jolla

San Diego

Coronado

✳ Excellent Retirement
△ Good Retirement
● Adequate Retirement
○ Other Towns of Interest

CALIFORNIA

Area of Detail

XV.

SOUTHERN CALIFORNIA—

IT'S AS GOOD (AND AS BAD)

AS PEOPLE SAY

Northern California is like a tweedy, pipe-smoking Easterner who is not quite sure what to do with all that sunshine. Proper Northern Californians look down their noses on their free-spirited, sun-worshiping, casual-living neighbors to the south. Southern Californians couldn't care less.

Southern California is a curvaceous pin-up girl, soaking up the sun, concerned with looking beautiful and enjoying life. Gregarious, happy, enthusiastic, Southern Californians know they've found the answer, that their way of life beats anything else under the sun, and they live in God's country.

God's country begins at a line north of Santa Barbara, and fills the bottom third of the state. It includes some of the famous tourist areas such as Los Angeles, where real estate prices have been rising 20 percent a year, to off-the-beaten-path areas like Hemet and Escondido, where retired persons can enjoy the famous sunny climate and still have enough money left to eat California's delicious fruit and vegetables.

I've lived in California and visited it many times, yet every time I come back I rediscover how *friendly* the people are. No matter where you go in Southern California you feel at home; just about everyone comes from someplace else and is interested in meeting people. Clubs and senior citizen centers abound, offering retirees a multitude of activities and ways to meet people. For years California was the destination of retirees from all across the country; the state is experienced in welcoming seniors. California is a leading state in providing services to seniors—breaks in taxes, good medical facilities, and excellent adult education programs.

But the flood of seniors has slowed during the past years as the state has become too urban, with smog and traffic problems. The cost of living isn't made for Social Security checks, and retirees can't always find the housing they need or can afford. Purse-snatching youths have plagued seniors in some urban areas, and job opportunities have shrunk.

That's the bad side. But there are still a lot of good reasons for retiring in Southern California—if you know *where*. There is housing, climate, and recreation to suit all tastes and pocketbooks—as long as you don't limit your looking to the well-publicized touristy areas where prices are prohibitive. As a rule of thumb, the coastal regions tend to be more expensive and bathed in cooling and refreshing fog the year round. Expensive areas include La Jolla, Santa Barbara, Santa Monica, and the "ritzier" sections of Los Angeles. Other coastal areas such as San Diego, Laguna Beach, Long Beach, and other beach towns share the same climate but cost less. Inland, in such areas as Hemet, Riverside, San Bernardino, there is a 4-season climate and living costs are lower.

There is *still a smog problem* in California, particularly in the Los Angeles basin. Smog is air pollution at its worst—a combination of smoke, dust, fumes, vapors, gases, and ash. It causes eye irritation, breathing difficulty, headaches, and other problems. The chief culprit is the automobile (in Southern California there is 1 car for every 2 people—the highest rate of car ownership in the world). Although all cars sold in California must have strict emission controls, so many cars are driven so many miles every day that smog remains a problem. Despite the strictest air pollution laws in the nation—tougher even than federal requirements—the smog battle is far from won. San Bernardino and Riverside are probably the worst cities for smog in California.

In general, the beach cities come out best in the clean air department. There are literally dozens of delightful beach communities on the Southern California coast. Starting with Santa Barbara on the north, cities such as Ventura, Pacific Palisades, Santa Monica, El Segundo, Manhattan Beach, Redondo Beach, San Pedro, Long Beach, Sunset Beach, San Clemente, Laguna Beach, La Jolla, and San Diego generally offer mostly year-round smog-free climates. The reason isn't hard to figure out. California normally enjoys a breeze *off* the ocean which simply sweeps the air pollution from the beach cities inland. On those relatively infrequent days when the wind decides to sweep in the *other* direction, though, watch out!

My advice on smog: Avoid communities such as Burbank, Glendale, Van Nuys, Pomona, Hollywood, Pasadena, Altadena, Monterey Park, El Monte, Riverside, San Bernardino, and *all* other Los Angeles area cities inland from the coast.

One of the causes of smog is also one of the reasons life is so interesting in Southern California—the incredibly good roads. Freeways run everywhere, whisking drivers from the Pacific beaches to desert sands or mountain peaks in 2 to 3 hours. There are peaceful mountain towns virtually cut off from the world that are less than an hour from busy lowland cities bustling with shopping centers, medical facilities, and senior citizens groups.

The other side of the coin—a car is a necessity almost everywhere, except for some parts of San Diego and a few other places where public transportation is adequate.

Another of Southern California's faults is the *earthquakes.* The most famous problem area is the San Andreas fault, 50 miles inland from Los Angeles. It last heaved violently in 1857 when Los Angeles was a dusty adobe village, and not much harm was done. Today a movement could be catastrophic. There have been several moderate-to-strong quakes in the last 120 years in the Los Angeles area—most recently in 1971—causing some damage and loss of life, but they have occurred along secondary fault lines. When or whether the San Andreas fault will act up again, and how much damage it will inflict, remains to be seen. In the meantime, headlines predicting imminent disaster—which, so far, has not come to pass—will continue.

The Famous Climate—Good and Bad

Generally, you get the sun you came to sunny California for. The sun shines 293 days a year in Los Angeles; 243 days in San Diego. The coast tends to be cool and foggy, but just a few miles inland it's warmer and sunnier. The deeper inland you go, the more of a 4-season climate there is, with hotter summers and cold, crisp nights.

In the San Diego and Los Angeles areas, the temperature varies from

90° to 100° F. in the summer to around 60° to 70° (sometimes 80°) in winter, although the thermometer drops as much as 30 degrees at night. Inland, in the Hemet area, the mean temperature is 49.2° F. in January and 98.4° F. in July, with temperatures dropping as much as 30 degrees between day and night. But most of the year you can count on generally good weather in Southern California.

I'll never forget my first visit to Santa Monica—in August. Cooled by the ocean breezes that never stopped blowing from the Pacific across the street, the temperature hovered in the low 50s—sweater weather. One chilly day I called a friend who lived a few miles away in the center of Los Angeles. While I huddled in my turtleneck, he had been *sunning* himself in his backyard where it was 86°.

A few miles can make all the difference in climate here if there's a mountain, valley, air pocket, or other natural configuration in the way. Friends once bought a "dream" home in an attractive community only to discover after they moved in that the breeze never stopped. Howling gusts blew every day, preventing them from barbecuing and enjoying the outdoor life they had expected in California. They had moved into a wind pocket—caused by a peculiar arrangement of mountains in the area. They sold at a loss and moved a few miles away where the wind rarely blows.

Also, watch out for the coastal areas if you're bothered by humidity. It ranges from 40 to 60 percent—no problem for most people, but a bane to sinus, asthma, and arthritis sufferers. Look into the drier inland areas, where humidity usually stays *below* 40 percent.

What about the desert areas, which are still heavily promoted in California? Desert living is definitely not for everyone but has tremendous appeal for many. The climate is *very* dry almost all year long. About 9 months of the year are balmy and delightful, but the summer months of early June to early September are blazing hot. Before air conditioning, most people simply abandoned desert areas until after Labor Day. Now, with autos, offices, shops, and homes all beautifully air-conditioned, desert dwellers simply shift to shorts and bikinis and spend the summer clustered around their swimming pools!

Palm Springs and Palm Desert are two of the best known of the desert communities, but there are many others. Most of these communities are still relatively smog-free year-round.

What about temperatures? A quick look at the following *average* temperatures from the U.S. Weather Bureau gives you an idea:

	JANUARY		APRIL		JULY		OCTOBER	
	Aver. Max.	*Aver. Min.*	*Aver. Max.*	*Aver. Min.*	*Aver. Max.*	*Aver. Min.*	*Aver. Max.*	*Aver. Min.*
Barstow (desert)	59	31	77	45	101	67	80	47
Indio (desert)	70	39	86	57	107	78	91	58
Long Beach (coast)	65	40	71	49	83	61	78	54
Los Angeles (downtown)	65	47	71	53	83	63	77	57
San Diego (coast)	65	46	68	54	76	63	73	58
Santa Barbara (coast)	64	43	68	48	76	56	74	51

But there's a lot more to climate than temperature, and there's more to moisture than humidity. Rain determines the seasons in most of Southern California, except in the mountain areas, where snow falls in the colder months at the higher elevations. Other than the mountains, Southern California has a 2-season climate, wet and dry. The dry months are from April to October, when the weather is warm. The rainy months, which are cooler, are normally from November through March. Though the yearly rainfall totals in some Southern California areas may not sound impressive (no more than 12 to 15 inches a year in most of Los Angeles and San Diego and 12 inches less in the desert), the rain can, and on occasion does, come in cloudbursts. Rain tends to materialize suddenly and to be extreme—either a drizzle or a downpour.

As dry as it is for 6 to 8 months of the year, Southern California usually welcomes a rainstorm. Water is literally a matter of life or death for the entire southern part of the state. Water is drawn to the Los Angeles area mainly from 3 sources: the Owens Valley, the Northern California mountain areas, and the Colorado River. Without these outside sources, southern California, with two-thirds of the state's more than 21,000,000 people, wouldn't last a season. There's not enough fresh water locally to support even a fraction of the present population.

When looking for a home in Southern California keep these unique rainfall characteristics in mind. That odd-looking dry-as-a-bone gully just behind your dream house *could* and probably *will* on occasion turn into a stream bed for a raging torrent of water. Every winter in Southern California, *some* homes are washed away from their foundations. Avoid low-lying areas which could be flooded. Also avoid remote hilltops if surrounded by trees or shrubs. These plants have adjusted to prolonged dry spells by building up oily substances that make them *highly inflammable* in case of a fire.

The Cost of Living—Going Up

Although it's possible to live cheaply in California, don't count on it. Housing costs have been going up 20 percent a year and more in Orange County (between Los Angeles and San Diego), West Los Angeles and, to some extent, in San Diego. Food costs about the same as in the New York City area. However, the savings are big on climate-related items—lower fuel bills, gas and electricity, no need for winter clothes, less home maintenance (no storms, less repainting), lower car upkeep (no snow tires, antifreeze, winter wear and tear). There are a number of big discount stores with big bargains—chiefly in the metropolitan areas.

Taxes—Big Breaks for Seniors

California still has one of the best senior citizens (age 62 or over) property tax refund laws. If your household income is $12,000 a year or less, you can get a cash refund on property taxes paid on your *residence* (not business or income property). Refunds are on a sliding scale, ranging from 96 percent at the highest to 4 percent at the lowest, based on the first $8,500 of assessed value. And the Senior Citizens Tax Rent Assistance Law authorizes refunds to renters 62 years or older whose total household income is $12,000 or less. For further information write Franchise Tax Board, Senior Citizens Program, P.O. Box 1588, Sacramento, CA 95807.

California also allows homeowners, age 62 or older, with combined household incomes not exceeding $33,600 to delay all or part of the tax on their homes. The state pays the tax and puts a lien on the property; interest of 7 percent is charged each year of the amounts postponed. The amount isn't payable until the home is sold or the owners die, in which case their estate or heirs would pay.

And thanks to the recently-passed Proposition 13, property taxes, both commercial and residential, are limited to *1 percent of the property's market value in 1975*, plus a small fraction to pay off existing bond issues. Tax increases on property are limited to 2 percent a year until the property is sold, at which time it could be reassessed to reflect prevailing market value.

State Income Tax—California personal income tax brackets are adjusted each year for the amount of inflation over 3 percent. The tax is levied on the entire taxable income of California residents and on the income of non-residents obtained from sources within California.

In 1983, rates range from 1 percent on amounts to about $3,000 for single taxpayers (about $6,000 if married) to 11 percent on amounts over $25,000 if single ($50,000 married). Married couples filing a joint return get a $64 credit, single persons $32. Married renters get a $137 credit, single renters $60. Surviving spouses get same credit as married couples.

For further information on tax write: Franchise Tax Board, Aeroject Center, Sacramento, CA 95876.

State sales tax—is 6 percent throughout the state. Grocery items and some minor products are exempt. Some communities levy an additional sales tax.

Housing—It All Depends

If you must live in the best section of the popular retirement areas— bring lots of money. The lowest-priced two-bedroom house in Orange County might sell for $100,000. But you can find housing for $50,000 and up at reasonable distances inland from the popular coastal areas.

Some of the best values (rents around $250 a month) are in the numerous retirement communities throughout Southern California. These are high-, medium-, and low-rise residential centers for seniors, *strictly* regulated by state and local authorities, with entrance requirements and rents based on income. They range from luxury-level life care to modestly priced straight rental apartments. Among their advantages—security, medical facilities, a wealth of recreational activities, freedom from house maintenance, and functional, modern design at sensible prices. The one restriction is that children aren't allowed on a permanent basis. In some you can either buy a unit outright or rent as long as you wish; many offer trial rentals for a few weeks or months. But there's often a waiting period for housing. Some new two- to three-bedroom housing starts at about $45,000 2 to 3 hours inland; the prices go up steadily the closer you get to the coast. In Los Angeles hundreds of people have camped out all night for the privilege of buying two-bedroom homes for $90,000 and up the next morning. In 1983 the median price of a house in California was around $125,000.

For general information on retirement communities and other possibilities in Southern California, write to:

California State Department of Commerce
1030 13th St. Suite 200
Sacramento, CA 95814

California Department on Aging
1020 19th St.
Sacramento, CA 95814

American Association of Retired Persons
215 Long Beach Boulevard
Long Beach, CA 90802

Or write to the local chamber of commerce if you have a particular city in mind (see later sections).

Mobile home living is a very popular life style in Southern California. California has over 2,000 mobile home parks, some built around lakes, many with a community center, golf course, and plenty of recreational activities. Mobile homes today—no longer mobile, since they are imbedded in a solid foundation—are surprisingly spacious and contain all the latest appliances. Average cost for a two-bedroom unit is $20,000 to $30,000. Mobile homes free you from maintenance expenses and property taxes, although state "vehicle" taxes on a $20,000 unit might run $250 annually. Many mobile home parks are true communities—attractive, well-planned, alive with clubs, get-togethers, a host of other activities—and are located within a short drive of movies, shopping malls, medical and cultural centers. There's a monthly land rental fee of from $75 to $150, which includes gas, water, trash pickup, and city services such as police and fire protection. Some newer parks are set up as condominium communities; you buy your lot and become a member of the park association, responsible for the maintenance of service and recreational facilities.

For further information:

> Western Mobilehome Association
> 3380 14th Street Suite 114
> Riverside, CA 92501

Medical Care—Some of the Best Anywhere

California now ranks second nationwide in the number of doctors, dentists, and nurses, and first in the number of hospital and nursing home beds. The state has 638 hospitals with a total of 123,090 beds. There are also 1,618 nursing homes with 115,560 beds and 2,527 personal care homes with 35,396 beds. However, a semiprivate hospital room averages $170.12 daily—$37 more than the national average (only New York is higher). There are some 47,223 doctors, which gives the state a doctor-to-patient ratio of 1 to 463—the best in the Sunbelt. California has long been an innovator in health care. It pioneered in group medical practice and health maintenance organizations (HMOs).

Culture—Just a Short Drive Away

It's hard to live anywhere in California without being near cultural activities. Symphonies, art galleries, museums, theaters, adult education courses, and other activities are nearly everywhere. The California state university—one of the best in the country—has branches throughout the state. Many offer a wide range of adult courses. Claremont, a few miles east of downtown Los Angeles, is the site of the famous Claremont colleges: Pomona, Scripps, Harvey Mudd, and others. Other local colleges, high schools, and community colleges offer programs for seniors.

Services to Seniors—Outstanding

With the 60-and-older population expected to increase by 25 percent between 1975 and 1985 (to represent 15 percent of the state's 21,185,000 population) legislators and other leaders have paid particular attention to this powerful political group. Most communities have senior centers, Golden Age Clubs, and chapters of senior organizations. In some areas these groups have obtained discounts on drugs, clothing, and other items. The California Department on Aging is especially active in planning many programs, including hot meal programs in local senior centers, churches, and schools. The California legislature has introduced a number of bills— particularly on nursing homes and home care—to aid the state's elderly. And California is the first state that allows people to make "living wills" prohibiting the use of respirators, dialysis machines, and other "unusual or artificial means" to sustain life during the terminal stage of an illness. The state has also banned mandatory retirement. And California's Supplemental Security Income (SSI) and Medicaid (Medi-Cal) are higher than in other states.

For further information on senior centers, area agencies on aging, or other local agencies, write to the local city hall or county courthouse.

1. SAN DIEGO—"NEXT DOOR TO EDEN"

San Diego (pop. 803,000 city; 1,650,000 county) is the most southern of the major Southern California retirement areas. It is about 25 minutes from Mexico.

Although I lived in California for years, and traveled throughout the state, it was years before I finally got down to San Diego. That seems to have happened to many people—as well as industry. While the Los Angeles and San Francisco areas were being developed—people pouring in, buildings shooting up, factories belching fumes, automobiles choking the streets —San Diego was left virtually untouched. As a result, today it is still very much like California used to be—clean, uncrowded, with very few of the smog, earthquake, and other problems that plague its more sought-after neighbors.

San Diego, founded by the Spanish, is the oldest town in California and was the capital of the state when it belonged to Mexico. Spanish influence is everywhere in San Diego—white homes with red tile roofs, even shopping centers in Spanish design. It's a delightful combination of the old and the new, a mixture of Spanish, Mexican, and American modern.

San Diego is big enough to have a great variety of facilities and entertainment, but not so big that you feel lost. Unlike other Southern California cities, San Diego has a good public transportation system.

One testimony to San Diego's attractiveness is that 1 out of every 10 U.S. Navy officers—most of whom are well-traveled—retires in San Diego. The hook-shaped harbor is one of the 10 best in the world. I saw what must have been a fleet of 100 ships tied up along the downtown wharves. It was a dazzling spectacle. Many of the bigger Navy ships hold open house on weekends; townspeople climb aboard to have a look, making for an interesting Sunday afternoon.

Another diversion is a jaunt to Tijuana, Mexico, a 25-minute drive away. Tijuana has grown from a dusty, fly-ridden, sleezy town into a booming metropolis with a race track, jai alai frontons, bullfights (don't go unless you have a strong stomach), and duty-free shopping—now even more of a bargain since the devaluation of the peso. You need no passport to cross into Tijuana. This is one of the busiest boundaries in the world with some 35 million crossings a year.

Climate and Environment. Located on the Pacific Ocean at the southern tip of California, San Diego County has nearly 70 miles of ocean shore, making water sports a favorite recreation, and water views a delight. There is a sizable amount of "clean" industry in the area—aerospace, electronics, research organizations, shipbuilding, tuna fishing. San Diego is also an agricultural center—citrus fruits, subtropical fruits, and flowers. Some famous research organizations are here—the U.S. Naval Electronics Laboratory Center and Mt. Palomar Observatory. Job opportunities for seniors are limited.

The climate is a big attraction. There is no sleet or ice, thunderstorms are rare, and snow has never been recorded. It rarely gets hot, and nights are cool. The average August maximum—about 81° F., the average January low—47° F. Rainfall is about 10 inches, mostly from December through March. Humidity averages 67 percent annually. Near the coast the air is moist (which is great for ladies concerned about their complexions, but could bother others suffering from asthma, sinus, or arthritis). About 5 or 10 miles inland it gets drier—also warmer in summers, cooler in winters. There is just about any gradation of climate you could want within a few miles of San Diego. I drove from sea level at the coast to an altitude of 6,000 feet—getting cooler and drier—within an hour.

Medical Facilities. San Diego has 28 general hospitals, over 60 nursing and convalescent homes, more than 1,800 doctors and 900 dentists. Among the outstanding health centers in the area: the Salk Institute for Biological Studies (devoted to, among other things, seeking a cure for cancer), Scripps Clinic and Research Foundation, the University of California, San Diego School of Medicine, and the Veterans Administration Hospital.

A semiprivate room averages $155.42 daily—about $15 a day below the state average.

Housing. Almost every type of housing is available, from retirement hotels with downtown convenience and marina-side condominiums in Coronado to adult community homes (for those age 45 or 50 and over) in Rancho Bernardo. Retirees have a choice of seaside homes, hillside homes with sea or mountain views, ranch-type homes in rural settings, condominiums, garden apartments, high-rise apartments with two-bedroom units starting at $45,000. Of special interest to retirees are two-bedroom condominiums starting at $55,000. Rental units are plentiful; average for an unfurnished one-bedroom apartment is $250 to $350 a month, a two-bedroom unit is $300 to $500 a month. There is a big choice of mobile home parks, some limited to adults. The newer parks offer community centers with group activities; most have recreational facilities such as a pool. Rentals are from $75 to $300; average space rental is around $125.

San Diego has an abundance of living accommodations expressly for retired persons: residential homes offering room and meals, facilities offering individual apartments with meals, lifetime-care homes with an entrance fee and a monthly fee for care, including hospitalization. Rentals are from $300 a month in some retirement hotels to over $2,500 a month in luxury retirement developments in such fashionable communities as La Jolla.

Desirable adult communities: *Rancho Bernardo,* with vast shopping, medical, and recreational facilities; *Sun Park* in the inland community of Lake San Marcos, 31 miles north of downtown San Diego, with an 80-acre recreational lake.

For more housing information, including names and addresses of specific developments, write:

"Community Guide to San Diego"   Special Service for Seniors
Security Pacific Bank   Dept. of Housing & Social Services
Box 2087   202 C St.
Los Angeles, CA 90051   San Diego, CA 92101

Cost of Living. Costs in San Diego are slightly lower than in Los Angeles. It will cost a retired couple over $9,000 to live on an intermediate budget in Los Angeles, but they could do so in San Diego for $8,772 a year. Seniors can take advantage of many free or low-cost city-sponsored events such as concerts, festivals, operas, and art exhibits.

Recreation and Culture. San Diego offers virtually unlimited year-round recreational and cultural activities. With its vast shoreline, water sports are big: swimming, surfing, boating, fishing (ocean fishing is free to qualified seniors, pier fishing is free to everyone). There are 15 fresh-water lakes nearby, many with campsites. There are 66 golf courses, 2 enormous parks, numerous neighborhood and community parks. Other activities—square dancing, crafts (classes offered by the city Recreation Department), and rockhounding (San Diego Mineral and Gem Society has frequent and interesting field trips). Spectator sports—professional football, basketball. And there's *whale watching* during the migrating season, when the enormous mammals cruise past San Diego viewing points.

In the cultural heart of San Diego, Balboa Park, are the Fine Arts Museum, Museum of Natural History, Aerospace Museum, Museum of Man, Space Theater and Science Center, and the Old Globe Theater, where a Shakespeare festival is presented every summer. You can also see plays, dance, opera, symphonies, and so on in the other theaters and auditoriums. Numerous events are sponsored by the city—concerts and operas in the parks, pageants, special exhibits, walking tours, sports events. Don't forget the San Diego Zoo, considered one of the best in the world—a must for visiting grandchildren.

Special Services for Seniors. Senior services are practically a small industry in San Diego. There are 180 senior citizens clubs in the county. San Diego's Sunday newspaper devotes 2 full columns to the "senior scene," as well as daily reporting of senior activities. And for $4 a year you can subscribe to *Senior World*, a monthly tabloid describing senior events and activities. For further information write: Senior World Publications, 4640 Jewell St., San Diego, CA 92109.

And for further information on San Diego write to:

San Diego Convention and
   Visitors Bureau
1200 Third Ave., Suite 824
San Diego, CA 92101

San Diego Park & Recreation Dept.
Senior Citizen Activities
Conference Building, Balboa Park
San Diego, CA 92101

This is a good place to start any inquiries about San Diego because they'll start *you* out with a Senior ID card that will save you money or get you in free at a lot of places.

Communities Near San Diego

A peninsula, linked to San Diego by the 2-mile Bay Bridge, *Coronado* (pop. 20,000) is home to many service-retired people. It has a small-town atmosphere, good shopping, and dependable public transportation in and out of San Diego. For the luxury-minded there are new high-rise, shore-line condominiums for sale or rent; also Coronado Cays, a new water-oriented home development on manmade fingers of land jutting into Glorietta Bay.

For further information:

Chamber of Commerce
Coronado, CA 92118

La Jolla (pop. 30,000) must be one of the most beautiful places on earth—miles of sandy beaches, clear blue water, spectacular shore caves for diving and snorkeling. The Salk Institute for Biological Studies is here, along with the Scripps Clinic and Research Foundation, Gulf General Atomic Research, and the Scripps Institute of Oceanography (don't miss the spectacular exhibits and underwater demonstrations). Other attractions include art galleries and museums, golf, tennis, fine restaurants, fine shops. The homes are handsome, but good two-bedroom units *start* at $150,000. La Jolla has 400 doctors. Residents use local and San Diego's hospital facilities, assuring good medical care.

For further information:

Chamber of Commerce
La Jolla, CA 92037

Del Mar (pop. 5,000) borders La Jolla on the north and is as aristocratic as its neighbor. Del Mar attracts the horsey set, and the thoroughbred racing season lures top stables and riders from everywhere. Del Mar offers surfing, swimming, boating, and fishing, and is surrounded by 12 golf courses. Seafood is a specialty at the outstanding restaurants (I particularly liked corbina—one of the fish from the local waters). Two-bedroom houses here start at $150,000. Del Mar has a medical clinic, 30 doctors in the area (assuring excellent medical care), and access to hospitals in the San Diego area.

For further information:

Chamber of Commerce
Del Mar, CA 92014

Solana Beach (pop. 4,000) is the next town north and is considered part of the San Diego beach complex. Solana Beach is lined with apartments and condominiums ($100,000 and up for two-bedroom units), many owned for investment purposes and rented out.

For further information:

Chamber of Commerce
Solana Beach, CA 92075

Rancho Bernardo (pop. 17,000) is a beautiful little enclave 23 miles from downtown San Diego, but with all the city services—police, fire, library, sewers, trash pickup, and regular bus service to downtown or the Mexican border (25 cents for seniors). Inland, Rancho Bernardo enjoys one of the best year-round climates in Southern California: January highs average 67° F., July highs 81° F. January lows average 44° F., July lows, 63° F. It's relatively smog-free with wonderful ocean breezes—except for occasional Santa Anas when the wind blows from the desert.

A planned community in the manner of Reston, Virginia, Rancho Bernardo is located on 5,800 acres of gently rolling valley facing the Laguna Mountains. It's divided into different areas: all-adult with two-bedroom single homes and condominiums from $60,000 to over more than $200,000, and family areas with no age limits and housing in the similar price range. Rentals are sometimes available at about $500 a month.

Rancho Bernardo offers good medical facilities, cultural and recreational opportunities, and delightful shopping centers including the Spanish-style Mercado with offbeat shops and boutiques. There's golf, tennis, riding, swimming, well-equipped community centers with craft workrooms, as well as drama groups, square dancing, bridge, and numerous activities, including public service groups. The cost of living may be a bit high, but it is less than you'd expect to pay for what you get in services and the delightful life style.

For further information:

Rancho Bernardo Information Center
Rancho Bernardo, CA 92128

San Clemente (pop. 24,000) is about 55 miles north of San Diego (61 miles south of Los Angeles), and it borders Camp Pendleton, the U.S. Marine base. Its main street teems with bars, backpackers, and "Baja Bugs" (souped-up VWs), creating a merciless din. However, San Clemente improves when you head back to the streets and the homes in the hills. Housing is more expensive here than in other coastal areas; two-bedroom houses, when available, sell from $100,000. Medical services are good: The San Clemente General Hospital of 116 beds and 2 other general-service hospitals have a total of 508 beds. There are some 50 doctors in the area— about 1 doctor per 440 residents. You'll also find a wealth of recreational activities: swimming, fishing, golf, tennis, skeet and trap shooting, lawn bowling; also some theater and light opera. There are 80 clubs in the area, including senior citizens groups.

For further information:

> Chamber of Commerce
> San Clemente, CA 92672

Laguna Hills (pop. 19,000). Up the coast, north of San Clemente, lies *Laguna Beach* (pop. 15,000) with *Laguna Hills* inland toward Mission Viejo, home of a Rossmoor Leisure World. There are 1,300 acres in Laguna Hills now being developed. Villas and condominiums cost from $60,000 to $200,000 for two- to three-bedroom units. You do the inside maintenance; the management takes care of the outside maintenance.

Laguna Hills includes all services and facilities, including department stores, a professional building, coffee shops, hotels and motels, restaurants, large markets, a tire center, post office, drug stores, a hospital, convalescent homes, churches, banks, and so on. There are 200 doctors in the area, providing adequate medical care. There is also a wide variety of activities, from horseback riding, golf, tennis, dancing, arts and crafts, and courses at a community college.

For further information:

> Rossmoor Laguna Hills
> 23532 Paseo de Valencia
> Laguna Hills, CA 92653

For further information on housing and facilities in the 26 cities within Orange County (which includes the area we've just discussed), visit or write the Home Shopper Information Center, 1477 S. Manchester, Anaheim, CA 92802.

2. ESCONDIDO AREA—RETIREMENT COUNTRY WITH A BIG "R"

Although only 30 miles northeast of San Diego, *Escondido* (pop. 57,100) merits attention in its own right. It is an important retirement city and the center of a highly desirable retirement area that caters to lower- and middle-income retirees. Retirees here often work to supplement their incomes. More than 133 manufacturing plants including some in electronics, sports equipment, aircraft manufacturing—National Cash Register, Singer Company, Sony, Burroughs, Teledyne Aero-Cal—plus other employers (schools, hospitals, insurance companies, department stores) provide jobs in the area.

Escondido lies in a sheltered valley with mountains climbing to 5,000 feet. Palomar Mountain, with its famed observatory, rises over 6,000 feet, yet the ocean beaches are only 35 minutes away.

Climate and Environment. Escondido enjoys about 280 clear, sunny days a year. Winter afternoons average in the middle 60s, summer afternoons in the high 80s. Temperatures reach over 90° F. about 44 days each summer. The surrounding mountains keep out extreme winds most of the time. Nights are generally cool all year. Humidity averages 40 to 50 percent during the day in winter to 90 percent at night. In summer it ranges from 35 to 50 percent during the day to 75 percent at night.

Medical Facilities. There is a comparatively new 300-bed general hospital, 140 doctors, and 58 dentists. In addition, San Diego's half-dozen top hospitals and scores of medical specialists are within an hour's drive.

Housing. Five suburban residential areas within 10 miles of Escondido offer two-bedroom homes priced from about $50,000 to $200,000. There are 30 mobile home parks (some of the finest in Southern California) ; also apartments and duplexes renting from $200 to $400 a month.

Cost of Living. Living costs here are lower than in most other areas of Southern California. An army of stores compete with each other, offering many more bargains than are available in isolated retirement communities.

Recreation and Culture. Besides year-round sports activities (5 golf courses nearby), Escondido has an excellent library, little theater and repertory groups, a philharmonic association, horse shows, square dancing, concerts, outing clubs, and all sorts of flower enthusiasts. It also offers an extensive adult education program—10,000-student Palomar College is only 10 minutes away. If you can't find what you're seeking in Escondido, downtown San Diego is only 45 minutes away.

Special Services to Seniors. The Senior Service Center is one of the best I've ever seen; big and well-equipped, it provides indoor recreation and other services for nearly 40 senior groups. Attendance averages over 3,500 a week. Most activities are free to all seniors. An extensive adult education program offers courses in schools throughout the area—all free to persons age 60 and over. There is also a broad sports and recreation program for seniors at the many parks, and a lunch program at the center.

For further information:

Chamber of Commerce
Escondido, CA 92025

Lawrence Welk's Country Club Village (pop. 1,000) is an adult retirement mobile home park with a golf course, clubhouse, hospital (8 miles away), heated swimming pool, shuffleboard, dancing. There is a fine restaurant and motel, but no apartments or condominiums. Mobile home spaces rent from $180 to $400 a month.

For further information:

Lawrence Welk's Country Club Village
8975 Champagne Boulevard
Escondido, CA 92026

San Marcos (pop. 16,000) is a small community some 3 miles west of Escondido and only about 10 miles from the ocean. San Marcos shares the electronics, aircraft, sports, and other industrial and manufacturing facilities of Escondido, assuring employment opportunities in the area. Some 5,000 retirees here live in mobile home parks in the area; rentals average $250 a month. Other costs are moderate. The climate is about the same as in Escondido, except for a little more morning and evening clouds and fog. *Lake San Marcos* is a manmade lake 1⅓ miles long. People who live on the lakeside have docks and boats, but anyone owning property can have a boat on the lake. The majority of homes are not on the lake, although many have a view from the gently rolling hills and winding streets. There are also homes around an 18-hole championship golf course (there are 12 other golf courses within a 20-minute drive).

A new development, *Villages of San Marcos,* is being leveled now, and individual homes will be built there for sale from $75,000 to $100,000. Condominiums, duplexes, and single-family homes already built at the lake development, ranging in price from $50,000 to $150,000 for lakeside sites, are on sale now. The 1,700-acre development includes an inn and a recrea-

tion center open to all residents. Many service organizations are represented in the area, and you can socialize at everything from dances to
hobby classes.

For further information:

Chamber of Commerce
San Marcos, CA 92069

Ramona (pop. 15,000) is in the opposite direction from San Marcos;
it is also opposite in personality—no industry. It offers "country living"
for those who like to raise citrus fruit, chickens, horses, vegetables, and so
on. The climate is a little cooler than in Escondido. Many ex-military and
former government employees live here. Two-bedroom houses sell for
around $75,000, and rentals, when available, average $350 a month for a
two-bedroom apartment. There is a 24-hour clinic operated by three resident doctors. Ramona has medical services available at a retirement home,
and access to medical and other services in Escondido and Hemet (see
below). Ramona is probably best known for the Ramona Outdoor Play, a
romance of early California that is in its fiftieth year. The play's worldwide
fame has attracted almost 2,000,000 spectators during the past 50 years.

For further information:

Chamber of Cemmerce
Ramona, CA 92065

3. INLAND TO HEMET—DISCOVERING
THE SAN JACINTO VALLEY

This is an off-the-beaten-path retirement area about 83 miles north of
San Diego and just 85 miles east of Los Angeles that is well worth looking
into. The San Jacinto Valley is a sunny, well-irrigated, rich valley (if you
like avocados you can grow them in your backyard), dotted with a number
of growing communities. One of the choicest is Hemet—a city that has
grown from a one-horse farming town to a thriving, modern, handsome
city serving a surrounding population of over 100,000. Far enough from
Los Angeles and Riverside, Hemet catches little of the smog that irritates
those two communities. What it does catch are many retirees escaping
Los Angeles with its big-city problems. The valley gets warm in the summer, but the nights are cool—and the days are comfortable most of the
year.

Hemet is filled with civic boosters who are proud of their city and the well-planned way it's growing. It has a palm-lined main street with wide sidewalks and attractive, modern stores; a new civic center; hospital, library, schools, and new homes that offer a lot of value for the money. A town planning commission keeps a watchful eye on community development, successfully avoiding the congestion and other problems less fortunate towns have succumbed to. Although the valley is flat and dry, without many trees, Hemet gets a good view of Mt. Jacinto, a nearly 2-mile-high mountain providing scenery and recreation. Hemet is an ideal spot for those who like the feeling of wide open spaces, yet the convenience of nearby big cities (Los Angeles and San Diego) and the ocean (85 miles away).

Hemet is a homogeneous community—practically everyone is in a similar income bracket, and practically everyone goes to church (there are 32 churches in town). There's little crime or juvenile delinquency. Over 4,000 people are enrolled in adult education courses—about the same as the number of children attending elementary school!

Climate and Environment. Many people with rheumatic and respiratory ailments come to Hemet for its warm, dry climate. The sun shines all year and there are about 10 inches of rainfall during the winter. The summers are warm, with average high about 95° F. But the nights are cool, around 55° F. April is the coldest month, the average high around 65° F. From January through March it's usually in the high 60s. Humidity ranges from 87 percent to 55 percent in January; 81 percent to 31 percent in July. The annual average at noon is 40 percent.

Medical Facilities. Besides a health center staffed by Riverside County, Hemet has a 252-bed general hospital, 5 convalescent hospitals, 67 doctors, 35 dentists.

Housing. Good housing is available for a lot less money than in the more well-known areas of Southern California. Individual two-bedroom homes start at about $45,000. You can also choose from mobile homes and condominiums, and a few retirement homes that provide 3 meals a day and personal service.

Art Linkletter's Sierra Dawn Estates is near here, a mobile home estate with a small golf course, swimming pools, hobby shops, and so on. Large mobile homes sell for $25,000 and up. At nearby Valle Hermosa Adult/Retirement Community, two-bedroom homes sell for $35,000 and up. Residential acreage sells for $25,000 an acre and up; farm land for $7,000 an acre and up.

Cost of Living. Just about everything costs less in Hemet and the surrounding areas than elsewhere in Southern California. Two-bedroom houses sell from $45,000 and two-bedroom apartments rent for about $300 a month. You can often buy fruits, vegetables, eggs, and chickens at road-side stands for a fraction of the supermarket cost.

Recreation and Culture. Tennis courts, golf courses, and lakes are available year-round. Because the terrain is flat, Hemet is a perfect place for cycling. There are 2 movie theaters, bowling, a library, a little theater group, a museum, the Ramona Bowl with outdoor concerts, and the Farmers' Fair in August, complete with a Western rodeo and championship competition. The nearby San Jacinto Mountains offer hiking, camping, and fishing.

Special Services to Seniors. Hemet has adult education courses, a special library program for adults, and home delivery of books for the ill or handicapped. Weston Park has a "rec" room for adults. There are several fraternal, social, and church organizations.

For further information:

> Chamber of Commerce
> 528 East Florida Avenue
> Hemet, CA 92343

Other Retirement Communities in the Area

Sun City (pop. 8,250) is a retirement community about 20 miles west of Hemet with rows of neat houses that lie under the desert sun. A mountain range looms in the background; lawns and shrubs carpet the foreground, and recently planted trees offer cooling shade. Sun City has a complete range of recreational activities—golf, hobby and craft shops, swimming pools, various clubs. It also has good values in homes (modern two-bedroom houses start around $60,000) low property taxes and a dry climate with temperatures in the 100s in summer (you need air conditioning). There are churches of all denominations, as well as most civic, fraternal, social, recreational, and religious groups. Sun City has 2 medical centers and 20 doctors, but you must travel to Hemet, 20 miles away, for general hospital care. A minibus operates in town on a regular schedule, and bus transportation is available to outside communities.

For further information:

> Chamber of Commerce
> Sun City, CA 92381

Riverside (pop. 155,000) is about 55 miles east of Los Angeles. Riverside is the key city of Riverside County; when I first visited it 30 years ago it was a clean, quiet, residential paradise. Unfortunately, smog has moved in and the city has taken on the grime and tackiness of some of the Los Angeles basin. Some older, wealthier residents have deserted the area, and you can find some good buys in two-bedroom houses in the $55,000 to $75,000 range. Hospital costs are lower here: $140.25 daily for a semiprivate room versus the state average of $170.12 daily. Medical care is adequate; there are some 350 doctors in the area. Riverside is rich in culture and recreation. It is home of the Mission Inn, a mission-style building which houses collections of art objects, bells, and pioneer relics; a municipal and an Indian museum; a March Air Force Base; Riverside International Raceway (for automobile testing and racing); and several colleges and universities—the University of California at Riverside, California Baptist College, Loma Linda University.

While Riverside still retains some of its former charm, be sure to check out the smog conditions if you plan to live in or near there.

For further information:

Chamber of Commerce
Riverside, CA 92501

Rancho California (pop. 4,050). The promoters say this is the only major agrarian development in the West. Built on nearly 100,000 acres, it spreads out for a total of 25 miles on either side of a highway. Vail Ranch was one of the last of the great cattle empires—before it was bought by Kaiser Aluminum and Aetna Life Insurance. Vail Lake, 850 acres, offers fishing, boating, and other water activities. Some 1,500 residential units have been built in five separate residential neighborhoods. Development includes apartments, condominiums, detached single-family units, and a 182-unit mobile home park. Prices start around $55,000.

For further information:

Rancho California
Rancho California, CA 92390

San Bernardino (pop. 110,000). Although this town is also plagued by smog at times, it does offer some retirement advantages. It is the home of Norton Air Force Base, which offers commissary and medical advantages to retired military persons. And it is the heart of Southern California vacation land, with 22 parks, swimming pools, tennis, golf, and other outdoor recreation. Cultural activities include the Civic Light Opera, San Bernardino Symphony Orchestra, 5 art associations, and the Arrowhead Allied Arts Council, blending year-round activities in the areas of stage, concert, and art programs. The average price of houses is around $60,000, and there are 15 residential-suburban areas within 10 miles of San Bernardino offering homes from $45,000 to $200,000. The area also has approximately 25 mobile home parks. Some 300 doctors practice here, assuring good health care.

For further information:

Chamber of Commerce
San Bernardino, CA 92402

Through the San Bernardino range runs Cajon Pass. This is high, beautiful desert country: windswept hills border the back of the San Bernardino range and flow across wide, sandy plains to other mountains of the Mojave Desert. The colors and vistas are glorious to behold, although there is no natural green, except where you find agriculture or irrigation of some sort.

Apple Valley (pop. 18,000) is one of the area's many ranches and resorts. Famous because of Roy Rogers and Dale Evans, the town rose out of the desert in 1946 and used its large underground water supply to create an oasis for retirement and vacation. There are complete shopping facilities and other services, including a medical clinic and 25 doctors in the area. The Apple Valley Inn is a complete resort complex with golf, tennis, riding, lawn games, heated pool, hayrides, dancing, and entertainment. Retirees live in a variety of housing. Some mobile home parks have average monthly rents of $125. More affluent retirees live on ranches ($5,000 and up an acre). More conventional housing is available in nearby Victorville.

Victorville (pop. 25,000) is a fair-sized city with all services. Prices for housing vary tremendously according to location and degree of comfort (you'll need air conditioning in summer and some heat in winter). Some retirees have moved into Westlake Village north of here and have found good two-bedroom housing in the $50,000 range.

For further information:

Chambers of Commerce at:
Apple Valley, CA 92307
Victoria, CA 92392

Palm Springs-Palm Desert (total pop. 32,000). To have a home here you have to be either a sun fanatic or rich enough to come out just for the winter. From November through April, the average maximum temperature is 90° F., from June through September it's over 100° F. Sometimes it rains; smog is an occasional problem. There's a good hospital, 300 doctors, elegant shopping, lots of recreation and cultural events. At the Palm Desert Country Club Estates, hundreds of expensive retirement homes (around $100,000 and up) border an 18-hole golf course. If you want to take a look, you can rent a one-bedroom "condo" for about $100 a day and up during the winter.
For further information:

Chambers of Commerce at:
Palm Springs, CA 92262
Palm Desert, CA 92260

4. "UP NORTH" TO LOS ANGELES

It takes less than 2 hours to drive from Hemet west to Los Angeles, but it's like another world—from a tranquil, unhurried, small town where everybody knows everybody to fighting traffic in the noise and congestion and anonymity of one of the world's largest cities. Instead of a neat, orderly main street there is chaos—cars going off in all directions, buildings of all shapes and sizes and states of disrepair, air choked with fumes and smog, crowds on the sidewalks, billboards, neon signs, urban sprawl.

Yet for all its disadvantages, there are a lot of good reasons to live in Los Angeles. It's an exciting city with plenty to do. And there are many beautiful areas in which to live, including nearly smog-free sections along the coast. The climate and weather much of the time are terrific, just like sunny California in the movies. And the city can be spectacular. I still get a thrill seeing the sparkling lights of the Hollywood hills at night and the footprints of once-famous movie stars in the cement in front of Grauman's Chinese Theatre on Hollywood Boulevard.

Climate and Environment. Los Angeles *County* comprises 78 cities with a population of over 8,000,000 people. This, plus the 4 other counties of the Greater Los Angeles area, totals over 11,000,000. The environment and climate vary depending on where in this vast area you live. Near the ocean the weather is cool—in the 60s and 70s in mid-summer, thanks to the ocean breezes. A few miles inland it can be in the 80s on the same day. Farther inland, in the San Fernando Valley, it might be in the 90s that day. Generally, you can expect mild winters (average 60.6° F.) and warm summers (average 72.5° F.), with a rainy season (annual total 6.54 inches) from November through February. Annual humidity averages 63.3 percent. Many parts of the area are still serene and beautiful—with Spanish-style homes or garden apartments built around a landscaped courtyard with a pool or fountain. There are beautiful shopping centers—overwhelming ones like Century City—palm-lined streets, gardens blooming with spectacular subtropical flowers. But many other neighborhoods are crowded and dangerous, victims of the same urban blight afflicting cities across the country. Some of the world's nicest places to live are in Los Angeles—and some of the world's worst.

Medical Facilities. Los Angeles has many excellent hospitals, including those connected with the medical school of the University of California system. Some 10,000 doctors and dentists have been attracted to the area by the combination of outdoor living and big-city stimulation. Los Angeles has 186 hospitals with 34,683 beds, and 424 nursing homes with 39,795 beds. A semiprivate hospital room averages $193.96 daily, about $20 more than the state average.

Housing. The Los Angeles area has practically every type of retirement life style—condominiums, retirement homes and hotels, mobile home parks, camper units, even houseboats moored more or less permanently in the vast marinas of the area. High- and low-rise rental apartments are available— from $300 to $500 a month. But if you're thinking of buying a house, you might be in for a shock. *Time* magazine, in its October 11, 1976, issue, reported this about the incredible real estate boom in Los Angeles:

Despite lashing rainstorms, more than 50 families last month camped out for days in cars and tents around the sales office of the El Toro Sunwood housing development near Los Angeles. Their purpose was to be near the head of the line when 34 new homes, going for $58,000 to $67,000 went on sale. Three weeks ago, 650 people turned up at the sales office of the Leisure World development in Laguna Hills, California, to participate in a lottery. Those whose names were drawn from a barrel had the privilege of paying up to $128,000 for one of the development's 132 new houses. In Huntington Harbor, a marina complex south of Los Angeles, Christiana Company recently offered 52 houses, ranging in price from $104,000 to $195,000. In all, 111 people showed up, and the firm also had to resort to a lottery.

Land Rush. These are but a few of the examples of the house-buying frenzy that is sweeping Southern California. Largely because of the region's improving economy and expanding population, the long pent-up demand for the limited available housing has resulted in scenes reminiscent of the Oklahoma land rush.

However, a few two-bedroom homes are available in the area from $50,000 and up.

For more information, write to:

> Chamber of Commerce
> P.O. Box 3696 Terminal Annex
> Los Angeles, CA 90051
>
> Southern California Visitors Council
> 705 W. Seventh Street
> Los Angeles, CA 90017

Inland, at varying distances from the coast where land is plentiful and less expensive, you are less likely to come up against the land rush. There are also a great many mobile home communities in outlying areas of Los Angeles (where rents average around $100 a month), and adult communities far enough away to still be reasonable.

Cost of Living. Once you've licked the housing problem, the cost of living can be surprisingly low. One of the big savings comes from the climate—you save on fuel, utilities, winter clothing, and winter upkeep of house and car. There are good buys in the many big supermarkets and discount stores (clothing and appliances especially). Eating out can be inexpensive—especially in some of the good Mexican restaurants. The big blow is housing. A resident of Los Angeles spends nearly 30 percent of his income on shelter compared to the urban average of 23 percent.

Recreation and Culture. You can find almost anything in the Los Angeles area: Learn how to use an awl, play a zither, listen to the best in rock-and-roll, hear a Chinese one-string fiddle or a 100-piece symphony orchestra; take any number of courses at the many schools and colleges; see plays, dance, opera; play golf, tennis, swim, ride, shoot, boat, and fish year-round. There are museums, art galleries, shopping centers, and places like Disneyland to take visiting grandchildren—and their parents.

Special Services to Seniors. The Los Angeles City Department of Recreation and Parks, Senior Citizen Programs, works with the Los Angeles Federation of Senior Citizen Clubs to help plan events, recreational activities, holiday parties, and keep them informed of current legislative issues of concern to senior citizens; clubs receive monthly mailings of information on discounts and special events for seniors. In addition, the program includes the Senior Citizen Nutrition Program, the Retired Senior Volunteer Program (RSVP) and Senior Companion Program.

For further information:

Los Angeles Dept. of Recreation and Parks
Senior Citizen Programs
City Hall East, 13th Floor
200 North Main St.
Los Angeles, CA 90012

All Around Los Angeles

There are so many possible places to live in and around the Los Angeles area that the only way to pick a place is to come out, rent for a while, and do some serious looking. Facts worth repeating: The farther inland you go, the warmer it gets *and the better values in homes.* To avoid smog your best bet is the beachfront cities— *Santa Monica* (90406), *Long Beach* (90802), *Seal Beach* (90740) (check the Leisure World here). Remember, the climate can change radically in a few miles—check carefully before deciding. Also, if you want to work after retirement, the Los Angeles area with all its industry and retail businesses has good prospects. To many people the problems of living in the Los Angeles area are nothing compared to all the activity and cultural stimulation it offers. You may agree.

5. COASTING ALONG TO BEAUTIFUL SANTA BARBARA

Santa Barbara (pop. 75,000 city; 175,000 metropolitan) is the northernmost retirement area of Southern California. Past Santa Barbara is Northern California—and a complete change of personality.

I never cease to be impressed by Santa Barbara—called "La Tierra Adorada" (the adored land) by its Spanish settlers. This famous community spreads out along the Pacific for miles of sandy beaches, and climbs tier upon tier up the mountain for nearly a thousand feet, offering spectacular views of sea, shore, and sun for the lucky people living in the hills.

Blessed with the best of the famous California climate, troubled only slightly by smog, Santa Barbara has long been a mecca for retirees—with a fair amount of money. There seems to be two classes of people in Santa Barbara—the rich (including plenty of young people) and the retired. And the retired need a reliable flow of money from pensions, Social Security, and investments. Don't count on working here to supplement your income; job opportunities are scarce, although volunteer opportunities are plentiful.

Climate and Environment. The average summer temperature range is from 56° F. to 72° F.; average winter is from 47° F. to 66° F. Rainfall is about 18 inches a year. Humidity averages 62 percent annually. There are over 200 clear days a year; most other days are only partly cloudy or have a morning overcast. The residential areas are quiet, charming, tree-lined (palm trees), beautifully landscaped, with white Spanish-style homes with red tile roofs. The hillside homes are dramatic and costly. Much of the town is rich in Spanish history and influence. Santa Barbara prides itself on its 280 excellent restaurants.

Medical Facilities. Four hospitals with a total of 842 beds serve the area; there are also many convalescent and rest homes. Four clinics specialize in outpatient diagnosis. More than 400 physicians and 145 dentists practice in the area. A semiprivate hospital room averages $157.50 daily, about $10 below state average.

Housing. Rental housing, both apartments and homes, is available; one-bedroom unfurnished apartments rent from about $300 a month, two-bedroom units from about $500. A wide range of homes, from conservative to ultraluxurious, is for sale. Two- and three-bedroom houses sell from $90,000 to $250,000. Many handsome older homes are located near downtown; new tracts are being developed in the suburbs. A respectable retirement home costs between $80,000 and $150,000. Best bets are the apartment club arrangements, where $75,000 buys a two-bedroom apartment with pool and clubhouse, near the beach. There are some excellent retirement hotels and residences, such as the New Carrillo (once owned by Leo Carrillo, the "Cisco Kid"). A monthly rate of about $500 provides a single person with a furnished private room and bath, weekly maid service, daily breakfast and dinner, free local phone calls, and recreation activities. There are also some attractive and well-equipped mobile home parks in nearby Goleta, Carpenteria, and Buellton—some with complete recreation facilities, and ocean and mountain views. Recommended are Rancho Goleta Mobile Home Park in Goleta and Rancho Club Mobile Estates in Buellton. Monthly costs are from $125 to $200. Rancho Club Estates has a lake in the park, as well as a pool and clubhouse.

For further information:

> Chamber of Commerce
> 1301 Santa Barbara Street
> Santa Barbara, CA 93102

Cost of Living. The cost of living is about the same as in the more prosperous suburbs of Los Angeles and other major cities. Food and other staples cost about the same as elsewhere, but rent, luxuries, and services are higher. The combined city and state sales tax is 7 percent (in most parts of Southern California it is 6 percent). Seniors get discounts on bus rides, theater tickets, meals and various goods and services.

Recreation and Culture. There's a lot more going on in Santa Barbara than in most cities of its size: antiques, art galleries, wine tasting, concerts, plays, lectures, little theater groups, a local symphony, performances by guest stars, courses and events at the local branch of the University of California, 3 museums and a big library. The city's adult education program offers approximately 100 courses. You can enjoy outdoor activities all year—tennis, golf, swimming, fishing, boating. There are public tennis courts, golf courses, and miles of free public beaches.

Special Services for Seniors. These are virtually unlimited, including Walk for Your Life (a 2½-mile stroll along the ocean boulevard 3 times weekly), choral singing, physical fitness classes, country and ballroom dance groups, potluck dinners, community singing, and a host of other activities. The Senior Citizens' Information Service at 1232 De La Vina Street, open weekdays, is staffed with volunteers ready to provide information on recreation, employment, health, education, housing, and other subjects of interest to seniors.

For further information:

Chamber of Commerce
Santa Barbara, CA 93101

Other Retirement Areas of Interest

Ventura (pop. 70,000) is about 27 miles south of Santa Barbara and right on the ocean. Ventura is not as elegant as Santa Barbara, but it could fill the bill if you want to work after retirement. It is home to 30 manufacturing plants—mostly in building materials, oil production equipment, and food products; both part-time and full-time jobs are available. Ventura is relatively smog-free. The city has 2 general hospitals with 622 total bed capacity, and 264 physicians and surgeons and 54 dentists to assure good medical care. Rental housing is plentiful, ranging from $200 to $400 for one- and two-bedroom apartments and duplexes. Homes in nearby suburbs sell from $45,000 to $150,000. There are 16 mobile home parks nearby; monthly rents range from $100 to $200.

For further information:

Chamber of Commerce
Ventura, CA 93001

SUMMARY

I like Southern California's diversity—all the things to see and do. There's no limit to the sports and outdoor activities available—as participant or spectator. The cultural attractions are vast—museums, theaters, concerts, adult education courses, clubs catering to every kind of interest.

The climate is excellent for the most part—especially in the smog-free areas. With the climate goes a casual, outdoor life style that is conducive to happy and healthy retirement living. You meet people easily; Southern Californians are warm and friendly, and make you feel at home. Clubs are everywhere and the welcome mat is out. There is a great variety of people from various places, and you can usually find a group you feel at home with—people who share your interests and outlook.

I like the interest that both the state and local communities take in seniors. California is a leader in offering special programs for seniors as well as tax breaks and other concessions. For information explaining the California tax laws and special concessions for seniors write:

California Franchise Tax Board
P.O. Box 1644
Sacramento, CA 95808

Senior Citizens Property Tax
Assistance
P.O. Box 1588
Sacramento, CA 95807

And, of course, Southern California has great natural beauty. You live near the ocean, beaches, mountains, palm trees, colorful flowers, and beautiful sunsets.

What *don't* I like? The smog and the other big-city problems of places like Los Angeles: congestion and crime. There's also a scarcity of housing and a high cost of housing when it is available. When you're living on a retiree's budget, 40 percent and more of your income is too much to spend on shelter.

Here are my personal ratings for Southern California's major retirement areas:

Excellent—Santa Barbara, San Diego (area);

Good—La Jolla, Coronado, Del Mar, Solana Beach, Ranch Bernardo, Ramona, Hemet, Rancho California, Sun City;

Adequate—San Clemente, Los Angeles (area), Palm Springs, Ventura, Lawrence Welk's Country Village, Riverside-San Bernardino, San Marcos.

RATINGS FOR SOUTHERN CALIFORNIA MAJOR
RETIREMENT AREAS

SAN DIEGO

LA JOLLA

DEL MAR

SAN CLEMENTE

RANCHO BERNARDO

ESCONDIDO

1 = Excellent   2 = Good   3 = Fair   4 = Poor   5 = Unacceptable

RATINGS FOR SOUTHERN CALIFORNIA MAJOR RETIREMENT AREAS

SAN MARCOS

Rating	Climate & Envir.	Medical	Housing	Cost of Living	Rec. & Culture	Spec. Senior Svces.
1						
2						
3						
4						
5						

RAMONA

Rating	Climate & Envir.	Medical	Housing	Cost of Living	Rec. & Culture	Spec. Senior Svces.
1						
2						
3						
4						
5						

HEMET

Rating	Climate & Envir.	Medical	Housing	Cost of Living	Rec. & Culture	Spec. Senior Svces.
1						
2						
3						
4						
5						

RANCHO CALIFORNIA

Rating	Climate & Envir.	Medical	Housing	Cost of Living	Rec. & Culture	Spec. Senior Svces.
1						
2						
3						
4						
5						

SUN CITY

Rating	Climate & Envir.	Medical	Housing	Cost of Living	Rec. & Culture	Spec. Senior Svces.
1						
2						
3						
4						
5						

PALM SPRINGS

Rating	Climate & Envir.	Medical	Housing	Cost of Living	Rec. & Culture	Spec. Senior Svces.
1						
2						
3						
4						
5						

LOS ANGELES (AREA)

Rating: 1, 2, 3, 4, 5

Columns: Climate & Envir. | Medical | Housing | Cost of Living | Rec. & Culture | Spec. Senior Svces.

VENTURA

Rating: 1, 2, 3, 4, 5

Columns: Climate & Envir. | Medical | Housing | Cost of Living | Rec. & Culture | Spec. Senior Svces.

SANTA BARBARA

Rating: 1, 2, 3, 4, 5

Columns: Climate & Envir. | Medical | Housing | Cost of Living | Rec. & Culture | Spec. Senior Svces.

RIVERSIDE-SAN BERNARDINO

Rating: 1, 2, 3, 4, 5

Columns: Climate & Envir. | Medical | Housing | Cost of Living | Rec. & Culture | Spec. Senior Svces.

1 = Excellent   2 = Good   3 = Fair   4 = Poor   5 = Unacceptable

HAWAII

KAUAI

Lihue

NIIHAU

OAHU

Honolulu

MOLOKAI

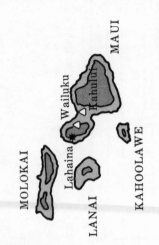

Wailuku

Kahului

MAUI

Lahaina

LANAI

KAHOOLAWE

Hilo

HAWAII

Kailua-Kona

Excellent Retirement

Good Retirement

Coastal Areas

Mountains

XVI.

HAWAII—

IS PARADISE WORTH

THE PRICE?

Almost everyone who vacations in Hawaii falls in love with it, many so deeply that they dream of retiring there someday. Some actually do. The Aloha State is filled with tales of seniors who pull up stakes and move to "paradise"—only to leave bitterly disappointed.

Why? Because paradise doesn't come cheap. The cost of living in Hawaii is the second highest of any state in the Union (only Alaska costs more), and that includes *all* the Hawaiian Islands, even those places that rarely see a tourist. The main villain is the cost of housing. Land is scarce, and most building materials have to be imported. Hawaii is odd because although it can be inexpensive to *visit*, it is almost prohibitively expensive to live there.

When I visited Hawaii I felt exactly like so many of the 3,000,000 or so tourists who come each year: What a marvelous place to retire, I thought. Who wouldn't like to spend his or her golden years on a beautiful island where orchids grow wild and the sun shines most of the time, where it rarely gets too hot or too cold, but stays balmy all year round, with endless beautiful beaches at one's doorstep, and clear, blue surf beyond? What a way to live—the leisurely, relaxed life style of an idyllic island combined with the best of American life—good medical facilities, safe water, all the modern conveniences! Now that's paradise.

Or is it?

The last state to join the Union (1959), Hawaii is the only state not on the mainland of North America: It's a string of more than 120 islands and atolls in the middle of the Pacific Ocean, about 2,400 miles west of the mainland, 5 hours or so by jet from California. Hawaii is also the southernmost state: Honolulu, the major city, is as far south as central Mexico. The total area of the islands is about 6,500 square miles—the size of Connecticut, Delaware, and Rhode Island put together.

About 80 percent of Hawaii's approximately 1,000,000 people live in or around Honolulu—and what an incredible *mixture* of people it is! There is an endless variety of facial types and skin tones, the result of generations of mixing of Polynesians, Chinese, Filipinos, Japanese, and Americans. The two biggest groups today are Caucasian (40 percent) and Japanese (30 percent); only about 15 percent are of chiefly Hawaiian ancestry. The population is very *young;* almost everyone seems to be in his twenties—I never felt so old! In fact, Hawaii's population is *younger* than most states'; *half* the residents are *under age 25.*

Hawaii depends on 3 major industries for its income: defense (salaries paid to military and civilian personnel at Pearl Harbor Naval Base and other military installations), tourism, and agriculture (chiefly sugarcane and pineapples). Hawaii supplies more than a third of the world's pineapples, and it is known for its lovely orchids, but its most important crop is sugarcane. Manufacturing here consists mostly of processing sugarcane and pineapples, but other industry has been developed, especially a garment industry, specializing in making casual and sports clothes. Hawaii's huge cattle ranches (the Parker Ranch is one of the largest in the United States) supply mainly local needs.

Four islands to pick from: Of the chain of islands that form the state of Hawaii, only four are sufficiently developed to be prime retirement centers (although *Molokai,* the "Friendly Isle," offers some possibilities). They are:

Oahu, the most developed of the islands; 80 percent of the population lives here, mainly in Honolulu, the largest city and the state capital, home of famous Waikiki Beach and Pearl Harbor.

Hawaii, the biggest island in *area* (over 4,000 square miles compared to 600 or so for Oahu), the *island* of Hawaii has its own international airport at its chief city, Hilo, second in importance to Honolulu.

Maui, virtually undiscovered by mainlanders until recently when a surge of resort hotels sprang up along its spectacular, once-isolated beaches, especially near its most visited city, Lahaina.

Kauai, just beginning to enter the 20th century. With its tropical flowers and stunning scenery, it's still for people who want to get away from it all.

Climate—Almost Too Good to Be True

Although it gets cold and wet the higher you go (people living on the slopes above Honolulu sit around roaring fires), where most people live it's sunny and balmy all year—a perpetual spring. In Honolulu the average high is in the low 80s from May through November, the high 70s from December through April. Highest temperature ever: 90° F.; lowest, 52° F. It's a bit cooler on the big island of Hawaii and a lot wetter in Hilo, the second city. Rainfall varies from hundreds of inches a year in the mountains and tropical areas to less than 10 inches in the lowlands (such as Waikiki). Humidity averages 70 percent annually. The Pacific trade winds provide Hawaii with natural air conditioning, but when southern winds take over, it gets warm, humid, and deenergizing. Fortunately, this doesn't happen too often or last very long. If you want winter snow, you'll find it atop the mountains on the island of Hawaii—you can even go skiing.

The Sky-Hawaii Cost of Living

The Commission on Aging *discourages* seniors from moving to Hawaii. Living costs are so high, they say, that most retirees can't cope unless they have independent means or an income of around $15,000 a year.

The biggest expense is housing, with food second. Food costs are about 15 percent higher than in the average mainland city and even higher in less developed areas far from Honolulu where transport costs are higher and there's little competition.

However, seniors age 65 and older may ride Honolulu buses free without restrictions, providing they apply for a free bus pass.

On the other hand, some people claim they eat cheaper than on the mainland because they've changed their eating habits and eat what Hawaiians eat—lots of fresh fruits and vegetables, lean meats and chicken, fish, rice, and noodles. It's not only cheaper, they claim, but healthier. If you must eat canned, packaged, and frozen foods imported from the mainland, it'll cost you a fortune.

There are some savings in Hawaii, though. The climate is so mild you can do without heating, air conditioning, or warm clothes. Clothing is so casual, in fact, you hardly need a clothing budget. Sports clothes costs less than on the mainland. Even cars and appliances are no longer sky-high—especially those coming from Japan and other Oriental countries. Some supermarkets and other stores now offer discounts to seniors.

Taxes. First, the bad news: There's a 4 percent "pass-along" sales tax, plus an income tax which, for heads of household, ranges from 2.25 percent on taxable income not over $500 to $5,757 plus 11 percent on taxable income in excess of $60,000. A credit is provided for the installation of a solar energy unit, and a general excise-tax credit for consumer, educational, and drug expenses, and for apartment rentals. The credit per qualified exemption ranges from $30 on income under $5,000 to $6 on income between $14,000 and $20,000. The tax rate on $10,000 taxable income is $647 plus 9.15 percent of excess over $10,000. As for property tax, homes are assessed at 60 percent of fair market value, and taxed at the rate of about $15 per $1,000 assessed valuation. Taxes on a $50,000 home (modest by Hawaiian standards) are about $450 a year.

Now, *the good news*. Seniors get some terrific tax breaks: a $24,000 property-tax exemption if you're over age 60; $30,000 if you're over age 70. This can cut your tax bill almost in half on a $50,000 home. Renters with gross income of less than $20,000, who have paid more than $1,000 rent for the taxable year, may get a tax credit of $20 multiplied by the number of qualified exemptions. The credit is doubled for a taxpayer or spouse who is 65 years or older.

And residents age 65 or older who have established residence in Hawaii before July 1976 get an exemption of any income received from property owned or traded or business conducted outside of Hawaii. If your income consists of Social Security and other tax-free pensions and extra money from sources outside of Hawaii, you might (if eligible) pay no Hawaiian state income taxes whatsoever.

Personal exemptions for seniors are $1,500 each, and there is a special $7,000 exemption for the blind, deaf, or totally disabled.

For more tax information, write:

Hawaii State Department of Taxation Office
425 Queen Street
Honolulu, HI 96813

Housing—Pay More, Get Less

Unless you're prepared to backpack and sleep in a sleeping bag on the beach like a number of young people I saw, you're in for a rude shock when you set out to put a roof over your head. Housing is not only costly, it's scarce. You'd be lucky to find a one-bedroom condominium for under $75,000. There's some low-income government housing for the elderly, but the waiting list is about 1,000 applicants long. There are a few retirement residences, mostly on Oahu—where apartments sell from about $30,000 to over $100,000, with monthly fees ranging from $350 to $600.

Medical Care—Good (When Your Doctor Isn't Surfing)

Several years ago when a friend took his family for a Hawaiian vacation, his 10-year-old son suffered a muscle spasm, but their hotel couldn't locate a single doctor. They were all out surfing, said the girl at the desk. They had to take a cab to a clinic in Honolulu where a young, tanned doctor took care of the boy—and then spent most of his time discussing surfing!

Generally, Hawaii has fine, well-equipped medical facilities in the urban areas. More than half the 31 hospitals (4,726 beds) as well as most of the 41 nursing and 101 personal-care homes are on Oahu, as are 800 of the 1,386 doctors in the islands. The average daily rate for a semi-private hospital room in Honolulu is $135.84, about $3 above the national average.

Seniors should check carefully before settling in "untouched" areas —they may be untouched by modern medical facilities.

Recreation—The Big Bargain

Low-cost or free recreational activities abound throughout the islands. The law decrees that all Hawaiian beaches must be open to the public *without charge,* and thanks to the climate you can use them all year. Beach sports are big: swimming, surfing, sailing, fishing, scuba diving, shell collecting, hiking, or just soaking up the sun. Federal, state, and county parks offer a variety of recreational opportunities—camping, fishing, hiking, hunting, and volcano watching. There's also tennis, golf, riding, and other outdoor sports.

State senior centers—as well as some parks and recreation departments (especially in Honolulu)—sponsor a variety of free or low-cost craft and educational programs: You can learn to hula, play the ukulele, sew, make ceramics, cook, and be physically fit. Many senior citizens clubs offer activities: group singing, dancing, handicrafts, movies, speak-

ers, and excursions. Seniors over age 60 can take free courses when there
are unfilled spaces at the University of Hawaii. Seniors get *free* bus fare
on Honolulu's buses.

If you like to garden, Hawaii's the place. The rich, fertile soil combined with plenty of sun and enough rain can give nearly anyone a green
thumb.

Services for Seniors—Limited

A very concerned Commission on Aging monitors services for the
elderly in the state. Different agencies provide important senior services
on the 4 major islands: hot noontime meals at senior and other centers,
transportation and escort services, information and referral services, home-
maker services, nutrition and consumer education, health services, recreation and education. So far all these services except for information and
referral are on a *limited* basis. Senior citizens clubs and centers on the
different islands provide cultural, recreational, and social activities.

For further information, write:

County Executive
Honolulu Area Agency on Aging
51 Merchant Street
Honolulu, HI 96813

Director, Executive Office on Aging
1149 Bethel Street, Room 307
Honolulu, Hawaii 96813

Department of Human Concerns
County of Maui
200 S. High Street
Wailuku, Maui, HI 96793

Executive on Aging
Hawaii County Office of Aging
34 Rainbow Drive
Hilo, HI 96720

County Executive
Kauai County Office of Elderly
   Affairs
4396 Rice Street—P.O. Box 111
Lihue, HI 96766

1. OAHU—WHERE THE ACTION IS

Although far from the biggest in size, Oahu has more than 80 percent of the state's population. Most of that is in *Honolulu* (pop. 710,000
metropolitan), the largest city and the state capital as well as the center

of industry, commerce and finance, and destination of most tourists. Waikiki Beach, a strip of sand about the width of a Band-Aid on which tourists sunbathe shoulder to shoulder at the foot of towering resort hotels is in Honolulu. Many more beautiful, spacious beaches on the other side of the island are left to the natives.

I was amazed when I first saw Honolulu. I expected a sparsely populated, idyllic island with swaying palms and hula-dancing girls. I arrived at a bustling, noisy, crowded airport, fought my way through the throngs for a cab, and survived a jouncing, brake-slamming, horn-honking ride through traffic-choked streets. I found office buildings and stores instead of grass huts, natives in modern dress instead of grass skirts. Honolulu is a mixture of the old and the new, the beautiful and the shoddy. But what saves it from being just another crowded city are the beaches at its feet, and the mountains above. Looking up at famous Diamond Head, the dormant volcano, and the other impressive mountains behind the city with their white houses sweeping down the slopes like white-capped surf makes the buildings and congestion disappear.

Those homes, as well as other homes in delightful suburbs nestled in the slopes around the city, are just minutes away from downtown Honolulu. A few miles outside of Honolulu are sugarcane and pineapple fields, tiny plantation towns and rural villages, and a deserted coast with empty beaches and not a hotel in sight. For all its tourism, nearly 30 percent of Oahu's land is still used for agriculture. There isn't even a billboard to remind you that civilization is not far away—the law forbids them.

Climate and Environment. Honolulu has the best climate in the islands. It's sunny and balmy all year round except for occasional humid spells. A big plus for swimmers—the water temperature doesn't vary much from the air temperature. It averages 75° to 77° F. in March, 77° to 82° F. in August.

Medical Facilities. More than half of Hawaii's 31 hospitals are located on the island of Oahu. Oahu also has the bulk of the nursing and care homes for the elderly and 4 privately-run day care centers.

Recreation and Culture. There's plenty of year-round recreation in and around Honolulu: beaches galore for swimming, surfing, fishing, boating, all the water sports; 80 public tennis courts in Oahu (plus hotel courts), half of which are lighted at night; 23 golf courses; parks for picnicking, baseball, horseshoes, even bowling on the green; endless walking trails and scenic drives with spectacular views.

Oahu is the center of Hawaiian cultural life with the University of Hawaii, the symphony, theaters, about 20 newspapers (English, Japanese,

Chinese, Filipino, Korean, and so on), and some 200 churches to satisfy nearly everyone's religious needs—including Shinto, Buddhist, and a Chinese temple built like a pagoda. There are a number of free events— concerts by the Royal Hawaiian Band, sidewalk art exhibits, ethnic festivals.

Honolulu's Ala Moana Shopping Center is one of the largest and most fascinating in the world. The supermarkets have a variety of foods that boggle the mind. And so does the variety of shoppers—I saw women in muu-muus, saris, Oriental slit skirts, Japanese kimonos, bikinis, dungarees, shorts, you name it. Local foods are reasonably priced, but imported American products—breakfast cereals, canned goods, detergents—are almost 20 percent higher than the U.S. average.

Housing. Housing in Honolulu, like everywhere else in Hawaii, is expensive and scarce. One-bedroom condominiums *start* at over $50,000. The few low-income projects for the elderly have long waiting lists. Rental units are also scarce and rents are high. There are several retirement residences on Oahu, the 2 largest are *Arcadia* and *Pohai Nani* in the Honolulu area. Arcadia is a luxury high-rise building a few minutes from Waikiki, offering various size units, meals, personal services, and health-care protection. You'd need an income of $15,000 to $25,000 to retire here. Pohai Nani, minutes from downtown, offers cottages and apartments, and is less costly than Arcadia. Apartments start around $15,000 and monthly fees start at about $300. For up-to-date information, write to:

> Arcadia (Sponsor: Central Union Church)
> 1434 Punahou Street
> Honolulu, HI 96822

> Laniolu (Sponsor: American Lutheran Church)
> 333 Lewers Street
> Honolulu, HI 96815

> Pohai Nani (Sponsor: Pacific Homes Corporation)
> 45-090 Namoku Street
> Kaneohe, HI 96744

2. HAWAII—THE "BIG" ISLAND

Hilo (pop. 35,000) is Hawaii's second most important city and the major city on the island of Hawaii. It has neat residential streets with palm trees, white bungalows, and luxuriant gardens with spectacular flowers. The downtown area is neat and orderly. Hilo is a port city with a busy harbor; it is the shipping outlet for the island's bulk sugar and cattle industries. Yet the pace of life here is slower than in Honolulu; it's quieter and gentler.

Since Hilo is the commercial center of the island of Hawaii, it has the benefits of civilization: hospitals, supermarkets, daily newspaper, a library, a branch of the University of Hawaii, churches of different denominations, golf courses. At the same time it offers a marvelous outdoor life: hunting, fishing, hiking, and all water sports.

There are a number of annual events in the area—the Orchid Show, Rodeo, County Fair, and others. Visiting the orchid nurseries is a major activity; many of the residents, as their magnificent tropical gardens confirm, are avid gardeners. The tropical climate, with 137 inches of rain a year, lends itself to gardening.

In 1960 when the Hawaiian Islands were hit by a series of seismic sea waves, Hilo suffered the most. Sixty-one people were killed, and there was an estimated $50,000,000 in property damage. The destroyed areas are now a park; merchants and homeowners have rebuilt on "safer" ground.

You'll find some spectacular scenery within driving distance of Hilo—a tropical rain forest dense with luxuriant ferns, tropical flowers, and cascading waterfalls, and the Kilauea Crater in the Hawaii Volcanoes National Park. It's well worth the usually cold and wet drive to the crater, because when you peer over the rim you see jets of steam shooting up from fissures in the lava crust hardened after previous eruptions. Besides crater peering, the park offers many other recreational activities. Orchids grow wild alongside the road to Hilo, which is the orchid capital of America.

The Island of Hawaii offers many volunteer opportunities for seniors: 500 RSVP and 25 Foster Grandparent programs, most of them in Hilo.

In Hilo, reasonably priced housing is virtually nonexistent. What little there is has a long waiting list. Bus service in Hilo is limited, with special bus transportation to and from senior centers. The cost of living in Hilo is similar to that in Honolulu.

Kailua-Kona (pop. 800), also known simply as Kona, or the Kona Coast, is a popular tourist area on the western shore of Hawaii Island, across the island from Hilo. It has miles of sugarcane fields, cattle ranches, and coffee plantations, as well as miles of lava ash—the gray cindery remains of lava flows that overran the area. Volcanoes erupted here as recently as 1960. Rivers of molten lava burned crops and homes and covered miles of agricultural lands. Over the years, however, the lava ash turns into rich, fertile soil.

Kona, once the summer playground of the monarchy, is a charming and fashionable town filled with luxury hotels, boutiques, and quaint restaurants. People are warned not to go in the ocean here because of the dangerous undertow. However, the ocean is superb for fishing. Charter boats and commercial fishermen set out every morning and return with marlin, ahi (yellowfin tuna), mahamahi, and ono.

New hotels or condominiums are built constantly. There is a cluster of retirement homes where you might pick up something for $100,000 or so—if you're lucky. Or you might opt for a one- or two-bedroom condominium in Sea Village, starting at over $50,000. But average two-bedroom houses sell for around $100,000. Facilities for seniors are negligible, public transportation nonexistent, and if you need more than the normal medical facilities, or want to see a play, you'll probably have to fly to Honolulu, or at least make the trip to Hilo. Food costs are about 10 percent higher than in Honolulu. But the climate is excellent, far drier than in Hilo, and there are plenty of recreational activities—especially if you're hooked on deep-sea fishing.

For more information:

> Hawaii County Office of Aging
> 34 Rainbow Drive
> Hilo, HI 96720

3. MAUI—A TOUCH OF NEW ENGLAND

Slightly larger than Oahu, Maui is the second largest of the Hawaiian Islands. It's called the Valley Island because most of it is a deep valley isthmus (it once lay beneath the sea) between two volcanic masses. On it is the world's largest dormant volcanic crater, Haleakala. The island also has the world's largest sugarcane plantation. Temperatures here are slightly lower than in Honolulu, although humidity is slightly higher.

Much of Maui remains exactly as it was hundreds, if not thousands, of years ago—inhospitable mountainous terrain touched only by a few narrow, twisting roads, observation points here and there, and an observatory atop cold, windswept Haleakala. Tiny villages are clustered at the shore, with groves of coco palms shading the coral sand beaches. Some beaches have black sand—lava ash turned to tiny particles over the years. This was Hawaii before the white man came.

There are 3 fair-sized towns on Maui:

Kahului (pop. 11,186), just a few minutes from the small interisland airport, is a bustling, up-and-coming sea and air port with new housing projects, shopping centers, a cannery, a bulk-sugar loading plant, and other industry. Kahului's growth is largely due to the Hawaiian and Commercial Sugar Company, which is developing a modern community of low-cost housing units here. The project, a model of its kind, has provided over 1,000 homes for Mauians since its inception over 16 years ago. But don't expect to get into the project: There's a long waiting list. Shopping is a delight in Kahului, whether browsing in the attractive lanai shops built around a delightful patio and fountain, or visiting the marketplace of Kahului, the Kaahumanu Center, with 50 shops and restaurants. But housing here is scarce and medical facilities are limited. There are only 20 doctors in the area and 1 general hospital with limited facilities.

Wailuku (pop. 10,810) is Maui's main city and county seat. Nestled at the base of the West Maui Mountains, it is a charming bit of New England transplanted by the missionaries in 1837. It's a provincial town with a compact but growing business district. Housing here is scarce and medical facilities are limited. There are some 20 doctors in the area; medical facilities are shared with Kahului.

Lahaina (pop. 9,278), picturesquely huddled between the sea and 5,800-foot Puu Kukui, highest of the West Maui peaks, is an old New England missionary and whaling town. Lahaina is more redolent of history than almost any other island spot, and it has turned into a major tourist center. Its clapboard buildings, shutters, and widow's walks draw many visitors. Built by the first New England missionary groups in 1823, Lahaina later became the center of the whaling industry, and is now known as Hawaii's Williamsburg—thanks to the diligent efforts of its restoration and preservation committee. Lahaina is filled not only with charm, but with mobs of tourists—and a pack of boutiques and souvenir shops to snare their dollars. From Lahaina you can see the towering resort hotels lining the beach at Kaanapali, a famous resort area a few minutes' drive away.

Because Lahaina is so popular with tourists, it's a costly place to set up housekeeping. One-bedroom apartments rent for around $600 a month. Luxurious condominiums are being built, but no retirement communities. Public transportation is nonexistent. Medical and cultural facilities and senior services are limited. Recreation is plentiful as long as you concentrate on water sports—the beaches and the climate are wonderful.

For more information:

> Department of Human Concerns
> County of Maui
> 200 S. High Street
> Wailuku, Maui, HI 96793

4. KAUAI—THE "GARDEN ISLAND"

Lying all by itself about a 25-minute flight northwest of Honolulu, lush, tropical, untouched Kauai looks like the Hawaii of the movies. Any number of South Sea movies have been filmed here, including *South Pacific*. An endless garden of every shade of green from celadon to emerald, Kauai is thick with flowering vines, shrubs, and trees almost constantly in bloom.

Most of Kauai's action and commerce is clustered around the little sugarcane town of *Lihue* (pop. 5,000), the county seat and one of the oldest plantation towns in the islands. Lihue came into being as the center of a vast sugar plantation. It's an active town with a plantation store, mill, shopping center, library, hospital, concert hall, and several churches; a few miles in either direction and you're out of this world.

Smaller plantation towns on Kauai include Nawiliwili Harbor, the chief seaport with its large bulk-sugar plant, and the Haena region, with country cottages and small homes. Kauai is mainly spectacular scenery (tropical vegetation, mountain peaks, canyons, waterfalls) and agriculture (pineapple, rice, and taro fields, and cattle ranches). Temperatures average about the same in winter as in Honolulu (72.4° F.), but is about 1 degree cooler in summer (78.3° F.).

Kauai has year-round recreation—especially water sports—as well as camping and golfing. It is also a gardener's dream—the soil and rainfall (average 43.54 inches annually) produce a dazzling array of flowers and shrubs. Mile-high Mount Waialeale, at the center of the island, is one of the wettest spots on earth, with as much as 486 inches of rainfall a year. The University of Hawaii has a community college here. Medical facilities (3 public and private hospitals, 50 doctors) might be adequate for the average health problem, but for more specialized care you must fly to Honolulu. Public transportation is minimal. Reasonably priced housing is very scarce, and what low-cost housing there is is reserved for locals. The cost of living on Kauai is generally *higher* than in Honolulu.

The Kauai County Office of Elderly Affairs has published a "Directory of Services" for the elderly on the island which describes activities and educational activities, nutrition programs, RSVP programs, health screening, maintenance, and education.

For further information:

Kauai County Office of Elderly Affairs
4396 Rice St.
Lihue, HI 96766

SUMMARY

I like the leisurely way of life in Hawaii. It's nice to be able to live outdoors all year and to have beautiful, uncrowded beaches at hand, and clear, blue water. Except for the rainy areas, I like the Hawaiian climate —sunny and balmy all year, with just a few hot and humid spells.

There is an amazing mixture of people here, especially in and around Honolulu. Hawaii offers an education in getting to know people with different backgrounds—experiencing their foods, their customs, their different viewpoints.

For the most part, Hawaii is a bright and cheerful place to live—the flowers, shrubs, sun, moon, sky, ocean, the clothes the people wear . . . it's all colorful and pleasing to the eye and soothing to the soul. Hawaii gracefully combines the gentle pace of the south Pacific with American vitality and know-how.

Hawaii has so many good things going for it, it's too bad it costs so much to live here. All costs—especially housing—are very high. I can't see spending most of my retirement budget on shelter; I have too many other things to do with the money.

Another problem is distance. It's a long and expensive trip to the U.S. mainland, and seeing friends and relatives back home wouldn't be easy. But if you hanker to pull up stakes and start completely fresh with a whole new life style—and if you have the money it takes—I can't think of a better place to do it than in Hawaii.

Here are my personal ratings for Hawaii's major retirement areas:
Excellent—Lahaina on Maui and Lihue on Kauai;
Good—Honolulu on Oahu, Hilo on Hawaii, Kailua-Kona on Hawaii, Kahului on Maui, Wailuku on Maui.

RATINGS FOR *HAWAII* MAJOR RETIREMENT AREAS

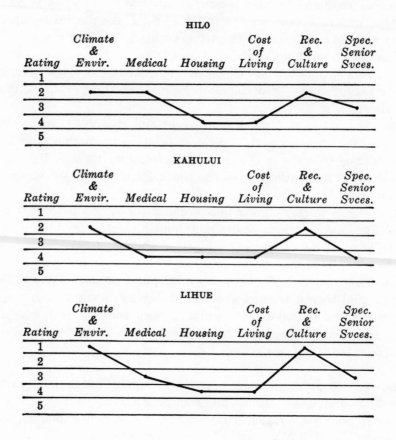

RATINGS FOR *HAWAII* MAJOR RETIREMENT AREAS

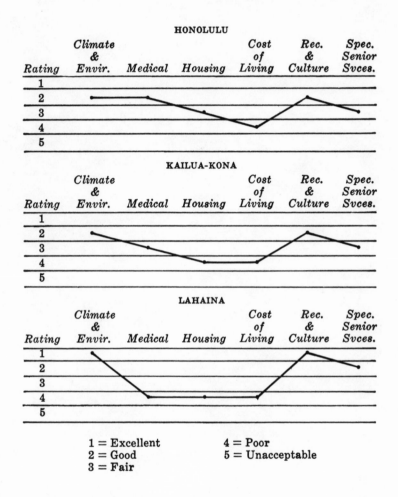

1 = Excellent   4 = Poor
2 = Good   5 = Unacceptable
3 = Fair

EPILOGUE:

FINDING YOUR PLACE

IN THE SUNBELT

1. THE ADVANTAGES

- *The Sunbelt offers a new frontier.* New people, environment, economics, and retirement activities. Seniors will wield much of the power. As we vote in larger numbers than younger people, we can cast enough votes to elect any candidate or swing any issue to our advantage. Thus, we can write our own political ticket in the Sunbelt. Also, the Sunbelt is changing, and change stimulates change. New people, new jobs, new ideas, and new activities generate an "anything can happen for the better" feeling in all areas. This opens up opportunities for all ages—youngsters with dreams as well as seniors with money.

- *The Sunbelt costs less.* With the exception of the Los Angeles area and the Hawaiian Islands, cost of living in the Sunbelt runs 5 to 10 percent below the national average. Living costs are especially low in rural areas of all the Sunbelt states and the coastal areas of Mississippi, Louisiana, south Texas, southern New Mexico, and southern Arizona.

- *The Sunbelt is healthier.* The Sunbelt's good climate makes fewer demands on your body and pocketbook. Diabetes seems to be more controllable in hot climes, and stress diseases—ulcers, certain heart problems, hardening of the arteries—are less frequent in warm zones. Sunbelt localities are frequently recommended for arthritis, rheumatism, emphysema, and sinus

319

and respiratory problems. Even retirees in good health feel better in the Sunbelt. It offers more of the "ideal" climate—around 66° F., with relative humidity of around 55 percent, and with a gently blowing breeze and beaming sunshine—than anywhere else in the U.S.

■ *The Sunbelt is generally more friendly.* While some "Southern hospitality" may be superficial, social life in the Sunbelt is centered more on people than places, and former status isn't important in a retirement community. The Sunbelt gives retirees an opportunity to meet new friends, and you can always find Midwesterners or Northerners who moved to your new home for the same reasons you did.

■ *The Sunbelt offers more housing at lower cost.* Homes cost less in the Sunbelt because they don't need full basements for central heating systems. Residents use space, floor, and wall heaters or heat pumps that cool in summer as well as heat in winter. Houses don't need as much insulation from the cold or even an enclosed heated garage—a simple carport serves nicely. Generally, $30,000 to $45,000 two-bedroom houses in the Sunbelt would cost $50,000 to $65,000 up north. And entertaining is less formal and less expensive with many activities centered outdoors—golf, tennis, lawn bowling, shuffleboard, boating, nature studies—that you can enjoy all year at low cost. *You should be outdoor-, sports-, or nature-minded to take full advantage of the Sunbelt.*

2. THE DISADVANTAGES

■ *Perpetual summer.* Though I prefer moderate temperatures, I also like distinct seasons to add variety. But mainly in northwestern North Carolina and Arkansas and in the high plateau areas of New Mexico and Arizona is there a four-season climate. As a Northeasterner, I am accustomed to high humidity in July and August, but experiencing such heat and humidity in the fall is a shock.

■ *Lack of transportation.* With few exceptions (perhaps Miami, Albuquerque, Los Angeles, Honolulu), public transportation in the Sunbelt is poor or lacking. *A car is a must.*

■ *An overabundance of insects.* Because average temperatures are higher in the Sunbelt states, annoying insects are more prevalent. Such pests range from cockroaches to mosquitos to fire ants. Snakes are more common too.

■ *Less emphasis on culture.* There seem to be fewer opportunities to enjoy classical music, museums, libraries, and art galleries in the Sunbelt states than in more cosmopolitan cities elsewhere in the U.S. However, there are good opportunities for continuing education in community and local colleges in the Sunbelt.

3. WHAT SUNBELT COMMUNITIES WOULD BE BEST FOR YOU?

To help you select the communities which are best for your needs and wants in terms of: (1) climate and environment; (2) medical facilities; (3) housing availability and costs; (4) cost of living; (5) recreation and culture; (6) special senior services, I recommend the following:

Climate and Environment

NORTH CAROLINA:
Southern Pines
Pinehurst
Hendersonville
Brevard
Tryon
Chapel Hill

SOUTH CAROLINA:
Myrtle Beach

GEORGIA:
St. Simons Island
Sea Island
Jekyll Island

FLORIDA:
Mount Dora
Vero Beach
Naples
Sarasota

ALABAMA:
Fairhope

MISSISSIPPI:
Ocean Springs

LOUISIANA:
Covington
Abita Springs

ARKANSAS:
Eureka Springs
Mountain Home

TEXAS:
McAllen
Kerrville

NEW MEXICO:
Santa Fe
Taos
Roswell

ARIZONA:
Cave Creek-Carefree
Prescott
Sedona

CALIFORNIA:
La Jolla
Del Mar
Santa Barbara

HAWAII:
Lahaina, Maui
Lihue, Kauai

Medical Facilities

NORTH CAROLINA:
Charlotte
Asheville
Chapel Hill

SOUTH CAROLINA:
Charleston

FLORIDA:
Miami
Sarasota
St. Petersburg

ALABAMA:
Fairhope

LOUISIANA:
New Orleans
Baton Rouge

ARKANSAS:
Hot Springs
Fayetteville

TEXAS:
Brownsville
Kerrville

NEW MEXICO:
Albuquerque

ARIZONA:
Tucson
Phoenix

CALIFORNIA:
San Diego (area)
Los Angeles (area)
Palm Springs

Housing Availability and Costs

FLORIDA:
Orlando
Clearwater (area)

ALABAMA:
Fairhope

MISSISSIPPI:
Ocean Springs

LOUISIANA:
New Orleans (area)

ARKANSAS:
Mountain Home

TEXAS:
McAllen

NEW MEXICO:
Roswell
Carlsbad

CALIFORNIA:
Hemet (area)

Cost of Living

FLORIDA:
Jacksonville
Orlando

MISSISSIPPI:
Ocean Springs

LOUISIANA:
Baton Rouge
Monroe

TEXAS:
McAllen

NEW MEXICO:
Roswell

Recreation and Culture

NORTH CAROLINA:
Chapel Hill
Tryon

SOUTH CAROLINA:
Myrtle Beach
Charleston

FLORIDA:
Miami
Sarasota
St. Petersburg

ALABAMA:
Fairhope
Mobile

MISSISSIPPI:
Biloxi

LOUISIANA:
New Orleans
Covington

TEXAS:
Corpus Christi
Austin
San Antonio
El Paso

NEW MEXICO:
Santa Fe
Roswell

ARIZONA:
Tucson
Phoenix
Prescott

CALIFORNIA:
San Diego
Los Angeles
Santa Barbara

Special Services for Seniors

NORTH CAROLINA:
New Bern
Hendersonville

SOUTH CAROLINA:
Myrtle Beach
Charleston

FLORIDA:
Orlando
Miami
Daytona Beach
Sarasota
St. Petersburg

ALABAMA:
Fairhope
Mobile

LOUISIANA:
Baton Rouge

ARKANSAS:
Mountain Home

TEXAS:
McAllen
San Antonio
El Paso

NEW MEXICO:
Albuquerque
Santa Fe
Roswell
Carlsbad
Truth or Consequences

ARIZONA:
Tucson

CALIFORNIA:
San Diego
Los Angeles
Hemet
Santa Barbara

However, my towns may not be your towns, and my needs and wants may not suit you. Only you know what you need, want, and can afford. To find your place in the Sunbelt I suggest:

1. *Write to the state units on aging* and to the chambers of commerce (see text) of the places that interest you. Specify what you want or need in the way of housing, medical facilities, recreation, special services, and so on. A friendly answer or no answer will give you an idea whether the welcome mat is out. Some towns may be too small to have a chamber of commerce. If so, contact a local realtor or bank.

2. *Subscribe to weekly or Sunday newspapers.* There's nothing like reading the local papers to find out what's happening and to get the pulse and flavor of a town. You can get names and addresses of papers through *Ayer's Directory of Publications* or *Editor and Publisher*—available at your local library.

3. *Visit the place off-season as well as in season.* A long visit will help you to get to know the people and the place. Find out its rhythms and the types of people it attracts ("birds of a feather" applies to retirement areas). Before buying, *rent or lease or swap* your present home as a handy place to retreat to if you find you really don't like your new community. Realize that it may take a year or two to go from stranger to neighbor, so be prepared for a settling-in period.

If you want to, you will find *your* place in the Sunbelt. I hope I've helped point the way.

INDEX

ABOUT THE AUTHOR

Peter A. Dickinson was born in Detroit, Michigan, and received his Bachelor of Arts degree in Journalism from Wayne State University. He has lived in various parts of the country, including Arizona and California, and his reporting for both newspapers and industry publications has given him access to thousands of people planning or living in retirement.

For the last eighteen years, Mr. Dickinson has been a pioneer in the field of retirement planning. He is the founding editor of *Harvest Years* (now *Retirement Living*) and the *Retirement Letter*, and he is a two-time winner of the National Press Club award for "excellence in consumer reporting." In addition to speaking and lecturing throughout the country, Mr. Dickinson acts as a retirement consultant to major corporations and has served as a Special Investigator for the U.S. Senate Committee on Aging. His most recent book is *The Complete Retirement Planning Book.*